THE SOCIAL LIFE OF
OPIUM IN CHINA

In a remarkable and broad-ranging narrative, Zheng Yangwen's book explores the history of opium consumption in China from 1483 to the late twentieth century. The story begins in the mid-Ming dynasty, when opium was sent as a gift by vassal states and used as an aphrodisiac in court. Over time, the Chinese people from different classes and regions began to use it for recreational purposes, so beginning a complex culture of opium consumption. The book traces this transformation over a period of five hundred years, asking who introduced opium to China, and how it spread throughout all sections of society, embraced by rich and poor alike as a culture and an institution. It is accompanied by a fascinating collection of illustrations, and offers a vivid and alternative perspective on life in China during this period, which will appeal to students and scholars of history, anthropology, sociology, political science, economics, East Asian studies, and to all those with an interest in China.

ZHENG YANGWEN is a Research Fellow at the Asia Research Institute of the National University of Singapore. She received her Ph.D. from the University of Cambridge in 2001.

T0382050

THE SOCIAL LIFE OF OPIUM IN CHINA

ZHENG YANGWEN

CAMBRIDGE
UNIVERSITY PRESS

CAMBRIDGE
UNIVERSITY PRESS

University Printing House, Cambridge CB2 8BS, United Kingdom

Published in the United States of America by Cambridge University Press, New York

Cambridge University Press is part of the University of Cambridge.

It furthers the University's mission by disseminating knowledge in the pursuit of education, learning and research at the highest international levels of excellence.

www.cambridge.org
Information on this title: www.cambridge.org/9780521608565

First published 2005

A catalogue record for this publication is available from the British Library

Library of Congress Cataloguing in Publication data

Zheng, Yangwen.
The social life of opium in China / Zheng Yangwen.
p.   cm.
Includes bibliographical references and index.
ISBN 0 521 84608 0 (hbk) – ISBN 0 521 60856 2 (pbk)
1. Opium habit – China – History.   I. Title.
HV5840.C6Z44   2005
306'.1 – dc22   2004057026

ISBN 978-0-521-84608-0 Hardback
ISBN 978-0-521-60856-5 Paperback

Dedicated to
Carol and Arthur Taylor

I think it could plausibly be argued that changes of diet are more important than changes of dynasty or even of religion.

George Orwell, 1937
The Road to Wigan Pier

Contents

Illustrations

Maps

Tables

Acknowledgements

I wish, first of all, to thank my teachers in Cambridge – Dr Tim Harper, Dr Hans van de Ven and Professor Chris Bayly – who have guided me since 1996. I thank Professor Peter Burke, who opened my eyes to the universe of social theory and culture studies. I remember the encouragement I received from Professors Ho Ping-ti, Jonathan Spence, Frederic Wakeman, Igor Kopytoff and Sidney Mintz in the early stage of this book. Professor Wakeman told me that he saw opium-smoking Chinese labourers in Havana, where he lived as a child, while Professor Kopytoff remembered opium-smoking Chinese ladies in World War Two Shanghai, where he lived as a Russian immigrant boy. I am very grateful to Professor Wang Er-min, who introduced me to material culture and unconventional sources, and to Professor Tony Guodong Chen, who shared with me the Chinese sources in the Jardine Matheson Archive. I thank Professor Alan Kors and the Bradley Foundation for the generous post-doctoral fellowship at the History Department of the University of Pennsylvania. Chairman Jonathan Steinberg, senior colleagues Nancy Farriss and Dan Raff and the Penn Economic Forum all helped to promote my work. I am most grateful to Professors Susan Naquin, Philip Kuhn, Benjamin Elman and Joanna Waley-Cohen, who took precious time to read my manuscript and shared with me their insights.

I thank Charles Alymer and Mrs Feng Nanhua of the University Library at Cambridge, John Wells of the Jardine Matheson Archive, John Moffett of the Needham Institute, the staff at Fu Sinian Library of Academic Sinica, Lily Kecskes of the East Asian and Prints and Photographs divisions of the Library of Congress, and Yang Jidong and Lee Pugh of the Van Pelt Library of the University of Pennsylvania. These professionals went out of their way to help me. I thank Taryn Kutish at Penn's History Department for polishing up my computer skills.

I could not have written this book without the funding of the Institute of Humane Studies, Oberlin College (my Alma Mater), King's College,

Cambridge and the Bradley Foundation. They gave me the means with which to travel around the world in the search and research of opium. I thank Dr Liz Gray, Maggie Cowen, Juliana Steiner, Nancy Jones and Dr Edward Castleton for reading my manuscript and polishing my English. I wish to thank Marigold Acland, Isabelle Dambricourt, Hilary Hammond and Mary Leighton of Cambridge University Press for their hard work. Finally, my gratitude goes to my parents in China, to Tove and Terje Mikalsen in Farsund, Norway, and to Carol and Arthur Taylor in Bronxville, New York, to whom this book is dedicated.

Introduction

The history of opium is a major theme in modern Chinese history. Books and academic careers have been devoted to its study. Yet the question that scholars of the opium wars and of modern China have failed to ask is how the demand for opium was generated. Who smoked opium, when and why? Recreational smoking was foreign to China, as was opium itself. How and when, then, did opium come to lodge itself within the sophisticated Chinese culture of consumption? Opium not only thrived, it spread like wildfire over the next few hundred years. This was during a period when western Europeans, the British in particular, were naturalising tea and sugar.

Opium has its own story. Historians have not set opium in its social and cultural context; they have not taken its consumption into account in the historiographies of opium and modern China. Some have dwelt on the opium trade, some on the opium wars, some on imperialism and others on the politics of control. The political history of opium, like the theatre of war, is only part of the story. However, the vital questions for me are, first, the point at which opium was transformed from a medicine into a luxury item and, secondly, why it became so popular and widespread after people discovered its recreational value. A full understanding of the root problem of the opium wars and of the role of the wars in the emergence of modern China is not possible without first explaining who smoked opium, when and why. This book studies the introduction of and the naturalisation of opium smoking; it makes preliminary conjectures as to why the Chinese embraced smoking and the use of opium.

I have chosen to look at opium biographically because, as Arjun Appadurai and Igor Kopytoff have argued, 'commodities, like persons, have social lives', that is, 'life histories'.[1] Commodities, be they houses or paintings, lead independent lives regardless of the change of their owners. We learn about them by studying their owners and their life histories. The social life of opium is indeed a biography of 'Mr. Opium' from his birth as a recreational item to his old age as a social icon. Such a perspective on the circulation of commodities focuses on 'the things that are exchanged', because, as Arjun Appadurai has said, 'their meanings are inscribed in their forms, their uses, their trajectories. It is only through the analysis of these trajectories that we can interpret the human transaction and calculations that enliven things.' With opium, the social significance of smoking was 'inscribed' in its vanguard consumers, who were the literati and the officials, and on the pipes packed with precious stones and symbolic designs. Chinese people of different classes, regions and times have endowed many meanings to opium, from luxury to necessity.

The 'genealogical method of anthropological inquiry' is revolutionary, as Kopytoff has pointed out. His example is slavery. Slavery began with capture; an individual was dehumanised, commoditised and later rehumanised when he/she was reinserted into the host group. Dehumanisation begins the biography of a slave; it also marks 'the diversion of commodities from preordained paths'. Opium was likewise diverted; from a herbal medicine it moved to become a luxury item. Diversion is 'frequently a function of irregular desires and novel demands'. This could not have been more evident with opium in 1483, when a medicinal herb became 'the art of alchemists, sex and court ladies'.[2] This diversion shaped the history of opium and indeed of China for five hundred years to come. 'A more theoretically aware biographical model', Kopytoff stressed, should be 'based on a reasonable number of life histories'. This book is the life history of opium as an aphrodisiac from the mid-Ming, as an expensive *yanghuo* or 'foreign stuff' and hobby among the scholar–official elite in the eighteenth century, and as a popular culture in the late Qing–Republican era and beyond. These histories tell us who smoked opium, when and why; they also help us to stitch together a much more complete picture of the Ming–Qing–Republican economy, and of its culture and society, and enable us to see both change and continuity in the culture of opium consumption.

This book examines opium from a cultural perspective because, as Daniel Roche has emphasised, 'Any object, even the most ordinary, embodies ingenuity, choices, a culture. A body of knowledge and a surplus of meanings are attached to all objects.'[3] Roche's example is clothing. 'Clothing speaks of many things at once, either in itself or through some detail. It has a function of communication because it is through clothing that everyone's relation to the community passes.'[4] The same can be said of other forms of consumption, including opium smoking. Roche emphasised that one should pay attention to the whole as well as to the parts; the signs that indicate minorities, the colours that can characterise social functions and member-ship of different groups, the cut, the material, the types of jewellery. For this, reference the smoking sets and accessories that accompanied opium smoking. Roche also advanced much more: 'the history of consumption must include analysis of demand, and therefore of the structuring of needs, the classification of consumers, the circuits of distribution and the spatial organisation of supply'.[5] To understand needs, we must understand 'the texture of our ordinary life', that is, 'the real weight of everyday life', or the 'history of what seems to have no history: material life and biological behaviour, history of food, history of the consumption of food'.[6] For the Chinese, opium smoking, like tea drinking, was material life and biological behaviour, a history of food and a culture of consumption.

Pierre Bourdieu is significant here. His influential *La Distinction: critique sociale du jugement* studied 'the science of taste and cultural consumption'.[7] Bourdieu applied this science to the consumption of the arts and music; I shall extend it to that of opium. Bourdieu saw taste as 'markers of class' and consumption as 'predisposed, consciously and deliberately or not, to fulfil a social function of legitimating social differences'. This was true with opium as its vanguard consumers, the literati and officials, enjoyed opium long before the 'ordinary' people heard about it. It was they who made opium smoking cultured and a status symbol; they who marked them-selves apart from those below them, legitimating their social differences. Bourdieu analysed the consumption of pictorial and musical works. 'A work of art has meaning and interest only for someone who possesses the cultural competence, that is, the code, into which it is encoded.'[8] An opium pipe carved with an epic poem and served by a highly literate courtesan was limited to and had meaning for those who could appreciate the poetry and exchange-coded language. Bourdieu had 'one foot in structural Marxism and the other in cultural studies'.[9] The case of opium supports this approach. Opium was an aristocratic luxury item during the Ming dynasty. It became a necessity during the late nineteenth century. The story of opium is the story of taste and distinction; it is also the story of politics and class formation.

One of the most influential works on consumption is Jean Baudrillard's *La Société de consommation: ses mythes, ses structures*. For Baudrillard, consumption is 'a language'.[10] Breaking away from a standard produc-tivist orientation, the post-modern social theorist believed that consump-tion was 'both a morality and a communication system, a structure of exchange'.[11] This was certainly true of opium smoking, where offering the smoke to friends, colleagues and guests involved a fundamental Chinese socio-cultural value in the late Qing–early Republican era. Regardless of whether one sanctioned opium or not, one must offer the smoke in order to be 'ti mian' (polite or fashionable), thus a Chinese 'morality', 'communication system' and 'structure of exchange' was created. Many sought to catch up with the Joneses; consumption became conspicuous. Consumption itself is subject to individual manipulation; it is also 'subject to social control and political redefinition'.[12] Parallels can be drawn to alcohol in general and vodka in particular. Opium is a perfect example of the political redefinition of consumption. When the rich smoked it, it was cultured and a status symbol; when the poor began to inhale, opium smoking became degrading and ultimately criminal. The lower classes made the consequences of smoking visible and social; the literati and officials had the power to reinterpret consumption. Consumption has never been a simple economic matter.

Mary Douglas proposed 'a distinctive anthropological perspective' in *Constructive Drinking*.[13] Anthropologists brought 'their own professional point of view to bear interestingly upon the same materials studied by specialists on alcohol abuse'. They argued that medical and sociological research exaggerated the problems. As Dwight Heath pointed out, 'Even practitioners of the so-called "hard sciences" acknowledge that social and cultural factors must be taken into account, together with physiological and psychological factors, when one attempts to understand the interaction of alcohol and human behaviour.'[14] I extend this distinctive anthropological perspective to opium because drinking and smoking are the obvious analogies. 'Drinking is essentially a social act, performed in a recognized social context'; so it was with opium smoking.[15] Many authors have studied the social context of consumption. David Christian's *Living Water* argued that vodka played a crucial role in Russian society on the eve of the Revolution. Thomas Brennan illustrated the 'positive uses of drinking' in pre-revolutionary Paris. And David Hardiman exposed the different political agendas injected into drinking in colonial India. Brennan's work is important because it challenged the heavily used accounts of the intermediaries, 'the three robes' – the clergy, the nobility and the liberal professions – their condemnation of taverns and consequently their influence on the study of popular culture.[16] Here, I will challenge the heavily used accounts of 'the Chinese robes'.

Deborah Lupton has furthered our understanding of the history of food and the culture of consumption. 'Food and eating habits and preferences are not simply matters of "fuelling" ourselves', she writes.[17] This was true of opium, since smoking did not fill one's stomach. 'Food is inextricably

interlinked with group membership as well as kinship', Lupton continues, and again, opium is a good example where friends and family gathered to share leisure through smoking. Food is 'the ultimate "consumable"
commodity'; so was opium.[18] George Ritzer has identified 'McDonaldization', a process whereby corporations cater to the 'lowest common denominator' of mass consumer culture.[19] The same happened with opium in the
late Qing, when smoking catered for the lowest Chinese common denominator – coolie labourers and peasants. Peter Atkins and Ian Bowler have
summarised recent trends in food studies. Where functionalists emphasise 'the utilitarian nature of food', structuralists focus on the 'broader and
deeper causes and meanings of food habits' and on how 'taste is culturally shaped and socially controlled'.[20] Opium smoking was utilitarian in
nature, but it was also socio-culturally conditioned. Structural functionalists such as Mary Douglas draw upon elements of both approaches. Douglas
has deciphered the grammar of the meal, a structured social event. I will
decode the syntax of opium smoking by 'mov[ing] away from a reliance
upon the production-oriented explanations of society, which [have] for so
long dominated materialism, towards a framework that can accommodate
considerations of consumption and lifestyle'.[21] This is pertinent to the study
of opium as a commodity and smoking as history of food and culture of
consumption.

The above-mentioned 'three robes' speak to sources, and they matter a
great deal in the study of opium. Many of those who wrote about opium
used sources provided by the court or government. These works were prohibitionist in nature and were the products of political redefinition. This
is essentially the same problem of which Brennan complained when writing about public drinking and popular culture in eighteenth-century Paris:
'information on the lives of the common people has always come from an
external and socially superior perspective. In this way the opinions of elite
observers have shaped historical accounts for generations by providing the
most accessible and coherent evidence.'[22] Seen through such eyes, the popular culture of public drinking was 'a major contribution to, and expression
of' the degraded nature of the lower classes, and the tavern was 'a symbol
of misery and debauchery'.[23] The perception of opium suffered the same
fate in the nineteenth century. Historians who used prohibitionist sources
provided by the government unwillingly, or willingly, perpetuated the prejudiced official line in their condemnation of opium. However, scholars
and officials themselves have cautioned us about the prejudice of official
histories: 'the sources of a historian are three: official history, family history
and unofficial history'.[24] Older generations of sinologists also warned about

the problem: 'Chinese history was written by bureaucrats for bureaucrats'.[25] This helps to explain why official history has a 'solemn ethical function, the duty of expressing "praise and blame"'.

Enlightened by such insights, I dived into the ocean of unofficial histories and unconventional sources, such as *biji* or *zaji*, that is, notes, jottings or miscellaneous and pornographic books. The more of these works I read, the more I found out about who smoked opium and under what circumstances. *Libianxian Zhiyan,* for example, revealed that opium was 'becoming a hobby among both the high and the low in the officialdom' in the middle of Jiaqing. Scholars and officials were opium's vanguard consumers; yet they condemned smoking in the 1830s when consumption needed a political definition. *Yin shu* or pornographic books are the most helpful; *huafanglu,* for example, is dedicated to the sex industry. These books expose the circumstances under which men and women smoked opium and how opium accompanied by sex has helped to galvanise the industry ever since the mid-Qing. The books demonstrate the value of unconventional sources and speak to the truth that unofficial histories complement official histories. Not only did I enjoy these delicious books, I also found more than enough material for my work, identified future research projects and learned to swim in the ocean of Chinese sources. Other helpful sources are the dinner and wedding menus of the late Qing–early Republican era, when entertainment included and was highlighted by opium smoking.

This book follows opium's journey from its birth as a recreational item to its old age as a social icon. The chapters that follow examine each social strata that have used opium and/or the circumstances under which they succumbed to it. From luxury to necessity, opium consumption went through many phases, from first introduction to its transformation in the fifteenth century; its popularisation in the eighteenth century; its urbanisation from 1800 to 1860; complete socialisation from 1861 to 1911; and its final decline in the twentieth century.

Chapter 1 traces the social life of opium back to the Ming dynasty, when opium was transformed from a medicine to a luxury item. The vassal states presented opium as a tribute to the Ming court, and it became an aphrodisiac for emperors and their leading consorts. This medicine-to-aphrodisiac transformation would survive the destruction of the Ming. Chapter 2 focuses on the seventeenth century. The empire changed hands, and tobacco smoking was naturalised. Here I situate opium in the larger context of its sister cultures – tobacco and snuff, and the four cultures of consumption, tea, cuisine, utensils and herbs. Just as the Ming's economy, culture and society helped the absorption of tobacco and smoking, the above-mentioned cultures of consumption provided the best soil from which opium was to grow. Chapter 3 studies the eighteenth century. Opium arrived in China via two routes: one as tribute; the other by way of sojourners of south-east Asia and participants of the Taiwan conquest. Opium was a natural addition to the Qing's economy, culture and society. In addition, high-ranking literati and officials helped imbed it into mainstream sex recreation. Chapter 4 examines the short reign of Jiaqing (1799–1819). Opium made its way to the interior with the help of compradors and corrupt officials. Meanwhile, smoking spread from princes to eunuchs. Jiaqing's reign saw opium permeate the literati and official establishments, its popularity and availability increasing.

Chapter 5 is devoted to the first half of Daoguang's reign (1820–50). Literati-artistic elite and officials exemplified opium smoking in the taste-making and trendsetting urban centres. They spread the gospel of opium, while smoking made its way from the top down to the middle and lower classes. Chapter 6 discusses the political redefinition of opium consumption on the eve of the first Opium War (1839–42). When men of letters smoked, opium was cultured; when the poor began to inhale, opium became a social problem. It led to prohibition and war. It also brought along a political discourse that continues to this day. China lost the war to Britain because she had already lost the war to opium. Chapter 7 centres on the 1840s and 1850s. These crucial interwar years saw the second Opium War (1856–60); they also saw a proliferation of smuggling, domestic cultivation and consumption. When wars were fought, opium led an enduring social life. Smoking facilities stood side by side with rice stores and tea houses in 1860. Like rice and tea, opium had become a Chinese necessity. Chapter 8 is dedicated to women and their lives with opium. Opium continued to live on as an aphrodisiac and galvanised the sex recreation industry in the late Qing and beyond. It helped the rich to escape boredom; it helped the poor to make a living. It generated jobs for women, but it also intensified their subjugation.

Chapter 9 dwells on opium-generated literature, be it praise, condemnation or narrative. 'Language is of critical importance in cultural transmission', Evelyn Rawski said; opium allows us to see this importance and the mechanisms of culture transmission.[26] Literature demonstrated opium's popularity and further instilled it into the Chinese psyche. Chapter 10 looks at the half-century after 1860. Opium consumption was completely socialised, as coolies depended on it to function and politicians used it to finance modernisation. It continued to sicken China; it also helped regenerate the Chinese economy, its culture and society as millions, from the

Empress Dowager to the ordinary man and woman, enjoyed it. Chapter 11 studies the cult and culture of opium in the late Qing–Republican era, when consumption became a refined popular and material culture. Opium was so chic and à la mode that it brought strangers together and entertained friends and family alike. It became a norm of social contact and exchange. Many individuals and households identified themselves with opium. Indeed, it ultimately identified the Chinese nation on the international stage. Chapter 12 focuses on the twentieth century, when opium became a political economy, as warlords, Nationalists, Communists and the Japanese battled it out for China. Whoever controlled opium could control China. What is more, opium's modern derivatives have come back to haunt China in the 1990s.

From aphrodisiac to material culture, from social identity to political economy, opium lived a colourful social life and played an even larger role in the theatre of modern China. This book tells the story of opium, and in so doing also addresses several 'black holes' in the study of China. First, opium is the history of an aphrodisiac and sex recreation. Although many have studied prostitution, opium widens our view of the Chinese 'art of sex'. Second, opium exposes mechanisms of culture transmission. From south-east Asia to China, western Europe and North America, opium spread in the same fashion. This kind of cross-language, cross-class and cross-continent culture transmission calls for more studies. Third, historians have ignored the inland march of opium. This book exposes opium's transportation to and distribution within the interior. Fourth, in their effort to assess the complexity of the Ming–Qing economy, historians have failed to study the important consumer trend *yanghuo re*, the craving for foreign stuff. Sandalwood, birds nests and singsongs came from or via south-east Asia, as would opium. Historians have also ignored *yanghuo*'s vanguard consumers – the court, the literati and the officials. They spread the gospel of *yanghuo* and helped to create the demand for opium. Fifth, many historians have fallen victim to official histories and perpetuated the fallacy that opium was a vice that 'enlightened Chinese wished to stamp out'.[27] This was the political redefinition of opium consumption.

Sixth, the circumstances under which women succumbed to opium varied dramatically. We must not generalise Chinese women; the story of opium exemplifies this assertion. Seventh, many have emphasised the devastating effect of opium in the late Qing, but few have seen that it was also a consumer, material and popular culture. Opium destroyed some, entertained many and delivered many more from their stresses and strains. A final 'black hole' concerns the Communists. Chen Yongfa believes that they cultivated opium in Yan'an in order to survive the economic crisis. I will argue that they were indeed one of the 'opium regimes'. 'Economic growth during the Ming-Qing could not have been significant if it did not produce a discernible impact on the lives of ordinary people.'[28] Opium enables us to see this discernible impact on the lives of ordinary Chinese. China's political and genealogical intimacy with south-east Asia facilitated the introduction of smoking and opium. It would not have thrived without the cash-cropping market town economy and indigenous cultures of consumption. The Chinese assimilated and redefined a foreign way of leisure, embedded it into their general relaxation and sex recreation. Opium smoking could not have come to a better place at a more opportune moment; it was a welcome addition to the Ming–Qing–Republican economy, culture and society. Opium's sinicisation took both exogenous and endogenous forces; the dynamics can be seen when these two forces met. Chinese historians will rise above the China-centred paradigm. *The Social Life of Opium in China* is a beginning.

CHAPTER I

'The art of alchemists, sex and court ladies'

This chapter follows the early life of opium, from 1483 up until the end of the Ming dynasty and the start of the Qing dynasty. In July 1405 a fleet of sixty-three treasure ships with more than 27,870 crew members and 255 smaller vessels left the port of Nanjing under the helmsmanship of the eunuch-admiral Zheng He. This was the third year of the Yongle emperor's reign (1403–24), and the trip was the first of seven epic expeditions Zheng would make with 317 ships between 1405 and 1433. The fleet called on many ports in the South China Sea and the Indian Ocean, from Surabaja and Chittagong to Calicut, from Hormuz and Jidda to Mombasa. In 1418 Zheng moored off the coast of Malindi with junks full of porcelain, silk, lacquer-ware and other fine art objects to trade for the things China prized: ivory, rhinoceros horn, tortoiseshell, medicines and precious stones. It was eighty years before Vasco da Gama would round the Cape of Good Hope. Zheng and his fleet were goodwill ambassadors of the Ming dynasty. The expeditions projected China as the benevolent Celestial Empire; they reinforced the role of the Middle Kingdom and strengthened China's ties with south, south-east Asia and the world beyond. The ties that were created were both political and genealogical, maintained by tribute when tribute was diplomacy and by coastal people when seafaring was a way of life. They would facilitate the introduction of new world produce, the peanut and tobacco for example, and would change the course of China. Old vassal states would continue to pay tribute to the Chinese empire, while new ones would be enlisted and would learn the ritual. Zheng's expeditions were important in the social life of opium, because when states selected the best indigenous produce to present as tributes to please the mighty Chinese emperor, a few would present opium.

CHENGHUA GUIMAO

This chapter traces opium's transformation from medicine to aphrodisiac in the late 1400s. Early Ming's rehabilitation allowed growth and spending, while peace and stability encouraged the redefinition of culture and tradition. What followed were a socio-economic transformation and a leisure revolution. Mid-Ming subjects welcomed, searched for and above all experimented with new ways of recreation. It was certainly natural that the mid-Ming court should lead this consumer revolution:

> Several overseas countries and *Xiyu* produce a medicine called *hepurong*; it is what we call *yapian* in Chinese. It looks like myrrha; it is dark yellow, soft and sticky like ox glue. It tastes bitter, produces excessive heat and is poisonous. It is mainly used to aid masculinity, strengthen sperm and regain vigour. It enhances the art of alchemists, sex and court ladies. Frequent use helps to cure the chronic diarrhoea that causes the loss of energy. Often less than three doses are enough. Overdoses will result in malignant boils, swelling and hard skin ulcers; it also helps with heat-related illness . . . During the year *Chenghua guimao*, Zhongguan Zhonggui were ordered to go to Hainan, Fujian, Zhejiang, Sichuan and Shaanxi where it is close to *Xiyu* to procure it. Its price equals that of gold.[1]

This excerpt from *Yingjing Juan* marks opium's initial medicine-to-aphrodisiac ('the art of alchemists, sex and court ladies') transformation. *Zhongguan* and *Zhongguanzhong* had been general terms for eunuchs; *Zhonggui* could be the official name, a combination of official title and family name of a eunuch. *Chenghua guimao* is the Chenghua emperor's nineteenth year, 1483 in the western calendar; *Xiyu* refers to the western part of China and inner Asia. Opium had been cultivated and used as a medicine since the Tang dynasty. Yong Tao, a scholar-official and native of Sichuan province, mentioned it in one of his poems: 'Pass dangerous brackets and surface to the loose slope, traverse all the plains and rivers as if I were already home. The sadness of a ten thousand-mile guest disappears today, the *minang* flower emerges in front of my horse.'[2] The sight of the opium or *minang* flowers assured Yong that he was approaching his home town. Guo Zhen, another Tang scholar-official who served in Sichuan, also wrote about the beauty of the *minang* flower. Su Shi, scholar-official of the Song dynasty and native of Sichuan, wrote about the common use of opium as a medicinal herb: 'Daoists often persuade you to drink the *jisu* water, but even a child can prepare the *yingsu* soup.'[3] *Yingsu* was another Chinese name for opium. *Jisu* or *Stachys baicalensis* was boiled and sold by the bowl on the roadside to passers-by to help prevent such acute afflictions as sunstroke in the hot summer. It was easier to prepare opium, even a child could do it.

This demonstrates how widely opium was used as a medicine and how easy it was to turn it into a decoction. Opium made medicinal history by combatting diarrhoea, dysentery, sunstroke, coughing, asthma, pains and other ailments at a time when people depended on herbal medicine for relief and even nutrition. Opium use was still medicinal in the Yuan dynasty. Li Gao (1180–1251), the 'magic doctor', stipulated clearly in his masterpiece *Shiwu Bencao* that opium was most effective for diarrhoea; so did Wei Yilin (1277–1347) in his landmark work *Shiyi Dexiaofang. Huihui Yaofang*, the Islamic pharmacopoeia translated into Chinese during the Yuan dynasty, gave evidence that opium was introduced as a medicine. Opium continued to be discussed and prescribed as a medicinal herb by later generations of physicians and herbalists, such as Xu Yongchen (d. 1380), Lan Mao (1397–1476) and Chen Jiamo (1486–1570).

Opium was undoubtedly no longer just a medicinal herb by 1483. From being an effective drug for diarrhoea, sunstroke and various aches and pains to becoming 'the art of alchemists, sex and court ladies', opium had transformed from *yao*, that is medicine, to *chun yao* in the dictionary of the Ming court. *Chun yao*, literally 'spring drug' or aphrodisiac, was medicine that helped to induce sexual desire, vitalise intercourse and control ejaculation or emission; the term 'spring drug' or 'spring formula' was used to symbolise lust and regeneration. The 'drug' could be administered as powder, pellets or syrup, and could be mixed with food and drink. The ability to control, according to Taoist philosophy and Chinese sexology, is the perfection of the art of sex. Joseph Needham's understanding was precise: 'The art of commerce with women is to close the hands tightly and to refrain from ejaculation, causing the sperm to return and nourish the brain.'[4] This was an art; it was also a science that attracted Taoists, herbalists and an enterprise that galvanised eunuchs and court officials. How opium could help to better the 'art of commerce with women' was not clear at this point; it would take decades of research and development. What was clear, however, was that opium had assumed a new role by 1483 if not earlier. What, then, were the circumstances under which eunuchs were sent out to procure opium? Was it the Ming court, if not the Son of Heaven himself, that gave the order? Who were the 'alchemists' and 'court ladies' in 1483?

The year 1483 sits in the middle of the Ming dynasty and would have been a 'year of no significance' if it were not for 'the art of alchemists, sex and court ladies'.[5] To outsiders China may have looked majestic, but internally the court was laden with sex scandals. The Chenghua emperor, who was on the throne, was devoted to a senior consort, Lady Wan. Wan had begun her imperial career as his nursemaid. At age 35, when the 18-year-old heir apparent ascended the throne, she became his senior consort. She bore him his first son; the infant was declared heir immediately but died within a year. Wan exhausted everything possible in her attempts to boost her appeal in competition with the hundreds of court women at Chenghua's disposal. The *History of Ming* commented thus on her endeavours: 'exquisite techniques and lascivious skills, ancestral hall prayers and palace observations, extravagant spending were countless'.[6] Wan was never to conceive again, however. Meantime, there was true concern about Chenghua's ability to produce an heir. Chenghua himself lamented so in 1476; so did his ranking officials and eunuchs. It was perhaps because of this that the emperor developed a passion for folk recipes. He collected them and on occasion even prescribed to some of his high-ranking officials. He liked herbalists and alchemists, especially those with secret formulas, and promoted them. *The Veritable Record of the Ming Xianzong Emperor* listed promotions to *Yu yiyuan*, the imperial hospital, and to the rank of *Yu yi*, imperial physician. No other emperor of the Ming dynasty had made so many such promotions.

Chenghua was often presented with 'sex manuals and works of pornography', as Frederick Mote reported.[7] Was this to 'aid masculinity, strengthen sperm, and regain vigour' or to enhance 'the art of commerce with women'? Shen Defu knew part of the story:

The corrupt habits of our dynasty's scholar-officials: *Zhengtong's* reign [1436–49] was steeped in licentiousness and *Chenghua's* reign [1465–87] was soaked in decadence . . . In Xianzong's [Chenghua] reign with Wan An and Lady Wan in the court, the habits were rotten to the core. Wan presented *mei yao* [another name for *chunyao*] to the Emperor and the Imperial Censor Ni Jinxian presented *yao* [abbreviation of *chunyao*] to Wan. The Capital Censor Li Shi and the Supervising Censor Zhang Shan passed on secret sex formulas and they both got their old jobs back.[8]

Such examples were many during the reign of Chenghua. Wan An was a *jinshi* (the highest of the three examinations in imperial China, equivalent to today's Ph.D.) of 1448; he took much advantage of the fact that he and Lady Wan shared the family name, and labelled himself 'your humble nephew'. He knew how to please Lady Wan, and rose to be a Grand Secretary. He purposely sorted out and promoted those who had *chun fang* or 'spring formulas'; the above-mentioned Ni Jinxian was only one of many. Among the most notorious were Wang Jing and Wang Chen, who were among those who were sent out in 1483. Wang Qi (1433–99) called Wang

Chen a 'sorcerer' and detailed the latter's extortion activities in Jiangnan. Other literati and officials of the period, especially those who worked in the capital and who had access to the court, wrote about the corruption in their memoirs. Yin Zhi (1427–1511), Chenghua's Minister of War and Junior Guardian to the Heir Apparent, was one of them. So were Lu Rong (1436–1494), Zhu Yunming (1460–1526), and a bit later Huang Zuo (1490–1566), Zheng Xiao (1499–1566), He Liangjun (1506–73), Li Rihua (1565–1635) and Cha Jizuo (1601–76). These memoirs confirm that eunuchs and officials were dispatched to source substances for making aphrodisiacs. They also reveal that Chenghua's private circumstances had become the 'ladder of success' for those who were ambitious.

Upon Chenghua's death reform-minded officials wrote to the new emperor Hongzhi, son of Chenghua, about the evils of the 'alchemists'. They detailed the wrongdoings of many eunuchs and officials, and asked for their removal. The report from Investigating Censor Xie Binzhong was to the point: 'The door of sycophant was wide open. Eunuchs and corrupt officials obtained appointments with unusual prescriptions, exotic practices, or pornographic instruments, paintings and calligraphy.'[9] The new emperor himself discovered many sex manuals and works of pornography that Chenghua had collected. He used them as evidence to rid himself of his father's ministers, especially Wan An. Hongzhi realised that his late father was not just an amateur alchemist, he had built up a battalion of 'imperial physicians' who were devoted to the research and development of such things as 'golden panaceas' and 'secret *yao* formulas'. However, it appeared that some of the panaceas and formulas had worked. Since Chenghua's fourteenth year (1479) court ladies had produced almost one boy every year. Hongzhi himself might have been a product of these drugs. The *History of Ming* openly discussed this: 'When Xiaozong (Hongzhi's temple name) was born, one part of his head did not have hair. Some say it was the effect of those drugs.'[10] Yet, Hongzhi did away with his father's officials and eunuchs. Many placed high hopes on the 18-year-old emperor. However, he reigned only seventeen years and died at age 35.

Mei yao and *yao*, in the extract above, were enigmatic abbreviations for *chun yao*. In China the making of *chun yao* had long been part of a much larger and richer tradition, an ancient science called *fangzhong shu*, 'the art of the bed chamber' or 'the art of sex'. Only a handful of scholars have ventured into this field: Robert Hans van Gulick worked on Chinese sex life; Joseph Needham studied the contribution of Taoist principles; while Ruan Fangfu, Liu Dalin and Li Jianmin have begun to systematically tackle sexology. Ruan maintains that China possesses the oldest sex literature, with such canons as *He Yin Yang* (Methods of Intercourse between Yin and Yang) and *Sunu Jing* (Bible of the Immaculate Girl) appearing before 168 BC. Later masterpieces (pre-AD 618) include *Yufang Mijue* (Secret Instructions of the Jade Chamber) and *Dong Xuanzi* (Book of the Mystery Penetrating Master). The study of *fangzhong shu* flourished during the Han and Tang dynasties, from 206 BC to AD 618. It split into two branches after this time: *fangzhong shu*, the original science that emphasised the art of sex and the prevention of disease; and *yunu shu*, 'the art of court ladies'. The study and research of *fangzhong shu* declined after the Song dynasty, when fascination and effort shifted to aphrodisiacs and the 'art of commerce with women'. The transformation of opium gives evidence to this shift.

The 'art of commerce with women' flourished during the Ming, as *Jinpin Mei*, *Roupu Tuan* and *Zhulin Yeshi* testify. Gulick believed that 'during the Ming dynasty the flowering of arts and letters, together with the phenomenal development of material culture, brought into being a refined art of living', one of which was 'the art of sex'.[11] He showed that there was a great demand for 'erotic literature' and that the printing of pornographic literature flourished. What marked the Ming period was the fact that officials and eunuchs, and not just Taoists and herbalists, joined this enterprise. The eunuch bureaucracy began to grow in Chenghua's reign and reached 'seventy thousand' by the end of the Ming.[12] Officials and eunuchs served the emperors and the court ladies, many pleasing them for their own ends. Novelties and aphrodisiacs were often presented. Some eunuchs gained so much power that 'of all the civil and military ministers of our dynasty, five out of ten would kneel when they see Wang Zheng, three out of ten for Wang Zhi and eight out of ten for Liu Jin'.[13] Eunuchs and officials made up the largest army of 'alchemists' in the mid-Ming. Frederick Mote pointed out that only five of the sixteen Ming emperors passed their fortieth birthdays; they either died young or suddenly. Could the 'spring formulas' to which they were addicted have shortened their well-cared-for imperial lives?

THE BOY EMPEROR

By 1483 opium was no longer a simple herb that even a child knew how to boil into a decoction for sunstroke. A more elaborate testament to opium as a court luxury can be found in the 1587 edition of *Da Ming Huidian* or *The Collected Statutes of the Great Ming*.

The country of Siam borders on the sea . . . In Hongwu's fourth year [1371] its King sent a tribute mission with a gold-plated letter and indigenous produces to celebrate lunar New Year. In the sixth year, he sent a mission again with a map of the country. In Yongle's first year [1403], the King sent another mission and it was decided that they would send missions every three years by way of Guangdong. In Wanli's seventh year [1584], they sent another mission with a gold-plated letter. The tribute items were: elephants, elephant teeth, rhinoceros horn, peacock tail feather . . . frankincense, tree fragrance, aucklandia root, *wu xiang* [black fragrance or opium], cloves . . . pepper . . .

The country of Java borders on the sea . . . In Hongwu's fifth year [1372] its King sent a tribute mission with a gold-plated letter and indigenous produce. In the fourteenth year, another mission was sent. In Yongle's second year [1404], its King sent a tribute mission. In Zhengtong's eighth year [1443], it was decided that they send tribute mission every three years. Since then, they came many times. Their tribute items have included: turkey, parrot, peacock, peacock tail feathers . . . rhinoceros horn, elephant teeth . . . sandalwood . . . *wu xiang* [black fragrance or opium] . . . myrrha . . . and pepper.

The country of Bengali is [in] east India. In Yongle's sixth year [1408], the King himself led a tribute mission. In the twelfth year [1414], the King sent a mission. In Zhengtong's third year [1438] its tribute mission came with a gold-plated letter. Their tribute items have included: horse, saddle . . . cloth, cotton . . . oriole . . . *wu xiang* [black fragrance or opium] . . . pepper . . .[14]

Opium was labelled *wu xiang* or 'black fragrance' by the editors of *Da Ming Huidian*, as Yu Zhengxie, a Qing court historiographer, decoded.[15] Indeed, many of the herbs and/or plants that were presented were called 'fragrance'. For example, benzoin (*Istyrax benzoin*) was called *anxi xiang*, sandalwood (*Santalum album*) *tan xiang*, and musk (*Chelonopsis moschata*) *she xiang*. The history of 'fragrance' is a specialised topic, and Lin Tien-wei is one of a very few historians who appear to have studied it. Lin believed that the fragrance trade flourished during the Song dynasty. One of the important books about fragrance, *Xiang Pu* or *Book of Fragrance*, was written during the Song. *Xiang* was both an imperial monopoly and a luxury, and vassal states competed to present the best and most exotic fragrances to China. Fragrances had many functions. Some were used to make beauty products, some were combined with foods, some used for air fragrance and pest control, some used in rituals, and some used to make medicines, including aphrodisiacs. As *Xiang Chen* or *History of Fragrance* written in the late Ming demonstrated, the commerce and culture of fragrance flourished during the Ming. *Wu xiang* demonstrated how the Ming court either perceived or how it was introduced to foreign opium. But were Ming court officials aware that this was a herb that could be found in at least Sichuan?

Was *wu xiang* deliberately coined to describe the transformed exotic opium? 'Fragrance' was attributed to opium. This affirmed the luxury status and feminine, if not explicitly sexual, facet of opium. It is a testimony to the changing nature of the substance. The commerce, culture and consumption of fragrance demand independent study.

What *Da Ming Huidian* did not specify clearly was the year and the quantities involved in each tribute mission. Yu Zhengxie had access to and read many Ming documents relating to maritime trade and diplomacy; his *Guisi Leigao* sheds light on the quantity of some tribute items presented. He remembered a gold-plated letter from the King of Siam to the Ming emperor; the Siamese mission asked to trade with China and desired twenty bolts of red and green yarn, and red and navy silk for this trip. To the Ming emperor, the Siamese presented 'tree fragrance 2000 *jin* and opium 200 *jin* [100 kilograms or 220.46 pounds]'. To the empress, they presented 'tree fragrance 1000 *jin* and opium 100 *jin* [50 kilograms or 110.23 pounds]'.[16] One hundred and fifty kilograms of opium in a single mission; this is indeed revealing. Yu did not remember the year of the mission. But neither the year of a mission nor the quantity of a tribute item are the most important insight we can gain from these sources. *Yinjing Juan*, *Da Ming Huidian* and *Guisi Leigao* all testify to the changing role of opium in mid-Ming. Although the date is uncertain for Bengal, and somewhat unclear with Java in 1443, the case for Siam is definite – 1584, the twelfth year of the Wanli emperor. This has at least put the case of Wanli into perspective, as we move towards the late sixteenth century.

Tribute items were the best and most exotic indigenous produce and products that were novel enough, and more than just worthy, to offer to an empire such as China. Vassal states tried to please the Chinese empire with their own luxuries. This was tribute; it was also diplomacy – keeping the barbarians under control. The Son of Heaven, his army of consorts and the extended royal family were the chief beneficiaries. The champion of them all was Zhu Yijun, the boy emperor who came to the throne at the age of 9 in 1573 and reigned under the title of Wanli until 1619. *The Veritable Record of the Ming Shenzong Emperor* shows that he often cancelled official functions and pre-scheduled audiences. He explained to his cabinet ministers in his seventeenth year: 'Your sovereign failed to keep audience last time because for almost nine *xun* [three months] now, the dizziness has not stopped and the internal heat of the two meridians of heart and liver has not been reduced.'[17] This was not all. He continued: 'I have also suffered from sunstroke, eczema, diarrhoea and my body is weak. The Empress Dowager is disturbed and has repeatedly told me to concentrate on recuperating in seclusion.' It seems strange that a superbly cared-for royal who never lifted a finger and who seldom stepped outside the Forbidden City should suffer all these commoner's diseases.

Wanli's dizziness and anxiety have fascinated historians and popular writers for over four hundred years. He began to complain about this incurable illness from his fourteenth year – a year after Siam presented 150 kilograms of opium, as *Da Ming Huidian* stipulated. This illness would stay with him for the rest of his life, despite intensive care and extensive treatment. Ray Huang's book describes Wanli's reign in his fifteenth year, while Carrington Goodrich and Fang Chaoying point out: 'after the eighth month of 1589 he ceased appearing at general audiences entirely for more than twenty-five years – until the fifth month of 1615'.[18] It was well known that Wanli favoured, like his predecessor Chenghua, a senior consort – Lady Zheng – and that he indulged in alcohol and *chunyao*. The fascination with Wanli centres around the true reason behind his long absence and the substance of the *chunyao*, which is, whether they included opium. Lei Jin carried on the debate about Wanli and opium in the late Qing–early Republican era. He wrote in *Rongchen Xianhua* or *Gossips from the City of Opium* that 'Ming Shenzong reigned for no more than thirty years. He did not summon his ministers because of *this thing*.'[19] The debate was reopened with *Jindu Shijian* or *Historical Lessons of Prohibition* published in 1997 under the auspices of the Ministry of Public Security and prefaced by its Deputy Minister. It attempted to deliver a final verdict on the case of Wanli:

The statement that 'the Ming Shenzong reigned for no more than thirty years and he did not summon his ministers because of *this thing*' is not empty language at all. *Dingling*'s underground palace [Wanli's burial ground] was excavated in 1958 and after laboratory tests, we found that the bones of Zhu Yijun [Wanli's common name] contained large quantities of *ma fei* [what we now know as morphine]. Occasional consumption of opium would not have such effects. This proves that he was an addict who often ate opium. If an emperor was like this, princes, dukes and ministers, relatives, eunuchs and officials must have been infected as well. The court contracted its evil first. No wonder during the reign of Chenghua, the Ming court sent out its eunuchs to so many places to buy opium.[20]

This revelation has put the case of Wanli in clear perspective. The Communist government opened the magnificent *Dingling*, Wanli's underground burial palace, and made laboratory tests on Wanli's bones to find out, among other things, whether he used opium. This was an extraordinary political undertaking, even if it was justified by other non-political motives. The discovery of what we now know as morphine in his bones, from a scientific perspective, does indicate that Wanli must have used large quantities of opium. This reminds us of the 150 kilograms of opium that Siam presented to his court in 1584. Yet this is just the tip of the iceberg of the puzzle; it does not reveal the way in which opium was consumed. While the court of Chenghua sent out eunuchs to procure opium at the price of gold, vassal states presented opium to the court of Wanli. Opium was omnipresent in the Ming court from 1483 to the reign of Wanli. The debate about the Ming emperors' access to and consumption of opium continues. The official Communist source does not tell us exactly how opium, as an aphrodisiac or as part of a formula, was used in the Ming court. For these answers we need to turn to contemporary men and to works of medicinal science.

LI SHIZHEN AND DA JINDAN

Bencao Gangmu or *Compendium of Materia Medica*, a milestone of Chinese medical science written by Li Shizhen (1518–93) and first published in 1578 (Wanli's sixth year), discussed opium as an effective herbal medicine for diarrhoea. It continued: 'it can help control the essence of men; ordinary people use it for the art of sex. Beijing has golden panacea for sale.'[21] Li Shizhen appeared to have put opium's medicine-to-aphrodisiac transformation into context. Opium could help retain the 'essence of men' that might be lost through ejaculation and involuntary nocturnal emission. This indeed speaks to the 'art of commerce with women'. Li is considered the founding father of modern herbal medicine. Was he sharing his own knowledge or simply relaying with the peculiar mention of 'ordinary people' what he had read or heard? One of his contemporaries knew about this golden panacea, and he was more straightforward about his knowledge. Gao Lian, a man of letters and leisure, wrote much about life and leisure. In *Zunsheng Bajian* or *Eight Discourses on the Art of Living* he included opium in *Da jindan*, the 'Big golden panacea'. The ingredients were: 'bezoar, pearl, borneol, musk, rhinoceros horn, *Calculus canis*, antelope's horn, catechu, *Sanguia draconis*, cinnabar, opium, amber, *Corallium japonicum*, eagle wood, aucklandia root, white sandalwood and use gold-plated coating'.[22] For direction, Gao instructed: 'pound into powder, add human milk to make into pellets big as gordon euryale fruit, use gold powder to coat, take one at a time, time does not matter, use pear juice to swallow'.

Gao explained that his big golden panacea could help to treat phlegm accumulation in the lung, food regurgitation from stomach, apoplexy, deficiency of the seven emotions, malfunction affecting fertility, consumptive diseases and other ailments. This deficiency of the seven emotions included that which was caused by excess of sexual intercourse, which would result in the incessant or excessive loss of 'the essence of men', that is, sperm or body fluid. This would cause a deficiency that manifested in the depletion of sperm and involuntary nocturnal emission. Since the 'art of commerce with women' called for the ability to 'refrain from ejaculation' and control nocturnal emission, Taoists and herbalists worked hard to find formulas that would help arrest or reduce incessant and excessive loss of male essence. Opium had been experimented with since Chenghua's time. By Wanli's time a preliminary consensus seems to have been reached. Another contemporary also wrote about the golden panacea. Gong Tingxian, a court physician who came from a family of court physicians, included it in his masterpiece *Gujin Yijian*, printed in 1589. Gong claimed that his panacea could cure everything from apoplexy and toothache to sunstroke and athlete's foot, and excess of sexual intercourse. Opium appeared in formulas designed to better 'the art of sex' in the late sixteenth century. Li Shizhen, Gao Lian and Gong Tingxian helped to put a historical claim in to medicinal and scientific perspective. They have furthered our understanding of opium the aphrodisiac, and indeed, carried on the transformation of opium.

Li Shizhen marked the watershed in opium's transformative process. Herbalists and men of medicine before him had discussed and used opium as an effective herb for diarrhoea, among them Lan Mao (1397–1476) in *Diannan Bencao*, Wang Lun (1484 *jinshi*) in *Bencao Ji*, Teng Hong (sixteenth century) in *Shennong Benjing Huitong*, Liu Wentai in his 1505 *Bencao Pinghui Jinyao*, Xue Yi (1487–1559) in *Bencao Yueyan*, Chen Jiamo (1486–1570) in *Bencao Mengquan* and Li Ting (sixteenth century) in *Yixue Rumen*. Many herbalists and men of medicine of Li Shizhen's time and later, while still discussing opium as a medicine, also prescribed it for the art of sex, among them Miao Xiyong (1546–1627) in *Shennong Bencao Jingshu*, Li Zhongli (1598 *jinshi*) in *Bencao Yuanshi*, Li Zhongxin (1588–1655) in *Yizong Bidu*, Gu Yuanjiao (b. 1604) in *Bencao Huiqian* and especially Zhang Jingyue (1563–1640), a master of medicine and an authority on sexology. Zhang was comfortable prescribing formulas containing opium for the 'art of commerce with women' in his milestone work *Jingyue Quanshu*. Volume 59 is devoted to *Gu zhen*, literally 'Strengthening the battle array', since sex was a battle between men and women. He listed sixty-six formulas, seven of which contained opium and one of which is simply called *Yingsu wan*, the 'Opium pill'.[23] If the message was still implicit in the late sixteenth century, it was certainly explicit by the early seventeenth century. Wanli's reign was crucial in the continued transformation of opium.

Herbalists and men of medicine intensified their research and develop-ment of opium in the decades that followed, as the Chinese empire changed hands. They would be explicit about opium the aphrodisiac, which figured prominently in their works. Zhang Lu (1617–99) detailed his understanding in *Benjing Fengyuan*:

Beijing has golden panacea for sale. It is said it cures cold and everything. Take one *feng* of *afurong* [opium], mix it with polished round-grained rice [kernel of *Oryza sativa*] into 3 pellets. Take one at a time. Don't take too much. Avoid sour and things with vinegar, otherwise the bowels would hurt . . . It is rarely used today except in the art of sex, it is really the best when it comes to control nocturnal emission and enhance performance.[24]

So did Wang Ang (1615–99) in *Yifang Jijie*. Volume 17 is called *Shouse Zhiji*, 'Prescriptions for Arresting Secretion', and one of them was titled *Zhenren Yangzan Tang*, 'Decoction for Reinforcing Internal Organs':

Opium shell, no stem and honey-roasted, three *liang* (50 grams) six *qian* (5 grams),
Medicine terminalia fruit (kernel), roast in fresh cinders, one *liang* three *qian*,
Nutmeg (ripe seed), roast in fresh cinders, five *qian*,
Aucklandia root, two *liang* and four *qian*,
Bark of Chinese cassia tree, eight *qian*,
Ginseng,
Bighead atractylodes rhizome, roasted,
Chinese angelica root, six *qian*,
White peony root, roasted, one *liang* six *qian*,
Prepared licorice root, one *liang* eight *qian*.
Each dose is four *qian*.
Direction: decoct in water for oral administration.[25]

Wang Ang furthered the understanding of opium. He seemed to have written the perfect prescription for the Wanli emperor's incurable 'dizzi-ness'. The 'internal organ' here refers to the kidney. Chinese medical science believes that the kidney is where the male essence, the body fluid and sperm, is stored. Sexual excess leads to the loss of body fluid and sperm; it therefore depletes and/or exhausts the kidney. This would manifest in such condi-tions as spermatorrhea, prospermia, dizziness and tinnitus, the latter two of which Wanli had constantly complained. Medicinal history since the Tang dynasty had proved that opium could help astringe the intestines to arrest diarrhoea; this unique astringent function was now extended to the 'art of commerce with women', that is, to retain and replenish the male essence in the kidney, therefore buttressing the organ itself. This was indeed revolutionary and the keystone of opium's medicine-to-aphrodisiac metamorphosis. But the process was gradual. Opium's connotation was undoubtedly sexual in 1483. Gao Lian had worked on the arrest and reduction of incessant and excessive loss of male essence in the sixteenth century. By the mid-seventeenth century Wang Ang was experimenting on the kidney, where this essence rested. His replenishment or reinforcement formulas lead us back to Xu Boling's claim that opium could help 'aid masculinity, strengthen sperm and regain vigour'.

Men of letters, medicine and leisure continued to research and develop opium use during the Ming. Their works mark the trail of opium as it continued to transform and gradually become demystified in the centuries to come. It is worth mentioning here that Wang Ang kindly acknowledged that the original formula came from Luo Tianyi. Luo (1246–83) was a student of the magic doctor, Li Gao (1180–1251). Luo inherited not only Li's philosophy but also his works. Rewriting, that is, copying from others with modification, was extremely common in the profession. Many simply changed or replaced one or two herbs or dosages in order to lay claim to a prescription. Wang turned around Luo's formula, and put opium at the top. What really made it an 'art of sex' formula was the fact that Wang placed and discussed it in a volume called *Guse yao*, 'Astringents and Haemostatics', while Luo had originally discussed and used it in a chapter entitled *Shixie men*, 'How to Cure Diarrhoea'. From Li Gao and Luo Tianyi to Wang Ang, we therefore see the journey of opium from medicine to aphrodisiac in a few hundred years.

OPIUM MANIA

Parallels can be drawn between so-called 'garden mania' and the dramatic rise in the use of opium during the late Ming.[26] Chen Jiamo (1486–1570) remembered that 'It [opium] is everywhere. Many families grow it in the garden to appreciate its beauty.'[27] So did Xu Chunfu, a court physician in the late sixteenth century: 'Many gentlemen cultivate flowers in their gardens today. Many more mix it with medicinal plants. How convenient should [the] situation arise. The opium flower can help cure diarrhoea and sooth coughing.'[28] Could this have been part of what Craig Clunas called 'the fruitful garden' or 'the represented garden'? Xu knew about more than just the medicinal value of opium: 'Take fresh opium capsule, pound it, boil and filter it with clean water in a clay pot. Take the juice and further filter it with water until it is totally wrought. Throw away the residue. Use gentle flame to dry it until it becomes something like paste.'[29] Otherwise, one could buy opium at the marketplace. Gu Yuanjiao (b. 1604), a native practitioner in Jiangsu, saw that 'some of what is sold in the marketplace today even has calyxes in it'.[30] An opium mania seemed to have gripped the Jiangnan region. Some still used opium as a medicine; some appreciated its beauty; others might have experimented with domestic aphrodisiac making. Gu Zhong (1565–1628) even fashioned a new dish out of opium. He wrote in *Yang Xiaolu* or *The Little Book about Good Living* that one could take the poppy seeds and make them into something like soybean curd, which he called *yingsu fu*, 'the opium curd'. Would opium have ended up in Chinese dishes if tobacco smoking was never introduced?

Among the 'many gentlemen' who grew or mixed opium with other plants in their gardens were Gu Qiyuan (1565–1628), Yuan Hongdao (1568–1610), Qian Qianying (1582–1664), Wen Zhenheng (1574–1636) and Zhang Dai (1597–1685). These men represent some of the most accomplished and influential men of letters and officials in the late Ming and the Ming–Qing transitional period. Gao Shiqi (1642–1704) sang the seductive praise of opium:

Beyond all the pavilions of hillsides and riverbanks there grows the *yingsu* flower. There are scarlet and pink, dark and plain purple, pale pinkish grey and light yellow; pure white and light green. One branch has thousands of calyxes and they are clustered together like trimmed silk. Legend has it that in the evening of the mid-autumn festival, girls should wear beautiful clothes and sow the seeds, for the blossoms of next year will be so luxurious and dazzling that nothing else in the whole world can match them.[31]

Opium was glorified in the context of feminine beauty and attraction. It spoke the language of lust and regeneration. This reinforced its aphrodisiac myth. The leading literary figure Gao Shiqi, like the Song dynasty scholar Su Shi, used the word *yingsu* rather than *minang* or *hepurong* for opium. *Yingsu* seemed more classical. Gao was not only a gifted writer and calligrapher, but also personal secretary to the Kangxi emperor. His *Beishu Baowenglu* was a book dedicated to 222 meaningfully chosen and carefully cultivated plants in his garden in Hangzhou. Kangxi paid a visit to the secretary's famous and lavish garden. Opium quite literally blossomed with a generation of literati, officials and the rich in the Jiangnan region. Knowledge of the medicine-to-aphrodisiac transformation filtered from the Ming to the Qing and from the court to the national elite, and a few decades of unrest did nothing to interrupt the accumulation and spread of the knowledge. Indeed, dynastic change seems to have allowed certain things to survive and thrive in an unnoticed way. The opium flower blossomed in the gardens of the learned. Some, Fang Yizhi (1611–94) for example, carried on the research and development. He gave hands-on instruction: 'When it is a green bud, use a needle to prick it ten or so times. Its liquid will come out; store it in china and use paper to seal the top. Expose it for twenty-seven days; then it becomes opium. It can control nocturnal emission.'[32]

The art of alchemists, sex and court ladies points us to opium's initial transformation in 1483, if not earlier. The context of its new role was clear by 1578 with Li Shizhen. The medicine-to-aphrodisiac metamorphosis was opium's genesis of lust and luxury, it is what anthropologists call 'diversion', that is, the diversion of a commodity from a specified path.[33] Indeed, the story is a perfect example of 'diversion', that is, from a herbal medicine to an aphrodisiac. The interpretation of an object is 'open to individual manipulation to some degree'; Chenghua's ministers and eunuchs alike manipulated the interpretation of opium. They redefined its role and rewrote its history. Igor Kopytoff also believes that 'the diversion of commodities from specified paths is always a sign of creativity or crisis'. Opium allows us to see the 'crisis' in Chenghua's life and the 'creativity' in Wanli's reign. 'Diversion is frequently a function of irregular desires and the novel demands.' Opium allows us see these irregular desires and the novel demands of the emperors. All kinds of sources – court, official, unconventional and medicinal – testify to the changing role of opium from the mid-Ming. Generation by generation, men of letters, medicine and leisure have guided us in opium's transformation. 'There is not a wall that does not let through wind.' The change of empire did not change the course of opium. Opium the aphrodisiac, or opium's 'diversion from its customary path', would survive the destruction of the Ming empire and go on to thrive under a new and alien regime.

CHAPTER 2

As the empire changed hands

Timothy Brook writes in the *Cambridge History of China* that 'the experience of life in China changed remarkably over three centuries of Ming rule'.[1] One of the changes was tobacco smoking. I devote this chapter to tobacco smoking, snuff bottles and to the four cultures of consumption in the seventeenth century, in order to illustrate the type of soil from which opium was to grow. We cannot understand opium without contextualising it within the larger context of its sister cultures: tobacco and snuff bottles, and the consumer cultures of cuisine, herbs, utensils and tea. These cultures of consumption blossomed during the Ming and Qing, as peace and prosperity allowed time and space for the redefinition of life and culture, both high and low. By the seventeenth century Chinese people had turned the tradition of cuisine into a philosophy, the practice of herbs into a science, the use of utensils into an art and the consumption of tea into a religion. Although opium the aphrodisiac was a knowledge that was limited to the learned in the seventeenth century, tobacco smoking was universally popular. Introduced a century earlier, the practice had become a Chinese consumer culture. China had always been a melting pot and Chinese culture a constellation of identities. Foreign commodities and ways of recreation, such as tobacco smoking, had enriched the economy, culture and society. The commerce, consumption and culture of tobacco highlight the significance of the Ming's maritime trade, economic growth and consumer culture.

THE SOCIAL LIFE OF TOBACCO

Opium smoking would have taken a much longer time to germinate in China if it had not been for tobacco smoking. Scholars generally agree that tobacco was found during Columbus's discovery of America. From Spain and Portugal, it spread quickly to the rest of Europe and to their new possessions in Asia, the Philippines for example. Men of letters and science in the late Ming put the time of entry at the reigns of Wanli and Tianqu, between 1573 and 1627. Yao Lu believed that tobacco came from the Philippines during the reign of Wanli (1573–1619). Zhang Jingyue (1563–1640) wrote that 'Tobacco was never heard of since antiquity; since Wanli, it started in *Min* (Fujian province).'[2] Fang Yizhi (1611–94) also believed that it came to China during Wanli's time, whereas Yang Shizong remembered that tobacco smoking was becoming very popular during the reign of Tianqu, 1621–28. This seems logical, given the Portuguese and Spanish conquests in south-east Asia at the time. Nonetheless, the estimate seems conservative when compared with an archaeological discovery in Guangxi province in 1980. Here, excavation work uncovered three porcelain pipes and one hammer used to imprint the date of manufacture. Inlaid on the hammer was 'Made in the twenty-fourth day of the fourth month of Jiajing's twenty-eighth year', that is, 1550, three decades earlier than the above Ming writers claim.[3]

The year 1550 means that tobacco smoking had found its way to China within six decades of Columbus's discovery of America. The debate about the exact timing of entry goes on, as do studies of the route of entry. Several routes are indicated by key sources and researches. One is via the south-east, from the Philippines and Taiwan to Fujian. Another is the south-west, from India, Burma and Indochina to Yunnan, Guangxi and Guangdong. A third one is the north-east, from Japan and Korea to Manchuria. The first two routes are well documented. This seems natural, given the prominence of the two regions and their peoples in maritime and overland trade. Other products of the new world came to these two regions first. Ho Ping-ti has studied the introduction of three American food plants – the peanut, the sweet potato and maize. He points out that the peanut came 'in the early and second half of the sixteenth century', the sweet potato decades before '1594' and maize 'two or three decades before 1550'.[4] He also discusses their three routes of entry. His research and insight puts the cases of tobacco and opium into perspective.

Ho believes that the peanut was introduced into China 'by way of the sea' to the coastal provinces of Jiangsu, Zhejiang and Fujian. The port cities he mentions include Zhangzhou, Quanzhou, Ningpo and Shanghai. The case of the sweet potato is more complicated. The gazetteers of Changle and Zhangzhou, two major coastal cities in Fujian, both claimed that the sweet potato was first introduced into their localities. Changle's gazetteer even pinpointed the native resident who brought the sweet potato back from the Philippines. 'In addition to maritime introduction', Ho continues, 'there might have been an overland introduction from India and Burma.'

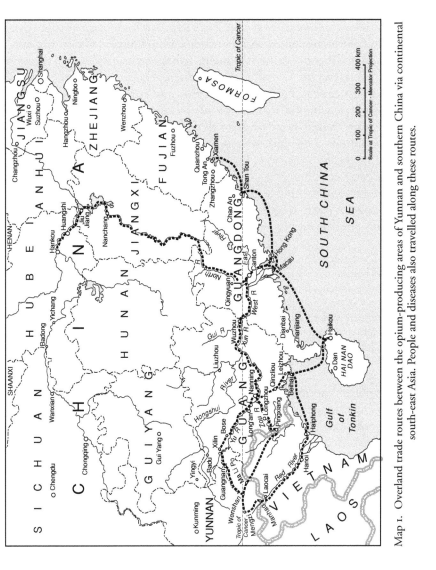

Map 1. Overland trade routes between the opium-producing areas of Yunnan and southern China via continental south-east Asia. People and diseases also travelled along these routes.

Dali, a prefecture in Yunnan close to Burma, recorded the sweet potato as a local product in the 1563 edition of its gazetteer; so did the provincial gazetteer in 1574. The case of maize is even more complicated, since the earliest reference to it appears in Henan. This central province was far from the south-east and south-west frontiers. Ho points to the various tribes that inhabited the mountainous regions running from southern Gansu and eastern Sichuan/Tibet to northern Yunnan. Tribesmen here often paid tributes to the Ming empire, travelling from western China through the central plains to the capital. Ho believes that this was 'fairly certain' because the early Chinese name for maize is *Yu mai*, 'Imperial wheat'. This overland tribute route should, however, not rule out a maritime introduction, as Ho Ping-ti cautions. The south-west and south-east frontiers saw the introduction of the peanut, the sweet potato, maize and tobacco; they would also see the entry of opium.

Introduced in the mid-sixteenth century, tobacco became 'the opiate of the people' in the mid-seventeenth century. Zeng Yuwang was fascinated with this phenomenon:

When I was thirty-six, I suffered the loss of my position. There had never been smokers before that time, only the Fujianese used it. Once in village Qin's *yamen* [local government office] headed by Wang Jiwei, I saw him smoke; I could not believe my eyes. Since Commander Li Chendun [anti-Qing] broke into the city gates, officers and soldiers all succumbed to it. It has extended to the common folks; eight out of ten is the proportion for the past twenty years. The son of Huang Junxian ate smoke in front of the salt-boiler at the south gate, he became tipsy and fell into the boiler; his body was decomposed instantly.[5]

The phrase 'eat smoke' here means the act of smoking, and the mention of 'Fujianese' reminds us of the south-east entry route. Zeng was a scholar-official who had lost his 'black gauze cap' with the fall of the Ming empire. He had returned to his home village of Qin, just outside of today's Shanghai. Years of absence had made Zeng fascinated with the local families he used to know and with things he had never seen or heard of before, such as tobacco smoking. The son of villager Huang was a salt worker, and salt making was a livelihood of the region. It generated a steady income, since salt was a government monopoly and an absolute necessity of the diet. Huang's family was middle class at best, but his son was not the only villager who could afford to smoke tobacco. People in the local government office smoked it; so had rebel officers, soldiers and eight out of ten 'common folk' for the past twenty years (the 1620s and 1630s). Tobacco smoking was not only common in the most populated stratum of the socio-economic hierarchy, it was also fully integrated into work and life. Ye Mengzhu shared not only Zeng's fate at the change of empire but also his fascination with local happenings. Ye knew the tobacco market well:

Tobacco originally came from Fujian. When I was small, I heard my grandfather say 'Fujian has tobacco; inhaling it can make one drunk. It is also called *baigan* [white spirit]; but we do not have it here.' During the time of Chongzhen [the last Ming emperor, 1628–44], someone from our town surnamed Peng got some seeds. He planted them right here, picked the leaves and dried them in the shade. Then he had someone, who specialised in this, to cut them into fine slices. He sold it to people from afar; but still the natives here never dared to taste it. Later prohibition orders came from above. The authority said that only bandits ate it to fight against cold and dampness; common folks were not allowed to grow it and merchants were not allowed to sell or buy it. Those who broke the rule would be charged with 'treason with barbarians'. Peng was the first to be reported and prosecuted. Cultivation was stamped out as a result. But by the beginning of Shunzhi [the first Qing emperor, 1644–61] everyone in the army used it. All of a sudden traders converged, cultivators multiplied, profits doubled.[6]

Since the end of the Ming tobacco cultivation had been quite profitable in Fujian and the Jiangnan region. Ye observed the production and price of tobacco, especially the fact that the price fell with the increase in local cultivation. The Ming's cash-cropping market town economy facilitated the cultivation and sale of tobacco and consequently the spread of smoking. Tobacco could not have come to a better place at a more opportune time. Profit-seeking farmers responded to a tobacco market that was expanding as fast as, if not even faster than, the actual practice of smoking. Local cultivation made local consumption cheap and nation-wide consumption possible. The late Ming scholar Yao Lu remembered: 'Today we have more than Lu-song [the Philippines], people take it [Fujian-grown tobacco] there to sell.'[7] From introduction to self-reliance and export, the naturalisation of tobacco in Fujian took less than a century. Not only was tobacco smoking naturalised, but it also laid the foundation for the entry of a sister product, as the pattern would repeat with opium in the south-east maritime and south-west overland trade regions in the nineteenth century.

The Manchus had been tobacco smokers before they entered China in 1644. This reinforces the north-east entry route theory. Emperor Taizong (1627–43) knew of the cultivation, sale and consumption of tobacco among his subjects in southern Manchuria. An edict of his sixth year (1632) stipulated that those engaged in its sale would be punished by death. He was so angry with an official who smoked tobacco that he personally laid out the details of the punishment. Evidence of tobacco as indigenous 'foodstuff' can be found in Manchu official histories and Chinese gazetteers by the late seventeenth century. Widespread cultivation and nation-wide participation in the recreation of smoking signalled the arrival of the tobacco-smoking culture of consumption and with it the unique *yan wenhua*, culture of smoke, which was modelled after and which thrived alongside *cha wenhua*, the culture of tea. Chen Cong was a child during the Ming–Qing transition. He saw the new consumer culture unravel in the early Qing, as he grew up: 'small tables were set out on the street side, with smoking sets and a bowl of water. Those who came to eat, after they finish inhaling, would rinse their mouth with the water, throw the money on the table and walk away.'[8] Chen also noticed that the price of a smoke was the same as the price of tea in tea houses and restaurants. Cheap, convenient and similar to a cup of tea taken over a break, a pipe of tobacco fitted in seamlessly with the daily lives of ordinary Chinese people. They had turned a foreign mode of recreation into a Chinese way of relaxation and a popular culture. The introduction and naturalisation of tobacco smoking demonstrates the capacity of the Ming–Qing economy to assimilate foreign products, and also the assimilating and redefining power of Chinese consumer culture and Chinese society at large. The social life of tobacco can be said to speak for the social life of opium.

'CHANGES OF DIET'

In less than a century Chinese people had naturalised tobacco smoking. Tobacco smoking and tobacco cultivation had become so visibly a part of Chinese life that both were now catching the eyes of European travellers. John Bell travelled from St Petersburg to Beijing in the 1710s. This is what he saw as he approached the capital:

> I saw also great plantations of tobacco, which they call *tharr*, and which yields very considerable profits; as it is universally used in smoking, by persons of all ranks, of both sexes, in China; and, besides, great quantities are sent to the Mongols, who prefer the Chinese manner of preparing it before every other. They make it into a gross powder, like sawdust, which they keep in a small bag, and fill their little brass-pipes out of it, without touching the tobacco with their fingers. The smoke is very mild, and had quite a different smell from ours. It is reported the Chinese have had the use of tobacco for many ages.[9]

Tobacco smoking was as Chinese as could be in the eyes of a European traveller, even though it was most likely introduced to China later than it was brought to Bell's British Isles. Tobacco smoking was quite popular in England in the late 1590s, as Paul Hentzner, a German traveller, observed:

At these spectacles (bull and bear whipping), and everywhere else, the English are constantly smoking tobacco; and in this manner – they have pipes on purpose made of clay, into the farther end of which they put the herb, so dry that it may be rubbed into powder, and putting fire to it, they draw the smoke into their mouths, which they puff out again through their nostrils like funnels, along with it plenty of phlegm and defluxion from the head. In these theatres, fruits, such as apples, pears and nuts, according to the season, are carried about to be sold, as well as ale and wine.[10]

Bell's and Hentzner's observations raise some interesting questions. Pipe smoking was popular in sixteenth-century England. It bred a culture and a cult of its own in the Dutch golden age, as Simon Schama has shown. Tobacco smoking was fashionable in western Europe and South Africa, in Java and Japan in the seventeenth and eighteenth centuries. However, nowhere did pipe smoking continue to develop and thrive in the same way as would opium in China. Why did pipe smoking die down in such places as Britain and Japan and yet continue to blossom in China in the centuries to come? What, in other words, was so unique about China that the Chinese alone continued their redefinition and indeed sinicisation of pipe smoking? The answer is multi-dimensional, complex and even controversial. From the perspectives of commodity and consumption, Sidney Mintz's work on sugar has set one standard for answering some of the questions. To understand the case of sugar and tea in Britain is to understand, at least theoretically, the case of tobacco and opium in China. Mintz discussed how 'a particular people become firmly habituated to a large, regular and dependable supply of sweetness'.[11] Sugar was prised as a luxury by the nobility and the wealthy when it was first introduced from the West Indies:

While king and archbishops were displaying magnificent sugar castles and mounted knights, the aspiring upper classes began to combine 'course paste' men-of-war with marzipan guns to achieve analogous social effects at their festive table. Some of these people were probably only newly ennobled; others were prosperous merchants or gentry. The techniques used to impress their guests and validate their status through consumption continued on a downward percolation.[12]

Sugar, at this stage of consumption, was the story of Pierre Bourdieu's 'taste' and 'distinction', and of Thorstein Veblen's 'conspicuous consumption'.[13] Bourdieu saw taste as a 'marker of class' and consumption as 'predisposed, consciously and deliberately or not, to fulfil a social function of legitimating social differences'.[14] This was obvious with sugar consumption in its early stage; it would be even more so with opium smoking in its early days. Sugar, in its later life, would become the story of class formation and politics, as Mintz argued. A cup of tea with sugar fitted in with the tempo of working-class life, because it was introduced just as work schedules quickened, the movement of people from rural to urban areas accelerated, and the diet of workers looked 'both calorically and nutritively inadequate and monotonous'.[15] Tobacco played the same role for Chinese working people in the seventeenth century and beyond, as would opium from the mid-nineteenth century onwards. From an upper-class luxury to a proletarian necessity, Mintz argued, the introduction and naturalisation of sugar went through two important phases: 'intensification' or 'ritualisation', and 'extensification'. The former is 'the incorporation and symbolic reinvestment of new materials', since 'ritual has to do with regularity' and 'a sense of fitness, rightness and validation'. The latter denotes the transformation of these new materials into 'something ordinary'. In China, tobacco had undergone 'extensification' as the empire changed hands, while opium was in its 'intensification' phase, as men of letters and medicine invented new symbols for it and invested it with new values.

Mintz built on the works of others: 'Culture must be understood "not simply as a product but also as production, not simply as socially constituted but also as socially constituting". One decodes the process of codification, and not merely the code itself.' Naturalisation, be it of tobacco, tea or sugar, is a process; we understand it by decoding the symbols and values attributed to the commodities and their consumption. Mintz emphasised that 'meanings – what the foods meant to people, and what people signalled by consuming them – were associated with social differences of all sorts, including those of age, gender, class, and occupation'. This applies to sugar, tea and tobacco as well as opium. The naturalisation of sugar and tea took the collective power of a people who, rich or poor, shared a language, culture and identity. So did tobacco smoking. As Wang Shizhen (1634–1711) marvelled, 'from the nobility and gentlemen down to slaves and women'.[16] This would be the same with opium. The naturalisation of tobacco in China is similar to Britain's indigenisation of sugar and tea. The British naturalised sugar 'over the course of less than two centuries'; so did the Chinese with tobacco and soon with opium. These commodities illustrate two larger issues: globalisation and indigenisation. The world was already global when the British drank tea and the Chinese smoked tobacco. It was, as John Lee called it, 'the age of global integration'.[17] 'I think it could be plausibly argued that changes of diet are more important than changes of dynasty or even of religion', George Orwell wrote in 1937. The story of tea and sugar in Britain and of tobacco and opium in China support this conviction. Daily life and ordinary behaviour reveal much about the history of food, culture and the politics of consumption.

Returning to tobacco and China, Chinese smokers redefined smoking; they also reinvented *yan qiang* or the 'smoking gun'. There were *han yan*, the long-stemmed pipe; *shui yan*, the water pipe; and *dou yan*, the short pipe. Affection for pipes was not distinctively Chinese. As Simon Schama has pointed out, Dutch smokers also refashioned the smoking pipe. Indeed, 'a subgenre of still life painting' was devoted to 'tobacco pieces', especially the pipe. The same was true of tea drinking, as sub-industries and an entire culture came to flourish in Europe, especially in Britain. It was also true of tobacco in China. Smoking inspired many literary works, and Chinese men and women, rich or poor, had their tobacco pipes with them as they posed for photographs (see illus. 1). But although tobacco smoking was prevalent among all classes of society in the late Ming, there were marked class differences when it came to the consumption of *yan*. Whilst tobacco was 'the opiate of the people' in the late seventeenth century, something called *bi yan*, 'nose smoke' or snuff bottles, swept the Qing court and high society. Wang Shizhen knew it well:

The smoke that the country of Lu-song [the Philippines] produces is originally called *danbagu* [tobacco], nicknamed golden-slice fragrance, which I have already detailed in [a] previous volume. Recently in the capital Beijing, some made it into a nose smoke. It is said that it could sharpen one's eyes and keeps disease at bay. It is stored in bottles made of glass. The shape of the bottle varies and so does its colour: red, purple, yellow, white, black and green, etc. They can be clear as crystal and red as fire; they are extremely exquisite and enjoyable. Use an ivory spoon, take it to your nose and smell it, and then put it back into the bottle. This is manufactured in the Inner Court. Common folks try to copy it but they can never achieve that.[18]

Wang was no ordinary observer of the cult phenomenon. Born into a powerful clan and a *jinshi* of 1658, he served both the Shunzhi and Kangxi emperors. What made him a historical figure was his literary talent. He was indisputably the leading poet of his day. Chinese literati and Qing nobles indulged in 'nose smoke' not only because it was regarded as an art form and the bottles themselves regarded as *objects d'art*, but also because it was elitist. Whilst the lower classes were satisfied with a few puffs of tobacco smoke in between their chores, men of letters and leisure derived poems out of the 'nose smoke'. Dubbed *yan*, tobacco was smoked and snuff bottles collected. It is important to understand this dual aspect, because opium consumption would be a combination of the two: it was both smoked

Illustration 1. Manchu ladies of the Qing Palace were warned to stop opium smoking during the late Qing. At this time the water pipe was as necessary as fans and handkerchiefs.

and its opium sets collected. The collection of *objects d'art* has a long and extremely rich history in China. Snuff bottles are endowed with all the virtues and exquisiteness of a collectible: utility, size, durability, artistry and history. They are works of art, and, importantly, they please all the senses. Snuff bottles belong to a dictionary of curios and to the culture of *yan*; they also form their own genre. The elegant shapes and artistic designs fitted perfectly with the sophistication of Chinese connoisseur art, which was the domain of the elitist literati and exclusive royals.

The art of snuff bottles deserves more than just a few words here. Works of art were inscribed both on the surface and on the inside of glass bottles. Bottles were made from metal, glass, jade, stone, porcelain, ivory, lacquer and many more materials. Those crafted in Qianlong's reign were the most refined and valuable. On these bottles were depicted jewelled palaces on the mountain of the immortals, celestial birds and animals, the stars of the Milky Way and caves of peach blossom. The imperial factory itself manufactured bottles for the exclusive use of the royal family. Kangxi and Qianlong bestowed snuff bottles upon their favourite princes, officials and foreign ambassadors. Officials and courtiers, like their counterparts in the Ming who presented aphrodisiacs, also used rare snuff bottles to please the emperors and to gain favours. Qianlong became the biggest collector and possessed several thousand bottles, many of which can now be found in the Palace Museum in Beijing and Taipei. Despite such popularity, the origin of snuff bottles in China remains a mystery. Mainland historians have argued that they were introduced by Matteo Ricci. Could they have been another foreign import or invasion? As the debate goes on, there is no doubt that the inscription art of snuff bottles had set not only the precedent but also the standard for opium pipes.

THE SOCIAL LIFE OF TEA AND JIANGNAN DECADENCE

The culture of *yan* blossomed as the Chinese empire changed hands. Whilst ordinary people enjoyed a pipe in between and after their work, the elite derived style out of snuff bottle appreciation. Although tobacco smoking and snuff bottles were different, both symbolised status and recreation of some kind. Different classes of consumers absorbed *yan* into their diverse lives. Its consumption was growing into a consumer culture. So what was it about the indigenous Chinese culture that made the culture of *yan* so welcome and natural to both the elite and ordinary people? It is not possible to fully understand the general phenomenon of smoking and the particular case of opium without situating them within the larger context of Chinese biological behaviour, material life, the history of food and the culture of consumption. This is a large claim for sure, but some preliminary conjectures can be made. The story that follows puts opium smoking into perspective with the four Chinese cultures of consumption, the consumer and material cultures of tea, cuisine, herbs and utensils.

Ji could drink. Since she came to my household and saw that I could take but what a banana leaf could hold, she gave up. Every evening, I would keep company with my beloved with only a few cups. But she loved tea just like me and we were both addicted to *jiepian*. Every time she took half a pod of *guzi*, she chose the best because a single cicada's wing could make a difference. She boiled it with a gentle flame and faint steam, slender kettle and long spout. *Ji* would gently blow and tend it herself. Every time when I chanted Zuo Si's poem 'To the Tender Girl', the sentence 'blowing while facing *ding li* [ancient tripod cooking vessel]', *Ji* would smile. The boiling tea made shiny bubbles like crab eyes and fish scales. This was the time to prepare the china, to select a spot sanctified by the soul of the moon and the spirit of cloud. This was superb and delightful. Under the moon and in front of the blossoms, serene and facing each other, we tasted the tea. Fragrance arose from the dark liquid, it was really as if the lily magnolia was morning-dewed and *yaocao* [grass in legends] were dancing with waves. This was the essence of *LuLu* [Lu Tong and Lu Yu]. *Dongbo* once said 'it is not the jade bowl [the moon] that upholds *Emei* [goddess of moon]'. My life was filled with pure happiness. It lasted nine years; it also alas finished in nine years![19]

The narrator above is the princely Mao Xiang (1611–93), who came from a prominent Jiangnan family. *Ji* was an exceedingly beautiful and talented courtesan who became his concubine and 'died' in this book. Their love story and *Ji*'s death have continued to fascinate many. Mao was also one of the many men of letters and leisure who cultivated opium in his garden. Mao and *Ji* are the quintessential *caizi jiaren* or 'talent and beauty' of Chinese history. They defined pure happiness through tea consumption. Selection was vital, 'because a single cicada's wing could make a difference'. Heating with 'gentle flame and faint steam, slender kettle and long spout' was a culinary art and science, and *Ji* 'would gently blow and tend it herself'. It was a ritual since 'when I chanted Zuo Si's poem "To the Tender Girl" ...*Ji* would smile'. *Ji* was a highly literate classic beauty, the perfect companion for the lettered rich. The 'shiny bubbles like crab eyes and fish scales' did not just make their mouths water; it electrified their senses. The ritual was holy, since they were 'to select a spot sanctified by the soul of the moon and the spirit of cloud'. Yet the climax was still to come: 'Under the moon and in front of the blossoms, serene and facing each other, we tasted the tea.' Mao and *Ji* experienced the celestial pleasure that only existed in heaven. Whose life would not be filled with pure happiness on being purified as such? Mao and *Ji* open our eyes to the ritual of tea, the philosophy of food, the art of utensils, the science of herbs and ultimately 'the art of sex'.

Mao and *Ji* indulged in the most expensive luxury tea of the time – *jiepian*. The process of selection and heating, that is, the art of cooking, the manner of presentation and the style of tasting were the same with opium smoking. Did opium smokers model their practice on the culture of tea? Did the existence of the larger Chinese cultures of consumption dictate the way in which opium was to be consumed? The social life of tea speaks for opium. Tea was discovered in China in ancient times. Like opium, it was used as a tribute when warring states fought against and appeased each other. The unification of China in 221 BC helped to spread its consumption and cultivation. Tea was considered medicinal and recreational. It dispelled sleepiness, reduced thirst and some praised it as the fountain of inspiration. It brought beauty and talent together; it also generated literature and business. It was a necessity for ordinary people, a ritual for the rich and learned. Symbols and values of different kinds were invented and attributed to it. It enriched Chinese culture, and its uniqueness was distinguished. The culture of tea flourished in the Tang dynasty, and Lu Yu's *Cha Jing* or *Bible of Tea* sanctified this tradition. This book gave birth to protocols and standardised social contact and exchange. Governments taxed tea as they did salt. Tea generated revenues for rulers and a livelihood for the ruled. The Mongols and Arab traders helped to introduce it to central Asia and far beyond. It became synonymous with China and the Ming dynasty saw its initial globalisation; it appeared in European royal courts and rich households and the Qing dynasty saw its Europeanisation. Tea distinguished China in faraway lands; it brought China closer to the world.

Tea was China's gift to the world. It was part of the Chinese culinary tradition and the culture of consumption. Tea was the seventh necessity of a Chinese household, alongside fuel, rice, oil, salt, soy sauce and vinegar. Smoke, that is, tobacco and later opium, would join the list to become the eighth necessity. Like food, tea embodies the cosmology of the Chinese culinary tradition and the culture of consumption. Claude Levi-Strauss used the work of H. C. Conklin on a Philippino tribe to argue what he called 'the raw and the cooked'. Conklin believed that 'The Hanunoo regard as a "real" food only that which is prepared for human consumption by cooking.'[20] This would be true with many cultures. 'Hence, ripe bananas which must be eaten raw are considered as "snack" foods. Real food such as pre-ripe bananas, root crops, cereals, cucumbers, tomatoes and onions are never eaten raw.' In other words, 'a *meal* must include cooked food. In

fact, meals are usually enumerated by the term: pag'apuy, "fire making".'
The insight of Conklin and Strauss can be extended to China and the case
of opium. 'To cook' is *kai huo* or *kai lu*, 'open fire or open stove' in many if
not all parts of China. Tea and food must go through fire, that is, *be* cooked,
before they can be enjoyed; and they involve fragrance, taste, colour and
shape. It was not simply a process of turning the raw into the edible. It
was the mythical and cosmological difference between nature and culture,
between barbarism and civilisation.

Deborah Lupton has furthered this understanding. She believes that
'cooking is not simply the application of heat or other technologies to
raw materials so as to render them more edible by changing their texture,
flavour or digestibility'.[21] Food is 'civilised by cooking, not simply at the
level of practice, but at the level of the imagination'. *Ji*'s gentle blowing of
the boiling tea and Mao's chanting of a classic poem put Lupton's insight
into perspective. The creative imagination that tea making inspired and the
drama endowed in the ritual made tea mouth-watering and soul satisfying.
This would come alive with opium consumption among the lettered. Like
tea and food in general, the opium paste must be carefully selected and
heated, that is, *be* cooked. This demanding process rendered the raw paste
smokable. That is why smoking was initially translated as 'eat smoke'. This
placed the act of smoking alongside eating, drinking and family dining.
Chinese culinary tradition and the culture of consumption had set the
stage for opium smoking, which would come to distinguish the Chinese
way of after-dinner entertainment in the late nineteenth century.

The consumption of tea demands the application, artistic or not depending on one's means and taste, of utensils. So would opium consumption.
Daniel Roche has pointed out that 'Any object, even the most ordinary,
embodies ingenuity, choices, a culture. A body of knowledge and a surplus
of meanings are attached to all objects.'[22] This was obvious with what *Ji*
used for boiling the tea – a slender kettle with a long spout. Like many
other objects, kettles are not merely physical objects, they are also endowed
with symbolic value. They are utensils; they are also *objects d'art*. Jan
Huygen van Linschoten saw that the Chinese and the Japanese cherished
their tea sets in the same way that Europeans treasured 'diamonds and
rubies'.[23] This would extend to opium pipes, as Chinese smokers, rich and
poor, adorned their pipes with precious stones or symbolic motifs. They
injected their own ideas and ideals on to their pipes. Some would treasure
them like 'diamonds and rubies' while others would become addicted to
them. They would fashion a most refined material culture around the pipes
and accessories of opium smoking. Tea and food can be medicinal; even

more so with opium. Chinese medical science believes that food and tea, like medicinal herbs, can help prevent and treat diseases. Food nurtures one's body and soul; so can tea and opium. Opium soothed the body and soul of many, from eunuchs and pain-ridden women to labourers. Opium in this context was a painkiller. It reduced pain, physically or psychologically, and helped suffering people. The act of taking from nature to nurture the body and the soul epitomises a Chinese philosophy – humankind's dependence and coexistence with nature. Men and nature complement each other; they can be in harmony.

Like food and tea, opium had played a role in the prevention and treatment of diseases. When its recreational value was discovered, it seemed a value-added situation. The combination of medicinal and recreational values would make opium smoking a most justifiable and pragmatic recreation. Tea can be enjoyed alone, but it is best consumed with food, as a recreation and with a companion; the same would be true of opium. *Yincha*, the tradition of having breakfast or food while sipping tea, set the precedent for dinner accompanied or followed by smoking. Men and women, friends and family, would gather to share their lives and leisure sanctioned by both nature and culture. Like tobacco and the 'subgenre of still life painting' it inspired in the Dutch golden age, the culture of tea begot other traditions, such as tea sets, tea houses and tea literature. Tea drinking was sociable. Tea houses became social institutions where local disputes could be solved and where, later, revolutions were hatched. It was even said to be where one could feel the spirit of a people and the soul of a nation, as the famous play *Teahouse* illustrates. This pattern repeated with opium, as both rich and poor relaxed over a few puffs and as foreigners came to identify Chinese culture with opium smoking. There is an intimacy implicit in the ritual of tea, the philosophy of food, the art of utensils and the science of herbs. Opium smoking would embody this in a unique way. It fitted perfectly with Chinese culinary tradition and the culture of consumption.

The story of Mao and *Ji* also points us to the larger topic of Jiangnan decadence – leisure in the Chinese style. Jiangnan, the lower Yangtze River delta region, was a land of wealth and culture. It had maintained the highest ratio of successful examination candidates and high-ranking scholar-officials. Talents such as Mao Xiang, came from Jiangnan, as did beauties such as *Ji*, and style such as *huafang* or luxuriously decorated leisure boats. Rice and fish were plentiful in the region; tea and silk were cultivated there. The whole country looked to the East and the East never failed to set the standards. The Kangxi emperor was fascinated with Jiangnan and toured it six times; so would his grandson, Qianlong. Tang Bin, Kangxi's

governor of Jiangsu, complained that Jiangnan's men of letters buried themselves in 'actors, drinking vessels, prostitutes and banquets, wine boats and
grand parties, expensive fruits piled tables and performances'.[24] A link had
developed between affluence and extravagance, between the culture of consumption and Jiangnan decadence. Yu Huai (1616–96) lived in Nanjing,
the heart of Jiangnan. He knew the place and its seasons well:

Jiuyuan [neighbourhood of prostitutes] faces *gongyuan* [place of metropolitan and
provincial examinations], they are across the river from each other. This was
designed for the beauty and talent. When it was the year of autumn breeze and
osmanthus fragrance, candidates from the four corners would gather. They would
ride the four-horse carriages, summon the prettiest and request the songs.[25]

Jiangnan decadence was to a certain extent the history of sex recreation.
It was written by a stratum of men whose lives were devoted, exclusively
or partially, to the cultivation of letters and leisure. They were sometimes
aristocrats and the lettered, and at other times the *nouveau riche*. As Dorothy
Ko explains, 'disenchanted with the thought of serving a corrupt court or
alien rulers, many well-to-do scholars shunned political appointments in
favour of domestic pleasures'.[26] Mao Xiang is an excellent example, as are
Yu Huai and Zhang Dai. Another is the celebrated Li Yu, who produced
plays, maintained a troupe of singing girls and wrote about everything from
chamber decoration and growing the poppy to when to have sex and how to
train concubines. Indeed, it was fashionable for the lettered rich in Jiangnan
to have their own troupes of singer–players and to write about the art of sex
and good living. Such scholars were the taste-makers and the trendsetters.
And they would soon become fundamental in creating the culture of opium
consumption. What standard they set for Jiangnan, Jiangnan set for the
whole country. The Chinese elite and the smoking-addicted public seemed
to be ready for something more sophisticated than tobacco. The seventeenth
century was no ordinary time in the history of smoking. On the one hand,
tobacco smoking and snuff bottles set the precedent for opium. On the
other, indigenous Chinese cultures of consumption provided the best soil
for it to grow. The foundations were well laid. And so it is not difficult to
understand why opium smoking would germinate so easily and blossom so
quickly, given other socio-economic conditions, such as availability, were
met.

CHAPTER 3

'The age of calicoes and tea and opium'

The eighteenth century has been described as 'the age of calicoes and tea and opium'.[1] By the eighteenth century opium-as-aphrodisiac could no longer be kept as a court or elite luxury and tobacco as 'the opiate of the people'. This chapter examines opium's introduction to a different level of society, its entry into mainstream sex recreation and the consumer vanguard. Many historians have emphasised the pathological effect of opium on the eve of the first Opium War (1839–42), but no one has explained under what circumstances it became pathological. Some conveniently point towards the previous century. But what is it about the previous reigns that contributed to the outbreak of opium smoking? It took time for the medicine-to-aphrodisiac intelligence to spread. It also took time for opium to become widely available. Above all, assimilation had to develop within the larger framework of existing Chinese cultures of consumption. The eighteenth century was a period when knowledge about opium was passed on to many people (in other words, accumulated and socialised). China's political and genealogical intimacy with south-east Asia in general, and with Taiwan in particular, was to play an important role. Sojourners to and from south-east Asia and participants of the Taiwan conquest both came back to the mainland with habits and memories of smoking. This was fundamental to the spread of opium, which involved not only maritime trade and what Chris Bayly called 'archaic globalisation' but also the wider Chinese diaspora and mechanisms of culture transmission.[2]

CHINA'S INTIMACY WITH SOUTH-EAST ASIA

The introduction of opium as a luxury item was intimately connected to China's maritime trade and to Chinese diplomacy. Tribute trade flourished after Zheng He's expeditions. The Bengalis, Siamese and Javanese valued opium highly. They sought to please the mighty Chinese empire with it, but they enjoyed it themselves as well. *Da Ming Huidian* testifies to

this, as do the memoirs of contemporary travellers. Pedro Alvares Cabral
noticed the high price of opium in Calicut in 1500. Tome Pires, writing
to King Manuel from Cochin on 27 January 1516, told of its social value:
'This is a great merchandise and it is customary to eat it in these parts –
the kings and lords in portions as big as a hazel-nut; the lower classes
eat less, because it is expensive.'[3] Peter Mundy, on his way from Agra to
Surat in March 1633, saw 'many fields of poppies of which they make
opium' and that they 'make a kinde of Beveredge called Post' and 'they
drinck it'.[4] Charles Lockyer observed opium's popularity among the Malays
and Acehnese in 1711: 'the Malayans are such Admirers of Ophium that
they would mortgage all they hold most valuable to procure it'.[5] John S.
Stavorinus travelled to Bengal, Batavia and Bantam between 1768 and 1771.
He remembered that 'the natives of all those countries are very fond of it
[opium], smoking it together with their tobacco, or chewing it unmixed'.[6]
From India to the islands of Indonesia, south and south-east Asians enjoyed
eating, drinking, chewing or smoking opium. But the issue here is not that
they enjoyed opium, but that the Chinese merchants and labourers who
travelled to and from and in many cases settled in these countries enjoyed it
as well.

As government-sponsored expeditions died out, tribute trade slowed
down from the mid to late fifteenth century. This opened the door to commercial guilds, enterprising individuals and pirates. They followed Zheng
He's route and opened new ones as well. Edmund Scott, a member of the
newly chartered English East India Company, spent three and a half years
(1602–5) in Java. He gave a detailed description of Bantam and the Ban-
tamese. He was certainly fascinated by the Chinatown in Bantam and the
Chyneses as *Javans*:

> They are very great eaters; but the gentlemen allow their slaves nothing but rice,
> sodden in water, with some rootes and hearbes. And they have a certain hearbe
> called *bettaile*, which they usually have carryed with them wheresoever they goe,
> in boxes or wrapped up in cloath, like a sugerloafe, and also a nutt called *pinange*;
> which are both in operation very hott, and they eate them continually, to warme
> them within and keepe them from the fluxe. They doe likwise take much tobacco
> and opium.[7]

Bettaile and *pinange* is the famous betel-quid, composed of areca-nut, betel
leaves and lime. The peoples of south-east Asia and Melanesia were invet-
erate chewers of betel – 'the characteristic relaxant central to the agreeable
social interaction that Southeast Asians valued'.[8] Chewing gave a distinct
red colour to one's teeth, which many viewed as most desirable. Betel was

used in rituals, weddings and as an aphrodisiac, since it sweetens the breath. Many women would not make love until they had done some chewing. It helped prevent diarrhoea, dysentery, eased hunger pains in long-distance travel and helped combat parasitic worms. The Chinese of south-east Asia learned to chew the betel-quid from the natives there, and they in turn introduced it back to China, probably as early as the Tang dynasty. Betel-nut chewing is still common in southern China today.

This culture transmission was to extend to opium, and herein lies the other dimension of opium's introduction or rather reintroduction to China. Seafaring Chinese, the merchants and labourers of south-east Asia, smoked opium as early as the natives there did. Not only did they enjoy opium, they also carried both the habit and the product with them when they returned to China. The *Dagh-Register Gehouden int Casteel Batavia* or 'Batavia Diary' of the Dutch East India Company registered the Chinese junks that called on Batavia and the goods that the ships, both Dutch, Chinese and others, carried with them when they left Batavia. The entries for April 1636 read:

April 4th. A junk from China, the fourth one, arrived here. It is loaded with all sorts of Chinese goods and has 330 Chinese passagers on board.

April 11th. A junk from China, the fifth one, loaded with all sorts of Chinese goods and 346 people entered our port. The name of its captain is Sicqua.

April 17th. Ships *Oudewaeter* and *Schagen* left here; *Oudewaeter* carried 55 people and the following goods:
   Japanese silver 10,000 *liang*
   Rixdollars (Meleka money) 8,000 *pieces*
   Various weaving products 51 bundle
   Red woollen cloth 1 chest
   Mirrors 1 chest
   Opium . . .
Its total value: 79,810 guilder 16 stuiver.[9]

Opium was carried into China this way. The trade was official, since it paid import duties in Zhangzhou as *Dong Xi Yang Kao* or *A Study of the East and West Oceans* detailed. The import tax for opium was 2 *qian* for every 10 *jin* (five kilograms) in 1589; it went down to 1 *qian* 7 *fen* 3 *li* in 1615.[10] The illustrious *Dong Xi Yang Kao* also tells us that the quantity imported was small, indicating individual carriers; and that the quantity steadily increased after 1589, following a reduction of its import tax. The ships and goods were headed for the Indonesian archipelago, China, Taiwan and Japan. For Leonard Blusse, the years 1636 to 1640 were 'the Honeymoon Years' of Dutch trade. Om Prakash has carefully studied the Dutch East India Company and the economy of Bengal from 1630 to 1720. Opium, he says, was a 'principal Bengal commodity the Company sold in the archipelago from the 1640s'.[11] The Dutch maintained this monopoly until the British broke it a century later. Dutch ships called on many ports and picked up any goods and people they could make a penny from. Indeed, this was how many Chinese travelled to and from China. Ivory, birds nests, sandalwood, tortoiseshell, tobacco and the sweet potato found their way to China in this way, as, naturally, would opium. Thanks to the Dutch, Java had plenty of opium; the island also had plenty of Chinese. Physician Engelbert Kaempfer arrived in Batavia in 1689. He saw opium-smoking shops where opium diluted with water was smoked with tobacco.[12] The Chinese in Java began to be noted for their opium smoking in the 1680s, as Luc Nagtegaal has noted. He attributes the spread of opium consumption in Java to the increased circulation of Chinese merchants and labourers on the island.

The cyclical sojourning of Chinese people in Java helped to spread smoking on the island. The cyclical movement of Chinese on the Malay Peninsula would also help spread consumption there. This would extend to their homeland, as they shuttled back and forth. It would continue in the late nineteenth and early twentieth centuries, when Chinese sojourners travelled to North America and Europe. These people would become famous for the 'opium farms' of south-east Asia, which were 'invariably Chinese', as Carl Trocki has pointed out. Opium, therefore, came to China via two routes – officially as tribute and unofficially through sojourners to and from south-east Asia. Hence, even if the official route was closed, the unofficial one was always open. Does this mean that the introduction of opium to China was inevitable, regardless of the official passage (since China's link with south-east Asia was not simply political, but more importantly genealogical)? My answer is *yes*, given the precedent tobacco set. This raises many questions, especially with regard to the Chinese diaspora. The origin and history of overseas migration has continued to fascinate many. Dynastic change and disasters of all sorts drove tens of thousands from the north and the central plains to coastal provinces. Some, Zheng Chenggong for example, rose to challenge the alien ruler, while others simply took to the sea. Taiwan was an excellent refuge, one that was easy to reach and return from should situations change. So were the Indonesian Archipelago, Cochin-China and the Malay Peninsula. The consequence of the Qing's continued Taiwan conquest was fundamental to the spread of opium on the mainland.

Zhu Yigui staged an uprising in Taiwan in 1721. Thousands of soldiers were dispatched to crush the rebellion. Lan Dingyuan and his brother led the campaign, and their methods were effective. Lan wrote extensively about Taiwan in his memoir; his observations were accurate because he was a native of Fujian, and hence shared the *minnan* dialect and culture of the Taiwanese. He wrote of the opium smoke: 'Boil it in a copper pan, the pipe is like a small club. Intemperate youth gather at night and eat it, it gradually became a custom. When taking it, serve a dozen or so dishes of sweets and fruits to company it.'[14] Of the accompanying facilities, he wrote: 'To allure new comers, first-timers do not pay. After a while one cannot resist and the whole family goes for it! It keeps you fresh at night and increases your sexual desire.' Many shared Lan's fate and fascination. Huang Shujing was one. He knew that 'The opium smoke is made with hemp, kudzu vine and shredded opium paste slices boiled in a copper pan. Mix opium with tobacco, take a bamboo pipe and stuff it with palm slices.'[15] He mentioned that opium was introduced from Batavia, and went on: 'The shops that manage this exclusively are called opium dens. The warm air goes straight into the diaphragm and one does not need to sleep much at night. The natives here take it as a tool to induce sexual desire.' Huang came from a family of high-ranking officials. As a provincial censor, his first contacts would be with the high-ranking officials on the island. Some might have told him about opium smoking, while others might have offered him a puff, if not a trip to a den. When it came to the details about how to set about smoking, the memory of Zhu Jingying was miraculous:

The opium smoke is from Batavia, Luzon [Philippines] and other ocean countries; it is a prohibited article by sea. Taiwan has many rascals; they mix it with tobacco and inhale it. It is said that it helps with the performance [during sexual intercourse] and one doesn't need to sleep much at night. When inhaling it, one must invite many people, take turns eating [smoking] it. Spread a mat on the floor on which everyone lies down, burn a lamp in the middle and then inhale. A hundred to several hundred mouthfuls is the amount. The pipe is made of bamboo, about eight or nine *fen* [2.99 cm] round, stuff it with palm slices and hair. Use silver to rim the two ends. Make a hole on the side, size it like the little finger. Use clay to shape a bowl like a kettle or gourd, make a hole in the middle so the fire can burn through. Inlay it to the hole, put opium above the hole, a little bit of paste [opium] is enough. Inhale it into the mouth until it is finished; it makes a *gege* noise.[16]

Did Zhu have an audience in mind, or was he simply relating his own experience? The attention to detail could only make us believe that he was sharing his own delight and insight. Zhu went on at great length to talk about indigenous produce and customs, such as opium smoking, in his memoir. Lan, Huang and Zhu all shared the same fascination; they also represented the different layers within the official establishment. Lan was a *xiucai*, a military official; Huang was a *jinshi*, a civil servant; and Zhu was a *juren*, from the middle echelon. It is important to understand where these three men stood in the social hierarchy, because scholar-officials loved to read, preface, critique and gossip about their colleagues' latest literary endeavours. This was not just a tradition, but also a necessity. Their writings substantiate the sexual mythology of opium, testify to one of its entry routes, and help to communicate and socialise the knowledge. Opium was limited to the coastal provinces and to those who were exposed to it in south-east Asia and Taiwan in the early eighteenth century. The Qing court could have used effective measures to curb the spread of smoking at this moment, when both knowledge of it and its availability were still limited. Yet, opium smoking spread quickly in Fujian after the conquest of Taiwan. Liu Shimin, the governor of the province, wrote to tell the Yongzheng emperor in the summer of 1729: 'Zhangzhou's magistrate Li Zhiguo informed me that the opium smoke is like an epidemic there. We should punish the traitors who possessed and sold it illegally.'[17] Liu mentioned a local merchant, Chen Yuan, who was found with 33 *jin* [16.5 kilograms] of opium. He asked the emperor to prohibit 'the opium smoke'. The Yongzheng emperor quickly issued the first edict prohibiting traffic in opium.

Opium also spread quickly in Guangdong. It can be found in the chapter on foodstuffs of the 1752 (compiled) *Aomen Zhilue* or *Brief History of Macao*. This work's two editors also call it 'the opium smoke' and write, 'it looks like mud and it boils and cooks into a smoke'.[18] Both the Fujianese and the Cantonese called opium 'the opium smoke', reminding us of the memoirs of Tome Pires, Peter Mundy and John Stavorinus. Their works demonstrate the evolution of opium consumption from eating and drinking to chewing and ultimately to smoking (mixed with tobacco at first). Edmund Scott's memoir tells us that mixed smoking had begun in at least if not earlier than 1602 in Bantan. This was standard service when physician Engelbert Kaempfer arrived in Batavia in 1689. Smoking was the way in which opium consumption was introduced to the mainland, as the Taiwan memoirs indicated. Huang Shujing claimed that the opium smoke was 'several times better than ordinary tobacco'. This indicates that the smoking of pure opium had now begun. This evolution would become a revolution with the entry of a formidable actor on the opium stage. The English East India Company had been trying to cut into the profitable trade from the Indian Ocean to the South China Sea against tough competition. By the early eighteenth century they seemed to have found a ray of hope in the shape of opium. Carrying opium from India to China became such 'a usual thing' among the servants of the Honourable Company that in 1733 its council wrote to warn them of the Chinese prohibition and penalty.[19] English competition did not escape Dutch eyes. Efforts were made to save the Dutch East India Company.

Luc Nagtegaal's research shows that 'the Dutch decided to confine them-selves to opium sales from their warehouses in Batavia, leaving Chinese traders to take care of distribution in the Pasisir'.[20] These tactics worked, since many of the smokers were Chinese. In addition, the 'Opium Society of Batavia' was established under Baron van Imhof, governor-general of Batavia (1742–9), and opium became a 'privileged trade' reserved to the Company under Jacob Mossel, Imhof's successor (1750–61).[21] The Dutch concentrated on wholesale trading in Batavia, leaving the Chinese to focus on retailing and distribution. The English were quick to learn. Sinnappah Arasaratnam studied the situation in close-by Riau, seat of the Johor empire. The English, and also the Portuguese, brought opium from Bengal, the *Bugis* (locals) bought it from them and then sold it to the Chinese. The Chinese were key to the distribution of Dutch-traded opium in the Indonesian island, despite the massacre of 1740; they were indis-pensable to English-traded opium in the Malay Peninsula. Here can be clearly seen the ascension of the English and the rise of opium as a most profitable commodity, coinciding with the expansion of the Chinese trade empire in south-east Asia. Ng Chin-keong's research shows that by the mid-eighteenth century many more coastal Chinese were shuttling to and from south-east Asia. These people established miner colonies in northern Vietnam, western Borneo, Phuket, Kelantan and Bangka, pepper export industries in Brunei, Cambodia and Chantaburi, gambier industries in Riau-Johor, sugar plantations in southern Siam, Kedah and Java, and trading enterprises in the Mekong delta area.

Both merchants and labourers operated and toiled in south-east Asia, and they returned to China to recruit and also to retire. The Chinese authorities encouraged this in 1754, stating that any Chinese with valid reason would be entitled to return home and to have his property protected. This led to an increased circulation of merchants, labourers and adventurers to and from south-east Asia. The period 1740 to 1840 was certainly 'a Chinese century'. Like the Taiwan conquest, the Chinese century was equally, if not more, fundamental to the further spread of opium on the Chinese mainland. In the meantime, the English were developing a much more sophisticated system with regard to opium. As Carl Trocki writes: 'In the years between 1773 and 1793, the East India Company, in its quest for a rationalized

monopoly over the opium trade tried a number of alternatives'.[22] Finally
'a workable opium system was devised that served both imperial and capitalist interests'. With the help of Governor-General Warren Hasting, the
Company obtained the monopoly over opium production in India. Trocki
has made a careful study of the history of opium cultivation, harvesting,
processing and wholesale in India. The famous 'Sudder factories' were
massive and elaborate, employing thousands in the business of cleaning,
drying, turning, cake-making and packaging. They auctioned the opium in
exchanges in Calcutta and Bombay, which were initially held twice a year
but which became monthly events in the nineteenth century. So-called
'country traders' purchased opium at these auctions, shipped it to China
and deposited the profit, the much-needed silver for the purchase of tea,
into the Company's treasury on the spot.

The trade between India, the eastern archipelago and China was known
as 'country trade', and it was conducted by both natives and Europeans.
The country traders were the 'independent English, and more often
Scottish, merchants who had established private firms in India'.[23] The
'country trade' kept the Honourable Company's hands clean and solved
its silver shortage problem – a perfect solution. The China supercargoes
of the Company, agents of the 'country traders', were key to its operation.
A supercargo was 'an officer aboard a merchant ship whose duty it was
to superintend the cargo and commercial transactions of the voyage'.[24]
Commander William Richardson, for example, arrived in Macao in July
1782 with 1,601 chests of Patna opium and was advised not to report that
his ship carried the chests.[25] The opium was safely disposed of with the help
of Sinqua and Puankhequa, two *hong* or government security merchants
who were to have extensive dealings with the commanders of the 'country'
ships and who would lay down the ground rules for later generations. The
trade and distribution of opium in Canton, as in Java and on the Malay
Peninsula, had much to do with the Chinese. From this time onwards,
English 'country trade' ships regularly carried opium and all vessels went
to Whampoa, a little island at the entrance of the Canton estuary, to
avoid Company intervention and Chinese suspicion. Thus began the infamous smuggling. The English had opened a new page in the social life of
opium.

THE QINHUAI, *HUAFANG* AND OPIUM

Merchant princes of the Indian Ocean and South China Sea, be they Dutch,
Chinese or English, had their eyes on opium just as its transformation

inside China was intensifying. Knowledge of opium the aphrodisiac from up and above was communicated down and below thanks to physicians and herbalists in the eighteenth century. Huang Yuanyu (1705–58) continued the work of his predecessors:

The opium smoke helps arrest secretion and control emission; it cures diarrhoea and proctoposis, spermatorrhea and nocturnal emission. *Bencao* says that opium is the *yingsu* flower. When it is in its full, prick the green bud, scrape out the juice, let it dry by itself; then it's called *afurong*. Today when foreign ships come to the Customs; they all carry it. In the central plains, rascals and spoiled rats, officials and their attendants, actors and courtesans, they all think that it replenishes them, strengthens their spirit, helps them sleep with women and beautiful boys, and that its effect is ten times out of the ordinary.[26]

Opium as an aphrodisiac was standard and common knowledge in the medical profession by the eighteenth century. Huang served the Qianlong emperor when the latter toured Jiangnan. Qianlong apparently liked him and even inscribed a horizontal board for his practice. This reminds us of the Chenghua emperor who promoted physicians and herbalists. Could Huang have prescribed something magic that prompted the emperor to bestow such an honour on him? Huang certainly was not alone. Xu Dachuan (1693–1771) also wrote about the magic of opium; so did Zhao Xuemin (1719–1805):

Guangdong has opium pills. It is made with Chinese caterpillar fungus, opium and Ginseng. This really is an aphrodisiac. This grass can strengthen *yang* [masculinity]. You can feel it when it enters the kidney. It protects the lung, benefits the kidney and replenishes the essential substance . . . It tastes sweet and is mild in nature. It helps reproduce the essence; it really helps to preserve our lives.[27]

Among the mid-Qing men of medicine who discussed or emphasised the aphrodisiac role of opium were Zhang Zhichong (1644–1722) in *Yixue Yaojue*, Nian Xirao (d. 1738) in *Jiyan Liangfang*, Shen Jin'ao (1717–74) in *Yaoyao Fenji*, Yan Jie, Shi Wen and Hong Wei in their 1761 *Depei Bencao*, Huang Gongxiu (1730–1817) in *Bencao Qiuzhen* and Chen Xiuyuan (1753–1823) in *Shifang Gekuo*. The opium–sex message definitely hit home in the eighteenth century, thanks to men of letters such as Lan Dingyuan and men of medicine such as Zhao Xuemin. Another watershed in the social life of opium had been reached. Like their counterparts in the Ming who researched and developed opium, eighteenth-century men of letters and medicine further refined and demystified the knowledge of opium. In fact, they carried on opium's medicine-to-aphrodisiac transformation. But how precisely did opium the aphrodisiac marry with the Chinese industry of sex recreation? *Xu Banqiao Zaji* gives us a picture of the industry in the 1780s.

The river-boats of the Qinhuai River are covered with awning above and sur-rounded by railings below. Lanterns hang at the corners, low beds are set in the middle. *Yu* [jar for liquid] and *lei* [ancient urn-shaped wine vessel] are decoratively placed; everything is exquisite. There is no curtain on either side so that it is easy to look out. When the boat sets out at sunset, the two oars move in unison. Wind of lotus assails the nostrils and the fragrance of snow-white lotus root stirs the heart. Songs charm the ear and ravishing women surround you. This is really a dream celestial world.[28]

The Qinhuai was no ordinary river. It was the cradle of the sex recre-ation industry. The 'river-boats' were luxuriously decorated leisure vessels called *huafang*. The Qinhuai flowed through Nanjing, the heart of Jiang-nan decadence. Zhang Dai, a Ming aristocrat who cultivated opium in his garden and who survived to the early Qing, knew the locale inside out: 'the Qinhuai river-houses are convenient for living, for socialising, for sex recreation. They are expensive, but the residents never waste a day. Painted boats, the sound of *xiao* (Chinese flute) and percussion come and go.'[29] Generations of men such as Zhang Dai frequented or kept residence on the legendary Qinhuai. In fact, it was a must among the learned and the urban rich; many wrote about its haunting beauties and celebrated the 'river-boats'. They left behind a genre of literature that sheds light on Ming–Qing elite life and sex culture. The Qinhuai catered to the lettered and the rich, as 'tea and smoke wafted gently in the air'.[30] This was a common scene: 'A smaller vessel with servants moves alongside, to fill the pipe or to take orders. They arrange meals, ordering from either individ-ual chefs or famous restaurants. The food is placed in fine red boxes and carried to the pier where they await collection by the boat.'[31] The 'smaller vessel' was the famous *yan ting* or 'smoke vessel'. It followed the master *huafang* and sold freshly filled pipes (initially tobacco water pipes) and other services.

Tobacco had laid the foundation for the entry of a sister product. Like tobacco, opium was a most welcome and most natural addition to the Qinhuai, or more precisely the sex industry it bred, the already popular 'smoke vessels' and most importantly the lettered and the rich it attracted. These were the socio-cultural forces at play in the interpretation of alien ideas and in the fashioning of new styles. Just as Jiangnan set the standard for the country, the Qinhuai River set the standard for the industry. By 1793 opium smoking accompanied by sex recreation on leisure boats had become a well-established industry in Canton. Shen Fu's memoir, *Fusheng Liuji* or *Six Chapters of a Floating Life*, details this:

> So we went to where the Yangzhou gang [of prostitutes] was. Opposite were two rows of boats, about a dozen. Everyone inside had [hair] buns, sprayed temples and light make-up. They were dressed in wide sleeves and long skirts; they talked and I could hear their words . . . I was asked to pick a prostitute. I chose a very young one. Her figure and appearance looked like my wife Yun, but her feet were extremely small and pointed; her name was *Xi'er* [happy girl]. *Xiufeng* [husband of Shen's cousin] called out to a prostitute named *Cuigu* [emerald girl] and the rest had their own old acquaintances. We let the boat anchor in the middle of the river and had a feast of wine and food for a few hours. I was afraid that I would not be able to control myself and insisted on going home. But the city gate was already closed. The gate of a sea town closed at sunset, I did not know that. After dinner, some laid down to smoke opium while others held their prostitutes in their arms to tease.[32]

These were the legendary 'flower boats'; they were Canton's *huafang*. Fu was a man of letters who came from a family of scholars and officials in the Jiangnan region. His father had spent his life working as a private secretary for high-ranking government officials. From his teenage days Fu had accompanied and assisted his father. The pinnacle of both their careers came when they joined high-ranking officials to welcome and entertain the Qianlong emperor during his imperial tour of the Jiangnan region in 1784. The Shens were good friends of the famous Chen family of Haining, in whose famous garden Qianlong dined. Father and son deployed their literary talents to make a living; they also engaged in business to supplement their lifestyle and to take advantage of their networks and travels, which extended from Jiangnan to Canton. Commerce was becoming more profitable than selling words and letters. The smell of money was blowing from Canton, and some of Fu's relatives had already moved to the city. These scholarly Jiangnanese and their Cantonese friends were well acquainted with the nightlife and prostitutes of Canton; going to the brothel was an institution among many scholars and officials.

The indigenous Chinese industry of sex recreation was absorbing a non-Chinese way of relaxation and putting it into context. Igor Kopytoff provides a theoretical explanation: 'in situations of culture contact, they can show what anthropologists have so often stressed: that what is significant about the adoption of alien objects – as of alien ideas – is not the fact that they are adopted, but the way they are culturally redefined and put to use'.[33] Opium was being culturally reinterpreted and socially redefined within and for the general public. This process was taking place not because

of the merchants and labourers who sojourned in south-east Asia and who
smoked opium; neither was it because of the men of letters and medicine
who wrote about the aphrodisiac magic of opium. The interpreters and
makers of culture and style were urban, lettered and sophisticated. It was
they who could afford opium and most important of all, who knew how
to best enjoy it. Smoking by the lowly seafarers did not make opium desirable. It was consumption by the educated urban elite that made smoking
fashionable. Born and bred in *Taiping shengshi* or the 'heyday of peace and
prosperity' under Qianlong, many of Shen Fu's peers indulged in sex and
drugs. Another contemporary, Yu Jiao, knew the situation well:

My friend, Yao Chunpu, bragged to me about the marvels of opium. He said that
it smelled fragrant and it tasted pure and sweet. When depression was drizzling
and melancholy settled in, you lie down facing the partner on the low bed with
a short lamp and take turn to inhale. At the beginning your spirit is refreshed,
soon your head is cleared and eyes sharpened. Then your chest and diaphragm are
suddenly opened and your mood is many times better. Before long your muscles
are softened and your eyelids closed. At this point, you doze off on the pillow,
detached from any thoughts as if you were in a dream world. Your spirit and soul
are calmed. This really is a paradise. I smiled and said that 'it looks like that but
it's not so'. Recently among the four classes of people, only peasants do not taste
it; many officials indulge in it. As for the brothels, everyone is equipped with it as
a bait to allure clients.[34]

   Qianlong's reign fostered a generation of lettered opium smokers who
knew how to put their experiences into words. They reinforced opium's
aphrodisiac role in sex recreation, and began to spread the gospel of opium.
Yu's memoir was a collection of short essays on his travels and encounters
from Beijing to Guangdong. He devoted a chapter to the prostitutes who
operated along the coastal urban centres, such as Chaozhou and Meix-
ian, where he lingered on in the late eighteenth century. His essays give a
good picture of low life in southern China. They demonstrate the educated
man's fascination with sex recreation, which was by now accompanied by
opium smoking. As Charles de Contant, a young French merchant trying
to make his fortune in southern China at the time, observed: 'la passion
des Chinois pour l'opium étant devenue un besoin'.[35] Contant saw that
the Chinese had a passion for opium and that this passion was becoming
a necessity. The people he came into contact with were mostly Cantonese
and southerners. His observation was original and his comment crude,
but he accurately predicted the future of opium. This 'besoin' or necessity
certainly did not escape the eyes of the Macartney ambassadors in 1793.
(The Macartney embassy of 1793 was Britain's first diplomatic mission to

the Qing court of Qianlong, Emperor of China.) Lord Macartney and his delegates were met and entertained by high-ranking officials in the Beijing–Tianjin area. George Leonard Staunton observed them carefully: 'As to eating, the Mandarines did indulge themselves in habits of luxury. They ate several meals, each day, of animal food highly seasoned, each meal consisting of several courses'; and 'they employed part of their intervals of leisure in smoking tobacco mixed with odorous substances, and sometimes a little opium, or in chewing the areca-nut'.[36] Opium smoking, like tobacco smoking to John Bell, was as Chinese as could be in the eyes of Staunton. Like tobacco, opium had become 'indigenous' in a matter of just one hundred or so years. On the mission's way to their fateful audience with the Qianlong emperor, Staunton reported: 'In the low grounds in the part of the country great quantities of tobacco are planted.' He observed how smoking was carried out: 'smoke is inhaled through bamboo tubes by the Chinese; and the practice is perhaps, more prevalent amongst them, than in any other country, as it extends to persons of both sexes, and to those of a very tender age'. He also noticed the age and gender differences of smokers: 'Girls not more than ten years old, or younger, coming from the houses near the road out of curiosity to see the strangers pass, were observed to have long pipes constantly in their mouths.' Late eighteenth-century China was a country saturated with all sorts of smoke and smoking. John Barrow, private secretary to Lord Macartney, noted: 'Tobacco is taken in powder likewise by the Chinese. A mandarin is seldom without a small ornamental phial to hold his snuff, of which he occasionally pours a quantity, equal to a pinch, upon the back of his left hand, between the thumb and index, which approaching to his nose he snuffs up several times a day.'[37] Barrow also noticed: 'It is not the only substance which is used in China to gratify this artificial appetite. Powdered cinnabar is often employed for the same purpose as opium and odorous ingredients are for smoking.'

Although the British ambassadors refused to kowtow, each of them received a refined snuff bottle from Qianlong. Even if the mission accomplished nothing, as some historians have argued, it at least gathered commercial intelligence about opium and smoking – opium was a luxury among the elite and smoking a necessity among the ordinary. Lord Macartney commented on the future of Sino–British trade: 'for the cotton of Bombay and the opium of Bengal are now become in great measure necessaries in China, the latter having grown into general demand through all the southern provinces, and the former being preferable to silk for common use, as a cheaper and pleasanter wear'.[38] Macartney's mention of 'all the southern provinces' echoes the experience of Shen Fu, Yu Jiao's friend, and also the observation of Charles de Contant. Opium smoking was becoming popular among the urban rich in the seafaring provinces by the late eighteenth century. It had made its way into one of the oldest and most profitable businesses.

Opium, tobacco and snuff were all called *yan*, and the culture of *yan* flourished during the reign of Qianlong, as both the high and the low, men and women, enjoyed the pleasures. Could this have contributed to what Kenneth Pomeranz has called 'the great divergence'[39]? The Qianlong emperor did not see much harm in smoking, and he indulged in snuff consumption. He only issued one edict, during his long reign from 1736 to 1799, to prohibit opium. Decadence, in the eyes of a sage, was as natural as the fact that 'rivers flow east'; therefore, 'who can block them and turn them westward'?[40] He enlarged China's map, doubled its population, patronised the arts and men of letters, and increased China's supply of silver, from 3 million taels (1760) to 16 million taels (1780). China itself had not seen such opulence and glory before; hence the emperor was dubbed 'the Son of Heaven whose like was seldom seen since antiquity'.

How can we make sense of eighteenth-century China, taking both its achievements and its disasters into consideration? Who was to blame for the disaster that was opium – Qianlong, the seafarers, Chinese cultures of consumption or the rise of western Europe? Perhaps empires live like human beings; they die either of disease, old age or disaster, be it natural or man-made.

From the 'art of alchemists, sex and court ladies' to the boat brothels of Canton, opium had filtered down from the mid-Ming court to the mid-Qing upper and upper-middle classes. From 1483 to 1793, three hundred years had seen the confirmation of opium the aphrodisiac. The eighteenth century saw its initial outward and downward diffusion. It also saw the rise of the English East India Company and opium smuggling. By the late eighteenth century opium had started to live a life of its own. This is the dynamism of commerce and consumption. Frederic Wakeman has asked whether China was 'essentially inert before the Opium War began in 1839'.[41] And Joanna Waley-Cohen has pointed out that 'it is obvious that at the dawn of the nineteenth century China's involvement with the wider world was already routine'.[42] The stories of tobacco and opium support their assertions. China was not only part of but also a major player in what Chris Bayly has termed 'archaic globalisation'. Timothy Brook believes that 'commerce had distinctive social and cultural effects'.[43] The stories of tobacco and opium allow us to see these distinctive effects. Where

China's political and genealogical intimacy with south and south-east Asia helped to introduce smoking and to reintroduce opium, Chinese consumer society and Chinese cultures of consumption helped to absorb a foreign way of recreation. The Chinese people naturalised tobacco smoking in the seventeenth century. They embraced opium smoking in the eighteenth century. They would sinicise opium in the nineteenth century.

CHAPTER 4

'A hobby among the high and the low in officialdom'

This chapter studies the downward penetration of opium from the literati-official establishment and its geographical spread inland in the first two decades of the nineteenth century.[1] Jaiqing's reign (1796–1819) was dwarfed by Qianlong's legacy; it was also overshadowed by the disintegration that followed. These years mattered greatly in the chain of events surrounding opium. Qianlong rebuffed the Macartney mission in 1793. But by the end of Jiaqing's reign in 1819 Britain had become the undisputed industrial and maritime power. I will trace the spread of opium during this period from two perspectives, class and geography. Opium smoking would work its way from the top down, from princes to eunuchs; it would also spread from the coast to the interior. In the eighteenth century the Chinese consumption of foreign goods, opium included, and its maritime trade were both in equilibrium, but by the nineteenth century a flood of free trade would break this harmony. The English East India Company, its 'cleverer than alchemists' servants and individual Englishmen would change the nineteenth-century global experience. Opium would enrich Britain and help them to build a most expansive empire; it would deplete China and hasten the downfall of the Qing dynasty. Opium smoking began to blossom in China at the same time as waves of free trade from Britain pounded the shore of Chinese consumerism. It fostered new generations of smokers.

PRINCE MINNING

Qianlong left China with 'ten enumerations', ten sons and many grandsons. One of his grandsons pleased him, in the same way he had pleased his own grandfather Kangxi, by felling a deer with a bow and arrow, like a real Manchu, on a hunting excursion with him in 1791. This grandson was made Prince of the Blood of the First Degree in his father Jiaqing's reign. Qianlong had indulged in snuff bottles; his grandson enjoyed smoking:

A new morning has begun with much free time. I sit alone in the study. It is the first sunny day after a spring snow, the sun and the wind in the garden and the trees are beautiful. I have nothing to do except reading and studying history. Bored and tired, I ask the servant to prepare *yan* and a pipe to inhale. Each time, my mind suddenly becomes clear, my eyes and ears refreshed. People in the past said that wine is endowed with all the virtues, but today I call *yan* the satisfier. When you desire happiness, it gives you happiness. And it is not vulgar like some of the popular customs today. As it expresses your thoughts, the drama and fun turn into eight rhymes.[2]

The author of this well-written piece of Chinese prose is Minning, the second son of Jiaqing and the sixth emperor of the Qing dynasty, who would reign under the title of Daoguang. It was written between 1799, when his father secretly chose him as Heir Apparent, and 1813, when he was made Prince of the Blood of the First Degree. The verses indicate years of study in Chinese; they also relate his experience of smoking. It is not clear, at this point in the extract, what Minning was inhaling. He called it *yan*, which by this time meant both tobacco and opium. This aside, the future emperor continues with the eight rhymes the *satisfier* inspires:

> Sharpen wood into a hollow pipe,
> Give it a copper head and tail,
> Stuff the eye with bamboo shavings,
> Watch the cloud ascend from nostril.
> Inhale and exhale, fragrance rises,
> Ambience deepens and thickens
> When it is stagnant, it is really as if
> Mountains and clouds emerge in distant sea.[3]

'Give it a copper head and tail' undoubtedly describes the opium pipe. Only an opium pipe has a 'tail' at the end, and more importantly an 'eye' on the side where the opium bowl sits and where the opium paste is inserted, tilted over the lamp, heated and smoked. Tobacco pipes have neither tails nor eyes on the side, rather, the pipe has a big hole at one end into which tobacco slices are laid, lighted and smoked. 'Stuff the eye with bamboo shavings' reminds us of Huang Shujing's 'stuff it with palm slices' and Zhu Jingying's 'stuff it with palm slices and hair'. Minning's fascination with the pipe is similar to that of the officials who worked in Taiwan. His appreciation compares to that of Yu Jiao's friend, who bragged about 'the marvels of opium'. The future emperor clearly enjoyed opium and was quite skilled in pipe making. Minning's smoking routines indicate that the habit of opium was tolerated in the royal chambers. No one saw much harm in its indulgence, certainly not Minning, whose reign would be plagued by this epidemic and whose name would become synonymous with the defeat China suffered during the first Opium War. Yet Minning's story is not simply that of a leisured Prince of the Blood in the 1800s. It is also about opium's availability and prevalence in the Forbidden City, and the immediate consequences.

Let me now turn to the servants, mostly eunuchs, who prepared the smoke. There is no doubt that they were exposed to opium earlier than most. The exact master–servant ratio in the case of a prince like Minning was about one to forty. Servants considerably outnumbered masters, and they knew a lot about the routines and interests of their masters. They dressed them, cooked their food, ran their errands and followed them wherever they went. And they prepared their opium smoking. Eunuchs played a significant role in opium's medicine-to-aphrodisiac transformation during the Ming. Qing eunuchs began to smoke opium from the early 1800s. We know this from court records. The Imperial Household arrested some eunuchs in possession of opium and opium pipes in the Daoguang emperor's eleventh year, 1831.[4] Interrogation revealed that the palace smoking gang included the head eunuch, Xiong Laifu, *Beile* or Prince of the Blood of the Third Degree, Kekesebuku, and many others. The eunuchs confessed that they had been smoking opium for almost thirty years. The case was difficult for the Imperial Household because Kekesebuku was the financier. He had cash and knew where opium could be procured. He sent his eunuchs to purchase opium, and he shielded them and their joint smoking within the security and comfort of his own palace. Who but the Son of Heaven himself could intervene when it came to the third highest of the twelve imperial nobles?

The eunuchs were merely the scapegoats. Did Jiaqing know about Minning and Kekesebuku's smoking? Jiaqing was certainly told about the existence of such practices, since in 1813 he instructed his cabinet ministers to draft details of punishment for those who smoked: 'Before only city rascals had opium and smoked it in private. But today attendants, guards and officials, they all take it. This is truly sickening.'[5] Jiaqing's statement is illuminating. His son Minning was not a city rascal by any means. But evil needed a definition. It had to come from below and outside, not from above and within. If Minning and Kekesebuku smoked it, their devious eunuchs must have led them. This was the opinion of the Jiaqing emperor. It would soon become the official line, and one which would influence the opinions of both historians and social scientists. The historian Edgar Holt, for example, believed that opium smoking was a vice that 'enlightened Chinese wish to stamp out'. Holt's book *The Opium Wars in China* (1964) helped perpetuate the narrow and prejudiced perspectives of official history. This is exactly what Thomas Brennan had seen in the case of public drinking in eighteenth-century Paris: 'information on the lives of the common people has always come from an external and socially superior perspective. In this way the opinions of elite observers have shaped historical accounts for generations by providing the most accessible and coherent evidence.' The political redefinition of opium consumption will be my subject in chapter 6 below.

'CONSPICUOUS CONSUMPTION' AND
'SHAME-ORIENTED CULTURE'

The case of the eunuchs is a good example of Veblen's 'conspicuous consumption'. Veblen pointed out that 'one portion of the servant class, chiefly those persons whose occupation is vicarious leisure, come to undertake a new, subsidiary range of duties – the vicarious consumption of goods'.[6] The eunuchs took up vicarious smoking of opium because their job was to light the lamp, heat up a small globule of paste, scoop it up and put it in the small bowl (the 'eye') on the pipe, and to hold the pipe until it is smoked. They were also to start the initial inhale, to make sure the paste was ready to smoke, to refill both the lamp and the bowl, and ultimately to rotate with their masters when the latter needed a break. Opium was smoked in rotation between two partners. Eunuchs would become skilled smokers. What they perfected at work, they could certainly enjoy in private. Opium was a rare and expensive item in Jiaqing's time. The middle classes of the Chinese interior might not even have heard of it. Eunuchs knew about it because they served princes such as Minning and *beiles* such as Kekesebuku. They were able to smoke it before many others because 'where leisure and consumption is performed vicariously by henchmen and retainers, imputation of the resulting repute to the patron is effected by their residing near his person'.[7] Their smoking bears witness to opium's availability and prevalence in the capital and its surrounding area and also among members of the imperial family. 'Conspicuous consumption' will be a recurring theme in the unfolding social life of opium.

Jonathan Spence has suggested that the institution of the eunuch and the royal hierarchy itself both contributed to the smoking of opium. He is certainly right. '[F]or the eunuchs and members of the imperial clan, there was a boring life in sheltered circumstances, without the possibilities of release that political power had given them in other times – for instance, the late Ming for eunuchs, or early Ch'ing for the Manchu nobles.'[8] Political frustration contributed to opium smoking, but the eunuchs' frustration was not just political. Contemporary writer John Barrow observed the eunuchs carefully: 'These creatures paint their faces, study their dress and are as coquettish as the ladies upon whom indeed it is their chief business to attend.'[9] He was fascinated by their sexual practices: 'there is scarcely one about the palace, whether of the class of porters and sweepers, or of that which is qualified for the inner apartments, but have women in their lodgings, who are generally the daughters of poor people, from whom they purchased, and are consequently considered as their slaves'. Could sexual frustration, like political frustration, have also contributed to their opium smoking?

Eunuchs faced verbal and physical abuse both inside and outside the palace. They often ended up as scapegoats for the many happenings that jeopardised the reputations of emperors, princes and court ladies. What they suffered from daily was socio-political oppression of an extreme kind. The fact that they were raided and punished for opium smoking, when princes and *beiles* all enjoyed it, was an example. 'Kill the chicken to frighten the monkey', as the famous saying goes. A few puffs of momentary indulgence and recollection in a hideaway with a few who shared the same fate must have helped to ease the suffering. Spence quoted the thought-provoking words of Charles de Contant. Contant was fascinated not only with opium smoking but also with why the Chinese, eunuchs in particular, had succumbed to it. He wrote: 'Le Chinois, lâche par nature, opprime, prive par sa constitution politique de toute espèce de société cherche sa consolation dans l'usage d'une substance qui par sa nature absorbe l'âme.'[10] Contant believed that the Chinese were by nature weak, oppressed and private due to their political constitution; they therefore sought consolation in a substance that consumed their soul. This was so because 'la prive des sensations douloureuse qu'un retour presque continuel sur sa situation presente ne faisait qu'aggraver'. They smoked opium because the private bitter sensation prevented their current situation from becoming further aggravated. In other words, it lessened their pain and helped them to carry on the burden of living.

Contant saw a direct link between political oppression and the Chinese addiction to opium. As Louis Dermigny was to paraphrase in his writing: 'il y a un lien étroit entre l'accroissement de la consummation de l'opium et les "progres du despotisme"'. He believed that the increase in opium consumption went hand in hand with political despotism. Tyrannical politics shaped the psyches and behaviours of a people. An oppressive political climate coupled with the introvert character of the Chinese people had led them to seek comfort and consolidation in opium. Opium smoking, in other words, gave solace by elevating the soul and allowing it to escape to a different world. People succumbed to opium under these circumstances. Opium in this context was anaesthesia of a socio-political kind. This was certainly a most original observation. And it is far-reaching, because eunuchs were not the only people who were oppressed. Many people, women and coolie labourers for example, were also exploited, both physically and emotionally. So did they also succumb to opium? This will be my theme in chapters 8 and 10. Contant raised an insightful question about opium consumption. What he alluded to would become the focus for anthropologists and psychoanalysts in the twentieth century, when debates began over the correlation between consumer behaviour and socio-political or socio-cultural constraints.

Westerners have often compared the evil of opium to that of alcohol in the West. Alcohol can offer temporary relief and detachment from life's frustrations. Stewart Lockhart, Protector of the Chinese in Hong Kong, gave evidence at the Royal Commission in 1893: 'Comparing the opium sot and the drunkard, I should say the drunkard is a man who makes himself a much greater nuisance to society than an opium sot.' Lockhart explained his reasoning: 'The opium sot, although he may be affecting himself physically, and perhaps mentally, does not make himself a nuisance to society generally; whereas the drunkard, as is well known, is not only a nuisance to his immediate surroundings, but very often to society in general.'[11] Many agreed with him. William Lockhart, who was a missionary in China for twenty-five years, was very clear about the boundary between individual harm and social evil: 'opium is personally hurtful to individuals. Alcohol is a much greater social evil.' He went further: 'as a social evil there is no comparison between the two. He that takes alcohol to excess is a nuisance to society, a man that smokes opium to excess subsides into quietness the moment he has had his pipe.'[12] Lockhart's observation exposed one socio-cultural constraint that could restrict consumer behaviour, and which helps us to understand at least one circumstance under which some Chinese people succumbed to opium.

'Nuisance to one's immediate surroundings' beckons more investigation. To be quiet and civil, that is, not being a nuisance to one's immediate surroundings, was and still is one of the many socio-cultural mechanisms that have kept the Chinese people, among others, under physical and moral constraint. This can be said to apply to many cultures. James R. Rush studied the Javanese, their opium consumption and their socio-cultural conventions. His research showed that many smoked opium because it 'altered outward behaviour so little. Unlike drinking alcohol, when smoking opium one could maintain decorum and be certain of one's public composure.'[13] The average Javanese smoker gave thought to the judgements of others before undertaking smoking. Indeed, it was not smoking itself but what it would do to their bodily behaviour that concerned them. This is extremely revealing. Socio-cultural norms constrained consumers like an invisible hand. Javanese smokers, in other words, feared or respected this invisible authority. They weighed the consequences of their opium smoking. So would many others, including the Chinese. This was the restraining power of socio-cultural constraint. In theory, it could be the difference between so-called 'shame' and 'guilt' cultures.

Shame as Deborah Greenwald and David Harder have pointed out is 'a self-conscious awareness that one is being viewed, or might be viewed, by others with an unflattering gaze'.[14] This seems to explain the Javanese case. Such awareness can 'constrain behaviour into channels that are socially approved of and/or culturally appropriate'. Javanese smokers consumed opium because smoking 'altered outward behaviour so little'; they considered it to be not socially disapproved of and culturally inappropriate. More importantly, 'shame makes the sufferer want to shrink away from others'. Smoking opium and dozing off on the pillow was not being a nuisance to one's immediate surroundings. And get it definitely was one way to shrink away not only from others but also from responsibilities and from the complicated world. This seems to echo the thoughts of Charles de Contant. To shrink away from frustration or life's difficulties was one motive behind opium consumption. Shrinking away can be self-defeating or even self-destructive. It is a response to or a reaction against outside forces, although it can be self-imposed at times. So what might these external forces be and why do they exercise so much power over individuals and their behaviour? Ruth Benedict's early work makes it clear:

True shame cultures rely on external sanctions for good behaviour, not, as true guilt cultures do, on an internalised conviction of sin. Shame is a reaction to other people's criticism. A man is shamed whether by being openly ridiculed and rejected or by fantasying to himself that he has been ridiculous. In either case it is a potent sanction. But it requires an audience or at least a man's fantasy of an audience. Guilt does not. In a nation where honour means living up to one's own picture of oneself, a man may suffer from guilt though no man knows of his misdeed and a man's feeling of guilt may actually be relieved by confessing his sin.[15]

An 'audience', real or imagined, is a powerful external force and the Javanese knew or imagined it well. The judgement of others is what is meant by 'external sanctions', unspoken but observed socio-cultural conventions.

These sanctions live with individuals who fear or respect these conventions and in societies that impose collective values upon individuals; they thrive in 'shame-oriented cultures'. The Javanese case demonstrates that they can constrain consumer behaviour. Greenwald and Harder continue their analysis of the cultural aspects of shame: 'shame seems to be closely associated with some specific domains of social behaviour, such as conformity, prosocial, and sexual behaviour'. For the Javanese, opium smoking gratified an individual desire. It also met with socio-cultural conventions. It was an undertaking that satisfied both needs. Although an individual counted for little, his or her responsibilities were many in a collective society such as China. Most would weigh up the consequences of their undertakings. The close association between 'external sanctions' and consumer behaviour will be the focus of chapter 11 below, when opium smoking became a norm of social contact and exchange in the late nineteenth century. Indeed, it is a recurring theme in the unfolding social life of opium.

WEN *JIANG* AND TAI *JIANG*

As the opium pipe passed from princes to eunuchs, it also spread geographically, to the north and to the interior. The opium-smoking officials who escorted the Macartney mission and the eunuchs confirmed opium's availability in the capital and its vicinity, especially Tianjin, from the 1790s to 1810s. When the political capital had so much opium, we can only imagine its prevalence in the capital of Jiangnan decadence. This can best be seen from the career of Mukedengbu:

The person of Mukedengbu, styled Shaoruo, used to be a Manchu Bannerman stationed at Jinzhou. He was the seventh son of the late Nanjing General Kuiyu . . . and he later climbed up to the Governorship of Jiangsu. He asked for an additional inspector to supervise taxation. He stated that since the *Dao* and *Fu* [provincial administrative units] had their own duties, it was not proper for them to co-supervise it. To prevent corruption and with the Emperor's consent, he would take up this responsibility. A term was four years and it was said that he received 300,000 *liang* of gold. He built great mansions in Nanjing, bought land/estates in the most prosperous areas along the river; he also had big capital in money-lending and salt transportation. He was the richest among all the inspectors in Jiangnan . . . The abundance of his opium stock amounted to several thousand *jin*. When the Taiping Revolutionary Army captured Nanjing, his opium was thrown out on the roadside and it was impossible to count them.[16]

Mukedengbu was a Plain White Bannerman who rose to be the garrison commander of Nanjing from 1814 to 1818. Not only was opium rare in those days, it was also extremely expensive. 'Several thousand *jin*' of opium amounted to tens of thousands of silver taels. Mukedengbu was a Manchu whose ancestors had fought for the Manchu dynasty. They had shed blood for the dynasty. Now it was their and their sons' turn to enjoy the fruits of their victory. The soldiers and generals who were known for their equestrian skills and marksmanship were either gone or fast disappearing. Now there was plenty of tea and time, silver and smoke. They came uninvited and they kept coming. Was there such a thing as 'the corruption and disdain of the Manchu official', as the writer titled the above story? Chinese decadence was eating up the strength of banner officers, demilitarising the Qing fighting machine starting from the top. It would soon envelop the whole apparatus. Mukedengbu's forefathers had 'fought for mountains and rivers'; surely his generation would only have to 'sit on the mountains and rivers'. Nanjing might have had a good deal of opium, but it was limited to the rich and powerful. Its neighbours in the south, however, had begun experimenting with opium *gao* or 'paste' and *jiang* or 'syrup' by the 1810s – a time that is much earlier than historians have been familiar with. Shi Hongbao remembered the situation in Zhejiang and Fujian provinces:

The opium that inland provinces produce are but paste made from the juice of the poppy. Guangdong has always had it. Towards the end of Jiaqing [1815–19], Zhejiang's Wen–Tai region also had it and they were called *Wen jiang* [Wen syrup] and *Tai jiang* [Tai syrup]. Recently Fujian's Funing Prefecture also had it; the part that matured into paste was called *Fu gao* [Fu paste] and the part that did not was called *Fu jiang* [Fu syrup]. The *jiang* was put in a jar and buried in the soil. The longer it was buried, the better it tasted compared to the barbarian's. If it was not buried long enough and left exposed, it could not be smoked.[17]

Shi's memoir yields much information about a fundamental discovery. The opium that Shen Fu, princes and eunuchs smoked came in through maritime trade. Opium could only be procured from foreigners. Zhejiang and Fujian peasants seem to have realised that China had what it took to make the opium paste, that opium did not have to be imported. This was revolutionary, because it meant that pioneering people could experiment making it from the medicinal plant that had been known since the Tang dynasty. The difference between syrup and paste was already known. Wen and Tai are two coastal prefectures of Zhejiang; Funing is the neighbouring prefecture in Fujian. A native of Zhejiang, Shi worked and travelled widely in the two provinces. Like Zhu Jingying, who wrote about how to smoke opium, Shi gave detailed instructions about how to make the smoke. Scholar-officials were indispensable in the spread of opium. Some noted that the paste and syrup made for good business.

Liang Shaoren (1792–1837), who was also a native of Zhejiang, wrote: 'Recently some have started to cultivate it in the inland area. In Zhejiang, it is called Tai *jiang*; in Fujian, it is called Jian *jiang*; and in Sichuan, it is called Shu *jiang*.'[18] Tai is the above-mentioned prefecture in Zhejiang and Jian a short name for Fujian. Liang added Sichuan to the list, whereas Bao Shichen (1775–1855) added Yunnan: 'Since Jiaqing's tenth year (1806), Zhejiang's Taizhou and Yunnan's indigenous people have all cultivated the poppy and made the paste.'[19] The scholar-officials mention the production of opium syrup and opium paste in four south-east maritime and south-west border provinces. Piecemeal domestic cultivation had begun. This is not surprising, given the precedent set by tobacco and other new world produce. It might have started even earlier than around 1806, perhaps as early as the late eighteenth century. This shows how quickly information travelled and how fast peasants responded to commercial intelligence. Profit-seeking farmers had switched to growing tobacco in the late Ming; their Qing counterparts switched to cultivating opium, and probably sold it as syrup or paste or most likely enjoyed smoking it themselves, mixed with tobacco or even pure.

It looked possible, given growing domestic cultivation in the 1800s and 1810s, that opium would repeat tobacco's naturalisation, since there was no prohibition at the time and since opium's poisonous effects were unknown to the public. But the process of naturalisation would take much longer. This was so partly because it would take time for the knowledge to filter through the vast agrarian society, and partly because *yanghuo re*, the Chinese craving for things foreign, was gathering momentum in the early decades of the nineteenth century. Foreign opium, one of the most popular and expensive *yanghuo* and soon to be called *yang yan* or 'foreign smoke', was considered superior to Chinese brands. Home-grown opium never surpassed its foreign rivals in terms of popularity, potency and price. It was thought to be milder than its Indian, Persian or Turkish counterparts. Hence, the wider consumer trend of *yanghuo re* can be seen as being at least partly responsible for preventing the extensive domestic cultivation of opium until the late nineteenth century, when foreign imports declined. *Yanghuo* is my topic in the next chapter.

Nowhere was opium more visible than in Canton. Here it enjoyed a natural advantage and had the largest army of smokers, as Zhu Fengchun remembered: 'The most addicted are found in Canton, today among the scholar-officials many indulge in such a Buddha. As to brothels and hostels, they are all equipped with it to allure clients.'[20] This situation can be seen elsewhere. Huang Yue, head of the Metropolitan Examination of 1820, knew the participants well: 'Students from Jiangnan and Guangdong went north for the examination in the spring. Their addiction attacked them during the examination; they died in the hall and their bodies were left on the roadside.'[21] 'Jiangnan' reaffirms the availability of opium and the prevalence of smoking in the provinces of Jiangsu and Zhejiang. The ritual of examination drew hundreds of students from the coastal provinces. They journeyed for weeks to reach the capital and the whole affair was one of anxiety, excitement and disappointment. Opium was the best thing to bring along, because it was easy to carry and profitable to dispose of. Smoking helped to dispel the boredom of study, refreshed one's mind and might even help produce the stroke of genius needed for success. Selling it at a marked-up rate in the north was easy, and it would bring in much-needed cash. Otherwise, one could always indulge in it oneself with a few fellow examinees.

   Examination students were not alone in carrying opium with them. Many provincial officials journeyed to the capital from the coastal regions. Their position offered them the best protection when they travelled:

Xingliang was a Lieutenant of the Plain Red Banner Cavalry in Canton; he worked under the Assistant Commandant Yongtai. In September of Jiaqing's nineteenth year [1814], the Vice Commander-in-Chief of Guangdong province, Xiaochang was going to Beijing for his annual mission and he asked Xingliang to accompany him. Xingliang thought that he could reap some profits by taking some opium with him. He gathered and borrowed one hundred and forty *liang* of silver, and bought fourteen cans of opium from a local man called Shi Er; the opium weighed eleven kilograms. He was afraid of being found and hid it at the bottom of his own chest.[22]

Xingliang was only one of thousands who took advantage of their official duties. Like Mukedengbu in Nanjing, he grabbed his small opportunities. This was not unusual, since corruption and other forms of extortion were common practices throughout the officialdom. The military and the civil pecking orders, as we have seen from the Taiwan conquest and the cases of Mukedengbu and Xingliang, helped to promote opium. They were directly responsible for an increasing awareness of opium and for its increased availability.

THE LONG MARCH OF OPIUM

Daniel Roche has pointed out that in order to understand the concept of consumption we should study 'the circuits of distribution and the spatial organisation of supply'. The examination-bound students and the travelling officials speak to Roche's point. They show us examples of opium's inland transportation and distribution. Opium's downward penetration and its spread into the interior were fuelled by two major factors: popularity and availability. A growing awareness of opium smoking was taking place among the general populace and a rise in smuggling met the demand. Economic historians have produced excellent studies on the opium trade. But foreign smugglers only delivered opium to Canton; it needed the Chinese themselves to transport and distribute it to the inland areas. The inward and upward long march of opium, along with its wholesale and retail in the interior, have not been explored. Non-professionals carried opium to the vast interior, but the bulk of its inland transportation and distribution rested with professionals – with commercial guilds. Their emergence was the direct result of the Ming–Qing socio-economic transformation and of the leisure revolution. Opium's transportation and distribution illustrates the power of the commercial guilds over the consumer economy, culture and society.

The commercial guilds of Guangdong and Fujian monopolised opium's wholesale, long-distance transportation and retail in the interior until the late nineteenth century. The Guangdong commercial guild was dubbed 'the vanguard of foreign trade' and the Fujian commercial guild 'the power brigade of sea commerce'. Henry Charles Sirr, a British diplomat, noticed the physical difference between them: 'The junks of Amoy have the peculiarity, namely, being painted a bright green colour at the bow; the inhabitants call their vessels *green heads*, to distinguish them from Canton junks, which being painted a brilliant red, are termed *red heads*.'[23] Commercial guilds and compradors pioneered the way into the interior. The scattered Chinese language material in the Jardine Matheson archive sheds much light on the way in which opium was transported to and sold in the interior:

So I decided to moor the boat on the river in *Yanping* [Fujian] and sent people everywhere to gather information. When there is a way, I will certainly go myself and buy packaged [versus loose] teas. *Xingli* [baggage] can only go as far as *Shaxian* [Fujian], I still have half and it is stored on the boat in *Yanping*. But we can not use *Shaxian* too much. If there is no other way to push local sale, I have to come back. Please do not send any more at this moment.[24]

The author of this note is Jardine's comprador Ahee, and opium in this extract was conveniently dubbed *xingli* or 'baggage'. Yanping is a market town near the tea-growing Wuyi Mountain. Ahee went there by boat on the Min River with his stock of opium. His job was to sell it in order to procure tea. The English could not do without tea; tea could not be procured without the Cantonese and the Fujianese. Just as the Dutch left the distribution of opium in Java to the Chinese there, Jardine Matheson left its own operation to the Chinese compradors. Rivers were important passages to and from the interior in Fujian. In the case of Guangdong, this was even more so. From Canton, opium travelled on three major waterways, that is, the East, the North and the West River (see map 1). Canton was connected with the whole country via local waterways and sometimes via land routes in between. The West River flows into Guangxi and Yunnan provinces. Archibald R. Colquhoun would observe smuggling along the West River in the late nineteenth century. The East River flows east into the greater Chao-Shan region. John Scarth was once there and saw the happenings on this waterway:

The Chaou-Chaou river is a large and important stream. Opium is conveyed from the above city into that province [Jiangxi]. We saw it being unpacked, and put into pillow boxes, rice-baskets, &c., quite openly, ready to be carried into the city. We were asked to go in by the opium dealers, but did not relish making our entry in such doubtful society. They appeared jolly, respectable sort of men, and were very civil.[25]

Chaozhou is where the shrewd Hakka people concentrated while Jiangxi led opium into the vast south-east interior. Migrants from the central plains, the Hakka had settled in the seafaring provinces. Industrious by nature, they were key players in China's maritime and opium trades. The North River was the busiest because it flowed into the Gan River of Jiangxi and the Xiang River of Hunan province, through which it joins the Yangzi (Yangtze) River in Hubei. The Yangzi, the mother river of China, is connected with all the major waterways of central China and also with the Grand Canal (see map 1). The North River flows into the small Hunan towns of Yizhang and Linwu via local waterways. This was the best way to and from Canton. Zhou Shouchang, a native of Hunan who later became Vice-Minister of the Board of Rites, went to Canton via this route. His memoir tells of the activities at the confluence of the Guangdong and Hunan waterways:

All along, rocks, shoals rise and recede with rapids, bank trees merge into shades. There are small tree stakes and wood stacks, field wheels and dancing waves, the sound of rowing boats and oars cutting water. They make one feel like an ancient man; they evoke the genius of poetry. But it is a great pity that in recent decades, Guangdong merchants have smuggled opium through this way; it is from here that they come to land in Hunan.[26]

Zhou went on to tell of how smugglers and bandits from both provinces overran the area. This would only intensify in the 1830s, when smuggling gathered momentum. The area would become the land and cross-land of criminals and opium. Yizhang and Linwu belonged to the larger circuit of Hengyang, seat of the circuit government and the major urban centre of southern Hunan. Hengyang is on the Xiang River. Rivers were vital. The regional urban centres such as Hengyang were even more so, when it came to storage and distribution. The sophistication of local commercial organisation and operation, and the ways in which opium was stored, advertised and sold in the vast interior, is well illustrated by the chapter 'Engagement in Trade' of the *Hengyang County Gazetteer*:

Heng yan's [Hengyang-grown tobacco] altar [guildhall] was established in Ming times, and its tobacco was sold throughout the country. The altar is in the north of the city. Shanxi and Shaanxi's big merchants who dealt in tobacco had nine *Tang* [Hall] and thirteen *Hao* [House]. The annual capital in and out of every one of them was more than tens of thousands . . . Looking back, it has only been for fifty or sixty years since Fujian's *yan* became popular; in comparison *Heng yan* is not good enough. All the *Tang* and *Hao* lost their business . . . And now there is the western barbarian's smoke-paste, it eats the country's wealth.[27]

Through Hengyang, the Xiang River flows into the Yangzi River in Hankou, the emporium of central China. Hankou's opium warehouses and wholesale stores were so notorious that Commissioner Lin would start his clean-up campaign from there when prohibition began in the late 1830s. Hunan sat on the crossroads. It was also the home of the famed *Xiangfei zhu*, the Hunanese mottle bamboo. The abundance of this much-loved bamboo would turn Hunan into one of the biggest opium pipe-making centres, and the Hunanese into some of the most skilled smokers. While commercial guilds were the most important players in the transportation of opium, urban centres such as Hengyang and Hankou were even more so in the distribution of opium. The short reign of Jiaqing saw the rapid penetration of opium smoking throughout the officialdom. This is best summarised by Dai Lianfen: 'In the middle of Jiaqing and in officialdom, it's becoming a hobby among both the high and the low!' The Chinese officialdom operated in both towns and cities. Their involvement in the spread of opium smoking was vital. The 'middle of Jiaqing' coincided with the 'opium rush' of 1813, when Indian commerce was opened up to all private English.[28] The rush was on: 'It is like gold, I can sell it at any time.'[29] The 'middle of Jiaqing' also coincided with the ascendancy of the British flag on international waters. Britain once again sent a mission to the Chinese court in 1817, 'to inform of the victories against France' and 'to place our concerns in China on a better footing'.[30]

The Amherst mission was considered a complete failure with regard to British trade privileges in China. Like the previous Macartney mission, it also gathered commercial intelligence on opium, as Clarke Abel reported:

No opium is exposed for sale in the shops, probably because it is a contraband article, but it is used with tobacco in all parts of the empire. The Chinese indeed consider the smoking of opium as one of the greatest luxuries; and if they are temperate in drinking, they are often excessive in the use of this drug. They have more than one method of smoking it: sometimes they envelop a piece of the solid gum in tobacco, and smoke it from a pipe with a very small bowl; and sometimes they steep fine tobacco in a strong solution of it, and use it in the same way.[31]

From the Prince of the Blood of the First Degree to eunuchs and 'the high and the low in officialdom', through students, military officers, compardors and guild merchants, opium was making its way to the masses and to the interior during the short reign of Jiaqing. The cash-cropping market town economy had once helped to spread tobacco; now it helped opium. Jiaqing tried to prohibit its sale and use, his edicts were few. At the grand celebration of his sixtieth birthday, in 1819, he bestowed exquisite snuff bottles upon his favoured princes and high-ranking officials. One of them was Huang Yue, the Minister of Rites, who enjoyed opium smoking, as I shall show in chapter 6. Snuff bottles were a symbol of elite culture and royal patronage, and production of them reached its zenith during Jiaqing's reign. Opium smoking was becoming popular and opium was becoming increasingly available. Yet it still did not constitute a consumer trend in the textbook sense. It would take the first decade or so of Daoguang to realise this. When availability was no longer an issue, consumption would be open to more, if not all, consumers.

CHAPTER 5

Taste-making and trendsetting

This chapter is devoted to opium's urbanisation and initial popularisation, in other words, to the birth of the opium-smoking consumer trend, in the 1820s and early 1830s. Scholars and officials had embedded opium consumption into mainstream sex recreation in Qianlong's time; they spread the gospel of opium in Jiaqing's time; they would urbanise it in Daoguang's reign (1820–50). Fuelled by the popularity of *yanghuo* and aided by the rise of smuggling, opium smoking spread quickly. The arrival of a consumer trend depended on the participation of the larger urban population and more importantly on the availability of opium. More individual Englishmen rushed to what Jacques Downs called the 'golden ghetto' of Canton after 1813, when Indian commerce opened up. They also found a better depot – Lintin. Soon a dynamic duo, William Jardine and James Matheson, would challenge the Honourable Company and see the 'termination of its exclusive right of trading with the dominions of the emperor of China' in 1834.[1] The consequences of free trade can be seen in the statistics. Opium imports stood at 4,244 chests in 1820, thereafter increasing yearly so that by 1839 the number had jumped to 40,200.[2] Opium was galvanising urban consumer society.

YANGHUO AND THE 'LEISURE CLASS'

Daoguang's first decade (1820–30) barely resembled Qianlong's heyday, yet for many, the good life went on. Not only did many smoke opium, many more also became increasingly fascinated with everything foreign. Liang Zhangju (1775–1849) remembered this vividly:

Chen Zhan said that the decadence of today's customs is not one that the prohibition of luxuries could resolve . . . Look at the place [where] I live. The luxury and delicacy of its carvings and the beauty of the utensils would be regarded as decadent in the olden days; but now they are just commonplace. *Wai yang* [outer ocean or foreign] things are the most fashionable now. For example, all without exception,

71

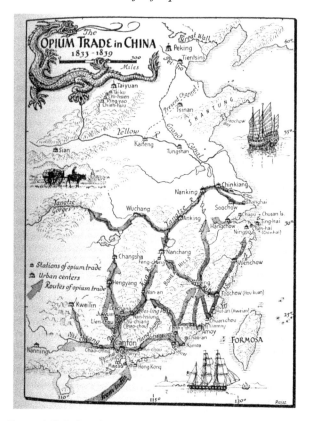

Map 2. Canton is linked to the Yangtze River and the Grand Canal via the rivers of southern and central China. This map shows opium's upward and inward routes along these waterways in the mid-nineteenth century.

houses, rooms, boats and carriages all contain glass-made windows, clothes and curtains are made from furs and feathers, even utensils and decorations are called *yang* copper, *yang* china, *yang* paint, *yang* linen, *yang* cotton, and *yang* blue, *yang* red, *yang* marten, *yang* otter, *yang* paper, *yang* pictures, *yang* fans, the list is endless. The southern provinces even circulate *yang* money [foreign silver]; they came from Japan, Liuku and England.[3]

Yang means ocean; it was used as a prefix for goods and things in general that came via the ocean. *Yanghuo* means 'foreign stuff'; it was the name given to the category that included opium. Liang did not mention that westerners were called *yang* people, their firms, *yang* guilds, and their matches, *yang* fire; opium was called *yang* smoke and soon became known as *yang yao* or 'foreign drug'. *Yanghuo* was very popular among the royals, literati and high-ranking officials in the eighteenth century. The late Qianlong–early Daoguang period was a time when more people, and not just the upper classes, joined in the appreciation of and consumption of foreign goods. The 1839 (printed) *Xiamen Zhi* or *Gazetteer of Amoy*, registered those *yanghuo* that arrived via Amoy in the 1820s and the early 1830s, among them *yang* carpet, *yang* handkerchiefs, *yang* glasses, *yang* harps, *yang* pens, *yang* matches, *yang* trees, *yang* pictures, *yang* bowls and many more. The comprehensive *Yuehai Guanzhi* or *History of the Guangdong Customs* registered all the foreign goods that came in through the Customs in Guangdong province, and their import taxes.

'We must examine Chinese acts rather than Chinese words', Joanna Waley-Cohen has emphasised.[4] *Yanghuo* had its origins in the Ming, when maritime trade brought a whole array of non-Chinese produce and luxuries to China. This trade intensified in the Qing, when 'the age of calicoes and tea and opium' bred newer generations of more sophisticated consumers. *Yanghuo* came from afar; they were rare, expensive and, more importantly, status tellers. A good example is the 'singsongs' – namely, a clock, watch or fantastically shaped mechanical toy, such as a snuff box that conceals a jewelled bird which sings when the lid is open. All were extremely popular collectibles among the Chinese elite. William Milburn was fascinated with the Chinese demand for *yanghuo*. He noticed the 'immense quantities of clocks and other valuable pieces of mechanism' imported into China, and was amused by the Chinese requirement for watches: 'they must be in pairs, to suit the taste of the Chinese'.[5] *Yanghuo* was the monopoly of the guilds of Guangdong, Fujian and Zhejiang. Many merchants had been operating in northern urban centres such as Tianjin since the eighteenth century. Linda Cooke Johnson has pointed out that 'More Fujian merchants were attracted to Shanghai in the Jiaqing and early Daoguang years.'[6] More *yanghuo* stores were opened. The 'Construction and Establishment' chapter of the *Extended Gazetteer of Shanghai County* recorded that 'In the beginning of Daoguang, all the *huatang* [fancy candy made of malt sugar] and *yanghuo* guild merchants of Fujian's TingQuanZhang prefectures all established their altar [guildhall] at *Dianchun tang* [spring-touching hall], near the north-east corner of the *Yu Garden*.'[7] The Fujianese were eager to cash in, the Cantonese even more so. A second Guangdong guild, which would become the infamous Swatow opium guild, was also established in Shanghai at this time. Coastal merchants saw *yanghuo*'s future in the north. The further north and inland you went, the rarer *yanghuo* were and the dearer they could be sold. The Tianjinese named the street where

Cantonese and Fujianese merchants operated their *yanghuo* stores *yanghuo jie*, 'foreign stuff street'. Cui Xu devoted a timely verse to it:

> All kinds of treasure come from ocean-going ships,
> Glass door shops open and compete side by side,
> Dutch, Indian, western foreigner's textile goods,
> Strange, exotic, and bewildering *yanghuo* street.[8]

The *yanghuo* phenomenon, especially the circulation of *yang* money, as mentioned by Liang, was a concern to many at the time. The Imperial Censor Huang Zhongmo complained to the new emperor Daoguang in 1822: 'Because people like to use *yang* money, the *yang* merchants use silver to do business, this led to the high price of tea in Jiangsu and Zhejiang; they also use *yang* money to buy *yang* stuff.'[9] Liang Shaoren and Zhou Shouchang both noticed the circulation of *yang* money and the popularity of *yanghuo*; so too did Lin Zexu and many other provincial officials. It was the beginning of the silver drain. *Yanghuo* was popular and profitable in the early days of Daoguang. Hu Shiyu knew the situation better than most. He observed: 'All things today, that which is expensive is called *yang*. Those money suckers in the city, regardless of where the thing was made, would add *yang* in front of it to show its preciousness.'[10] Indeed, how would northerners and inlanders know the difference? 'That which is expensive is *yang*' was a saying of Daoguang's time, and indeed opium was the most expensive. Yang Zhangsheng's *Jingchen Zalu* or *The Miscellaneous Notes on the Dust of Beijing* tells the story:

The number one celestial I knew was Yunxiang, surname Lin, who came from *Wu* [Jiangsu] to the capital to study at the House of *Songzhu*. The House was in decline, it could not survive and members were leaving. Some of its teachers and patrons recruited new young pupils; they called themselves the Small House of Songzhu . . . Yunxiang came at this time and lived at *Chuanjin tang*, also called *Hongbin tang* or 'Hall of grand guests' because many fine young men also lived there. In the first year of Daoguang [1821], *Ershuang-Sanfa* [new style of singing and performance] emerged from there . . . When Prince Yi Shen's birthday came in *xinmao* [1831], only the Small House of Songzhu was invited to the palace to entertain the distinguished guests . . .

Yunxiang was bravoed 'Good Boy!' The Small House of Songzhu suddenly became famous; their shows were full and filled with distinguished guests. His talent was unique . . . But nothing could make him happy . . . He wanted to quit when his three-year contract expired. His teacher was cunning; he sent for his father from *Wu* and promised 800 *liang* of gold for another three years. But Yunxiang outwitted him by hosting a famous dinner party when he invited the fine young men and raised 3,000 *liang* of gold to buy himself out . . .

From then on at *Meihe tang*, or 'Hall of plum and crane', the wine gatherings of the literati as well as conversations over tea and melon would always see Yunxiang present . . . This was happiness of a life time . . . But it seemed that his unknown illness was deeply rooted and it was taking its hold. After three months, it went out of control. On the day he died, his face was wet with tears and he swore to Buddha: This life was finished and in the next life he would never be an object of love again. Alas! Dead and gone! It first began with Zheng Xuechao of Xiangshan [Guangdong], who wanted to make Yunxiang happy and gave him the opium paste . . . That winter Zheng had guests from Guangdong who brought him that most celebrated thing and sold it to him at 240 *liang* in gold . . . Unfortunately Xuechao died and three days later Yunxiang died as well. It was the Twelfth Moon of the Fourteenth Year of Daoguang [January 1835, western calendar]. Yunxiang was only eighteen. All is lost! How sad![11]

'An object of love', opium at 240 *liang* in gold, the Pear Garden, as the performing art world was called, nineteenth-century China was an age of sex, drugs and rock-and-roll. What this story points us to is female imper-sonation and homosexuality or 'Passions of the cut sleeve' within the royal and literati/artistic circles of Beijing in the early 1830s. Female imperson-ation and sex recreation with male partners were Chinese traditions, and they flourished in the Qing. Lin Yunxiang was a superstar who had single-handedly revived the House of Songzhu with his female roles; his partner Zheng Sheren was a literati hanger-on from Canton. Female impersonators were usually handsome males who looked or behaved like females. At this time women were not allowed on the stage. Little is known about Zheng. He could have been the son of a distinguished or wealthy family. Otherwise, how could he have afforded such a leisured lifestyle and opium at 240 *liang* in gold? Lin and Zheng were good friends of the author Yang Zhangsheng, another native of Canton. Yang passed the *juren* examination in 1831, and he worked in the capital. This was ideal because it gave him a salary, time to study for the *jinshi* exam, and an opportunity to network within the political establishment. Yang came from a family who could afford his fees at the prestigious *Xuehai tang* or Hall of the Sea of Learning in Canton. He was fond of opera and wrote songs while waiting for examination results and career opportunities to come to fruition. He passed the *jinshi* exam, but was not awarded the title. Many believed this was because the Head Examiner, who happened to be his old teacher Ruan Yuan, did not approve of his decadent lifestyle.

This was the scandal of the examination season. Yang, as a result, gave himself up to 'wine gatherings' and 'conversations over tea and melon'. He returned to Canton after his friends died and wrote down what he saw and knew from Beijing. He compared himself and his friends to 'the dust of Beijing'. He was disenchanted with the political establishment and its conservative ideologues. His memoirs tell more than just the stories of his intimate friends and of nostalgia for life gone by. They extend to the wider topics of elite life, urban culture, public institutions and mechanisms of culture transmission. 'Sons of the Pear Garden', as actors were called, and men of letters were drawn to the cities, where their patrons resided and where the future lay. Some had talent, some were endowed with fortune, others enjoyed patronage. They mingled with their patrons from the court and with the political establishment. They could afford to hang around the political metropolis, and they fashioned and lived by a code that was all their own, as one of them detailed: 'In the winter months, gentlemen invited each other and gathered around the stove for drinking wine. They took turns to be the host and they called this "the club of cold-dispelling". Some went out of their way to have nine people and rotate every nine days because nine-nine is said to dispel cold.'[12]

'Nine' is phonetically similar to 'wine' in the Chinese language. The above was lettered recreation, and it was but one of many pastimes. Zhao Yi remembered his good old days: 'In the *Pear Garden* of Beijing, those with sex skills, gentlemen usually go whore them.'[13] Now they had one more excuse to 'gather around the stove' and 'go whore' in the bitter northern winter: there was opium. Opium was a perfect addition to this lifestyle. Prince Minning and *Beile* Kekesebuku had enjoyed opium in the 1810s, now the literati/artistic elite also enjoyed it. The kind of gathering described above became so notorious that Beijing surveillance officials began raiding suspected premises. Opium had come from Canton, and the Cantonese became its synonym in the north. The elite of the capitals had information about and access to opium. Their prestige and wealth created superstars like Yunxiang. In turn, Yunxiang's beauty and talent helped them escape to a world where there were no ascetic moral principles. Just as the birthday of a Prince of Blood could not be celebrated without opera ('the mania for opera', as Susan Naquin calls it), so the capital elite could not be without the most expensive *yanghuo* – opium.[14]

THE '5 PER CENT OR SO OF THE POPULATION'

The elite of the capitals and their royal patrons were, to a large extent, what Veblen calls the leisure class. Opium lived with them because they knew about it and could afford it. Cities such as Canton, Nanjing and

Beijing were where the leisure class resided, even though many kept their rural premises and ties, and where foreign commodities, such as opium, could be sold at a high price. Veblen's theory of the leisure class substantiates the position of opium in China. 'The ceremonial differentiation of the dietary is best seen in the use of intoxicating beverages and narcotics. If these articles of consumption are costly, they are felt to be noble and honorific.'[15] With the leisure class, opium became leisurely, urban, cultured and a status symbol, as Yang's memoir perfectly illustrates. It was leisurely because it lived with the rich and famous, urban because it lived among quintessential city-dwellers, cultured because it lived with men of arts and letters, and a status symbol because 'the consumption of these more excellent goods is an evidence of wealth, it becomes honorific'.[16] In the cities we see the urban origin of elite culture, and we feel the elite touch of urban culture.

Notions of the leisure class lead us directly on to 'the science of taste and of cultural consumption'. Pierre Bourdieu saw taste as 'the uncreated source of all "creation"'.[17] Opium at this moment in the history of China was a perfect example of this. The leisure class enjoyed opium long before the lower classes heard about it and the middle classes were eager to lay their hands on it. For sure, seafarers and some coastal people had access to opium. However, their consumer culture and society did not represent the mainstream. It would take moral authority to validate and sanction the consumption of opium. For the larger inland consumer society, however, opium was the 'uncreated source'. The leisure class was its creator, taste-maker and trendsetter. Such a process is both cultural and political. It is cultural because a new commodity is being defined and put in the indigenous theatre, political because what is appreciated will come to influence the consumer society. The leisure class would set the example as well as the standard for the general populace. Deborah Lupton believes that in a broader understanding, taste is 'a sense of style or fashion related to any commodity'.[18] Style and fashion were exactly what the Chinese leisure class had endowed opium with ever since the mid to late eighteenth century. But opium was unfamiliar to the larger consumer society of the vast Chinese interior at this juncture. The vanguard consumption of the leisure class made opium extremely desirable or 'honorific'.

Opium consumption at this stage is the story of Bourdieu's 'taste' and 'distinction'. Deborah Lupton furthers this understanding: 'Taste is thus both an aesthetic and a moral category.' It is a means of distinction, a way of subtly identifying and separating 'refined' individuals from the lower, 'vulgar classes'. This was obvious with opium smoking, as we have seen from

Shen Fu, Prince Minning and now the literati/artistic elite. The leisure class marked themselves apart from those below them through their opium consumption accompanied by sex recreation and topped off by opera, poetry and royal patronage. Opium was rare to find, expensive to obtain and elaborate to consume. All these are signs of taste and distinction. Perhaps it is not strange at all that Bourdieu's mid-twentieth-century French leisure class have so much in common with their counterparts in nineteenth-century China. Bourdieu established two basic facts from his survey, one of which rests on the conviction that there is a 'very close relationship linking cultural practices to educational capital and to social origin'.[19] This fits perfectly with the Chinese case, as we have seen from the social origins of the elite of the capitals. The Chinese leisure class included the aristocracy, the literati and high-ranking officials. They fashioned a language of 'taste' and social 'distinction'. They spoke it through their early opium consumption.

Opium at this stage resembled the social life of sugar in its early days. Mintz has argued that the introduction and naturalisation of sugar, that is, its evolution from luxury to necessity, went through two important processes. 'Intensification' or 'ritualisation', the first process, is 'the incorporation and symbolic reinvestment of new materials', since 'ritual has to do with regularity' and 'a sense of fitness, rightness, and validation'. 'Extensification', the second process, denotes the transformation of these new materials into 'something ordinary'.[20] Opium was living through 'intensification', as the leisure class of the early nineteenth century was engaged in the creation of new symbols and new values. This process had started in the late Ming. It intensified when smoking became 'a hobby among both the high and the low in officialdom' in Jiaqing's reign, reaching a certain zenith in the mid-1830s. What followed was the political redefinition of opium consumption, another process in the social life of opium. Opium consumption would enter 'extensification' when opium became something ordinary in the late nineteenth century.

Elite lifestyle, taste and the cities themselves both point towards the larger issues of urban culture, public institutions and the mechanisms of culture transmission, that is, towards consumer behaviour and popular culture in general. The elite, be they political, literary or commercial, converged in the cities, the cradles of style and fashion and refuges from boredom and constraint. And the cities beckoned to everybody. The national elite in Beijing helped to shape the urban culture of opium smoking in the capital. So too did their counterparts in the provinces. The year 1835 was not just when opera superstar Ji Yunxiang and his partner Zheng Sheren died of opium consumption. Hundreds journeyed to Beijing for the *jinshi* examination. Peng Songyu, a native of Hubei province, was one. Luck struck, and Peng passed it. He left for the remote province of Yunnan and joined the upper-middle-ranking officials there. New to Yunnan and office politics, Peng was surprised by an after-lunch scene in the office:

> When I worked privately for Zhang, the other six colleagues of mine all lived on opium. After lunch, they would each take a lamp and lie down; and they would bring their own pipes to share in the evenings. I worked around them for two years, but never tasted the smoke, my hands never touched the tools. All my friends tried very hard to persuade me but I was never moved. They all laughed at me and said that I was willing to suffer.[21]

The provincial scholar-officials of Yunnan had turned their lunch hour into indulgent sessions of opium smoking. They continued in the evenings. This practice had begun before Peng's arrival. Xu Zhongyuan, a native of Jiangsu, spent much of his official career in the south-west, especially in Yunnan, from the 1790s to the 1810s. Many of his colleagues smoked opium, as he detailed in his memoirs; two of them were addicted and died before 1827, when he left. By the early 1830s, Xu's old friends wrote to tell him that 'there was almost a shop to every few households'.[22] Yunnan was becoming the heartland of cultivation and consumption. Wang Pei Xun, a native of Shandong, also sat for the *jinshi* examination in 1835. To his great disappointment, he failed and was sent to work in the remote Sichuan province as a magistrate. He found comfort among the non-Sichuanese there. Zhao Guisheng, a native of Jiangsu who shared his fate and frustration, celebrated smoking in a poem titled 'Playful Verses to the Opium Smoke':

> The Hunanese pipe in the mouth,
> the lamp throws sunshine around,
> That unique odour exquisite rarity from sea trade,
> rises like steam and cloud.
> . . .
> The curved shoes below are like softened jade
> the lazy hands at the bed are as thin as a thread
> Intimate friends meet again when smoke rises
> how splendid![23]

Sichuan was nothing like Zhao's native Jiangnan, but he and others found happiness in opium smoking accompanied by sex recreation in this remote corner of the empire. Ru Yuanpu, a magistrate of Leshan, summed up its prevalence among the county-level officials of Sichuan in the 1830s: 'Opium, the peculiar smoke, makes you feel wonderful, so fashionable now, everyone turns on the lamp'. Li Songlin explained its attraction: 'secluded small room and bean-shaped lamplight, lowered curtains and slender figures'.[24] The private lives and interests of these scholar-officials confirms opium's prevalence in urban centres in the early 1830s. More importantly, these memoirs remind us of the aphrodisiac role of opium. Daoguang's local scholar-officials enjoyed and shared their poems inspired by opium; they spread the gospel of smoking through their words and deeds. These were the earliest smokers and the most visible patrons of their local smoking facilities. Some would shield the premises with their power, some would team up with the owners to make a profit, while others would make false raids and take the confiscated opium for their own use. Jiang Benzhi was one. Pan Lun'en (1786–1867) detailed this in *Daoting Tushuo* or *What I Heard on the Road*:

Hefei [capital of Anhui province] had an indigenous tiger called Jiang Benzhi. A plain and cunning man, he controlled the local government office and had friends in high places in the provincial administration. Anyone in the business of public entertainment, street performance, acrobatics and prostitution was under his spell. Prostitutes from afar, they could not move an inch without calling upon him first on their arrival.

At this time [1835–6], Li Dianzhuan [an influential scholar-official] was visiting his family in Hefei, he buried himself in poetry, wine, performances and women. Hefei had a similar character, the Gentleman Zeng. Zeng resigned from office and was a good friend of Li. Li must have famous prostitutes accompany him at dinner. Zeng also had his two favourite girls; they were beautiful and ranking among all the women in the business.

Li indulged in women; so did Zeng. They both had the *yang yan* [foreign smoke/opium] habit. Steeped in smoking, they never bothered to raise their curtain. The lamp was always lighted; and they smoked face to face with their women. Swallowing cloud and spewing fog, fragrance wafted and days were gone. At this time, there was prohibition. Jiang Benzhi ganged up with Li and Zeng, and used his office and connections. They went on unauthorised raids, confiscated opium and took it as their own. They caused a lot of trouble for others, their profit was very fat.[25]

Daoguang's scholars and officials were besotted with opium smoking accompanied by sex recreation, whether in Beijing, Yunnan, Sichuan or Anhui. Provincial officialdom made up the largest proportion of the political establishment and dominated local agendas, be they political, economic or cultural. What differentiated provincial officials from their counterparts in the capital was that they had many more avenues open to them for making money and better chances of breaking the law, since they themselves were the law-makers of their locality. With opium, this could not have been more real. John R. Watt emphasised the function of *yamen* 'as a major political institution', that is, 'the county *yamen* relates closely to the process of urbanisation in Chinese society'.[26] By this time, *yamen* related even more closely to the urbanisation and initial popularisation of opium smoking. The '5 per cent or so of the population', as Susan Naquin and Evelyn Rawski labelled them, pursued a life of examinations and public office.[27] They were the moral guardians of the Chinese people, and they worked and lived to interpret and uphold high principles. They were the symbols of culture because they defined culture. They did not just inspire others, they led them. The more they pursued their own lifestyles, the more they spread the consciousness and knowledge of consumption.

MECHANISMS OF CULTURE TRANSMISSION

The opium-smoking scholars and officials I have just mentioned were natives of eastern and east central China, but they worked in the south-west and elsewhere. Some might have picked up the habit in their home-town, some might have been exposed to it during examination seasons, while others might have learned it when at work. These people would be transferred again in their careers. Most would return to their home-towns for holidays and rituals, and/or when they resigned or retired. The frequent transfer of officials was common under Qing rule and was designed to prevent the cultivation of local power and corruption. *Huibi*, the so-called 'avoidance' policy, dictated that officials must not serve in their own home provinces. This undoubtedly contributed to the spread of opium smoking. Provincial officials spread the consciousness of consumption when they moved from city to city every few years and from workplaces to home-town each year. Susan Naquin and Evelyn Rawski have argued that 'the centralising influence of the Chinese state, whose administrative centres were overwhelmingly in cities, also affected public behaviour, family life, and personal morality. In short, urban culture was important not just for the 5 per cent or so of the population that actually resided in central places but for virtually all Chinese.'[28] This could not have been more obvious with opium consumption.

The '5 per cent or so of the population' smoked opium long before the lower classes were able to lay their hands on it. However, the effect they had on those around and below them was dramatic. Within their own families, sons and womenfolk began to emulate their smoking habit and personal morality, thereby spending more time and money on smoking accompanied by prostitutes. Indeed, the opium culture thus fashioned was important for 'virtually all Chinese'. Provincial officials helped to standardise the popular culture of opium smoking in the various regions, where people spoke different dialects and practised different customs. They and their institutions were the most effective mechanism of culture transmission. In addition, the circulation of commercial agents and agencies also increased. As *yanghuo* and *yang yan* became increasingly popular, more Cantonese and Fujianese expanded their operations in the north and the interior, while their counterparts from these regions set up their own businesses in the coastal provinces. As Naquin and Rawski observe, 'The circulation of officials and travellers through the empire and the increase in sojourners in the major cities spread consciousness and appreciation of different food.' Opium is a convincing example of this, as Aleqin'a, governor of Shanxi province, discovered in Daoguang's eleventh year, 1831: 'The people from Taigu, Pinyao and Jiexiu counties do business in Guangong and other southern provinces; they have contracted the opium habit and became addicted.'[29]

Aleqin'a did not know that this had already begun in the 1820s. The *Taigu County Gazetteer* recorded that the then magistrate, Chen Luhe noticed that those who did business in Fujian and Guangdong not only had the habit but also brought opium back to Taigu. Chen tried to persuade them to quit smoking and to stop bringing opium back to Taigu, but to no avail. Although Taigu, Pinyao and Jiexiu are small towns in south central Shanxi, their native sons travelled far. They were members of the famous Shanxi *piaohao* or 'banker guilds' that dealt with drafts or bills of exchange as business multiplied and the management of money became more sophisticated in the eighteenth century. They were China's modern bankers. It is likely that they picked up the habit of smoking opium in coastal urban centres such as Canton and Tianjin, where they sojourned and where they worked. The habit travelled with them when they returned to their home-towns. This, like the Taiwan conquest, was fundamental for the spread of opium in the vast interior, as more Shanxi natives travelled for the opium that Shanxi needed and for the bills that could be exchanged to buy more. *Piaohao* guildhalls operated in many big cities by the 1830s. Guildhalls were the rendezvous for native officials, scholars, students and merchants; they hosted parties and sponsored performances, and now they became the agency or agents of opium transmission. Taigu would become famous for the opium lamps and pipes its inhabitants fashioned well into in the early twentieth century. The city, however, would decline as a result of widespread addiction, which reduced productivity, and because of its widespread cultivation practices, which resulted in natural disasters.

'It is only at a relatively early stage of culture that the symptoms of expensive vice are conventionally accepted as marks of a superior status, and so tend to become virtues and command the deference of the community', Veblen continues his theory of the leisure class. Opium was indeed an expensive vice among scholars and officials, and their words and deeds commanded the deference of the entire urban community. The story of Taigu's banker sons is a convincing example. This was, in wider context, the situation for the whole country in the mid-1830s. The memorial from Song Pu, governor of Guizhou province, read: 'In the areas that neighboured Guangdong and Yunnan provinces, people did business with them, some have become addicted to this smoke.'[30] High-ranking officials from Hunan, Anhui and remote Manchuria wrote essentially the same thing. Li Zhaotang, a local scholar in Chixian, in Anhui province, remembered the case there: 'One began to hear the name of it in the beginning of Daoguang. It first started with the rich, then the lower classes began to emulate. Profiteers quickly furnished places for smoking; they operated in secret initially, but soon they opened businesses and sold the mud.'[31] Not yet a publicly pronounced vice, opium smoking was definitely the mark of superiority at this time. The mention of opium signalled one's worldly knowledge, whereas smoking denoted one's socio-economic status.

Sons of the Pear Garden, scholars, officials and merchants, these people are what Susan Naquin calls the 'urban communities'.[32] They helped spread the gospel of opium, as did the institutions to which they belonged. Opium smoking allows us to see the dynamics at work in these communities, and more importantly, helps us see the role of urban public institutions in culture transmission. Local dialect opera entertainment, for example, embodied many aspects of urban society and was in many ways the essence of collective or regional identity. Opera houses, performances and festivals, like tea houses and the marketplace, were socio-economic and cultural institutions. Zhao Shanlin's research shows that tea houses and restaurants were frequently used as theatres, as they competed for patrons and clients alike. This was certainly true with guildhalls. These venues and happenings were, as Barbara E. Ward put it, 'the most significant source of information about the believed-in historical past, the values and manners of the elite, attitudes and relationships between and among people of different status, and ideas of good and evil'.[33] They were the 'embodiment of Chinese culture and value', and they were often situated in the heart of towns and cities. Qian Yong (1759–1844) brilliantly pointed out the larger role of these institutions in Jiangnan:

Alas, the way to manage a country, the first important thing is to settle the poor. When Governor Chen Hongmo [Jiangsu] prohibited women from burning incense in the temple, the tourist business in the spring declined, coolies and boatmen could not make a living. When Hu Wenbo was governor, he banned theatre performances . . . *Jinchan* [marketplace in Suzhou] is a place where traders convene. It's crowded all the time and there were many theatres and restaurants. Everyday, performances would help feed at least several thousand people. This is something law cannot prohibit. What does prohibition do to the good management of the poor? Suzhou is a conjunction. It is a place full of temples, theatres, restaurants, leisure boats, brothels, cricket/quail fighting, and gambling, they are all places to feed the poor.[34]

Here is described the 'urban mosaic' of Robert Park, the 'urban facades' of Peter Burke and the 'public purposes' of Susan Naquin. Government offices, market squares, guildhalls, tea houses, theatres, *yanghuo* shops, brothels and opium dens – city centres served not just scholars, officials, merchants, sojourners and urbanites in general. They were where barbers, cobblers, coolies and prostitutes thrived, where street performances and quick snacks could be enjoyed, where celebrities might be spotted, and where gossip became news and news travelled. They drew the rich, the powerful and the talented; they also attracted the ordinary, the poor and criminals. The haves came to live and spend, the middle class to open their eyes, and the poor to beg and be fed. Urban institutions contributed to the management of the poor. They also helped to expose and transmit opium smoking. Cheng Enze (1785–1837), a scholar-official who travelled to oversee the Guangdong provincial examination in 1832, witnessed opium in front of the solemn examination hall. Cheng remembered this vividly: 'The efficacious grass *afurong* ranks with big money and expensive gifts, gentlemen spent ten thousand-gold to pass a moon-lit night with it, even beggars intoxicate themselves in it.'[35] He footnoted 'beggars': 'it is all over the place in Canton, even beggars have it (smoke or offer it)'. Cash or opium, there was little difference for a beggar, indeed opium could be more valuable. The public space in front of an examination hall was the best place to beg or sell. Examinees might need a larger supply, and there would be new recruits.

From opera stars in Beijing to beggars in Canton, many urbanites had access to opium in the early and mid-1830s. The poor in Canton took for granted what the upper classes in the capital and other inland cities greatly appreciated. Both opera and beggary are urban phenomena. A Canton correspondent of the *Chinese Repository* for 25 November 1835 described well the fusion of Sons of the Pear Garden, urban culture, the public institution and opium:

Happening to be at the side of the river today when a large theatrical boat had just arrived, its proprietor, or some one else in his stead, invited me on board – more for their amusement than mine. A short visit satisfied my curiosity. The boat was very crowded with people, and they were civil and polite, in their way. Most of them had been making large drafts on the 'black commodity', and four were then at their pipes. The company of players was engaged to perform on one of the public theatres tomorrow morning, and the manager was preparing a scheme of the contemplated performance.[36]

Such a scene was to become a tourist attraction, as foreigners went to see for themselves once they were in Canton. James Holman was one:

On our return to the shore we passed between a double line of large boats, that are constantly moored in the centre of the river, with the head and stern of each boat so close in line that you might pass along the whole, from one to another, without having occasion to go into a boat. These barges are called 'flower boats', a name they derive from the elegant and ornamental style in which they are fitted up, and carried and gilded. These boats, however, are nothing better than licensed brothels of the first order, for the exclusive use of the Chinese, foreigners not being permitted to trespass upon them with impunity. The ladies on board, however, do not appear to have any objection to the visits of strangers, if their sentiments may be speculated upon, from their outward signs, for no respectable foreigner can pass these boats without receiving signals of invitation. I have heard of one or two foreigners who were bold enough to venture on board, but who paid dearly for the experiment, although to what extent I cannot really say.[37]

Opium enhanced a city's attraction, and urban public institutions effortlessly advertised opium to the larger populace. The taste for opium and the trend of smoking were fashioned and promoted by the urban elite, be they scholars, officials or Sons of the Pear Garden, and transmitted to the interior by those who sojourned in the coastal and national urban centres. From the islands of south-east Asia to coastal China, from cities such as Beijing to provincial capitals such as Hefei, and later to the shores of North America and Europe, this was opium's mechanism of transmission. Opium smoking rested easily with scholars and officials and their literary and recreational pursuits. Indeed, it was evolving into a trend all of its own in the first decade or so of Daoguang's reign. Opium was part of the elite culture; it had begun to sweep across urban consumer society. The Jiaqing emperor had once complained about the 'city rascals'. But scholars and officials were the real 'city rascals'. They smoked opium long before the masses could lay their hands on it. They were what Arjun Appadurai called the 'message-sending' and 'production-moulding' forces. They appreciated *yanghuo* and helped generate the demand for opium. And what they appreciated came to influence their urban communities at large. This was the 'politics of value'.[38]

CHAPTER 6

The political redefinition of opium consumption

This chapter examines both the initial and the continual political reinter-pretations and discussions of opium, and also the arrival of the consumer trend or epidemic of opium smoking on the eve of the first Opium War. The year 1834 was a milestone in the social life of opium, because the East India Company's exclusive trading right in China ceased and the trade was thrown open to all so-called 'private English'. The *Chinese Repository* hailed it as the 'triumph of principles'.[1] When free trade triumphed, opium smoking became a pathological problem. When free trade failed, gunboat diplomacy was applied. Michael Greenberg's understanding of the political consequences was to the point: 'the most immediate result of the victory of the free-traders was to bring the power of the British state to bear directly on the China trade'.[2] The Chinese failed to realise that who they now dealt with were not only the private English but also subjects of Her Majesty. They called Lord Napier, the first British Superintendent of Trade, *Daban/Taipan* or Chief Merchant, and this meant that for the Chinese he could never represent a sovereign. The year 1834 did not bring the kind of victory the private English had hoped for. Free trade drew too many free-traders and too much wild speculation. James Matheson lamented in 1837: 'We are still pegging away here, pretty much as you left us and almost sighing for a return of the Company's monopoly in prefer-ence to the trouble and endless turmoil of free trade.'[3] The so-called 'Napier fizzle' and Matheson's lament heralded disaster.

CHINESE 'ROBES'

The arrival of the consumer trend of opium smoking depended on the participation of the general populace and, more importantly, on a steady supply of opium. Shipments stood at 18,956 chests in the 1830/31 season; they had jumped to 30,202 chests in the 1835/36 season.[4] Shipped opium facili-tated the participation of the larger urban community and fuelled domestic cultivation, which had started in the 1800s. This certainly did not escape the eyes of the scholar-officials. When they smoked it, opium was cultured and refined; when the lower classes began to lie down, opium became irksome, degrading and ultimately criminal. The story of opium was very different when the smokers were the lower classes or the 'inarticulate'.[5] Scholar-official Xu Zhongyuan commented: 'Intemperate and reckless youngsters, they are not a pity. But gentlemen have also succumbed to it. When I was in Yunnan [before 1827], Zheng Liu and Shi Qi were addicted to it and died of it.'[6] Xu's view is extremely revealing. 'Intemperate and reckless youngsters' reminds us of the 'city rascals' fashioned by the Jiaqing emperor. 'Gentlemen have also succumbed to it' suggests that gentlemen were the unwilling victims of the spreading evil. The undesirable habit of opium smoking stemmed from below and outside, not from up above and within. The Jiaqing emperor pointed his fingers at the 'city rascals' rather than at his own son, Prince Minning. Xu pointed his finger at the 'reckless youngsters' rather than at his own colleagues.

The connotations of 'city rascals' and 'reckless youngsters' were not simply troubled youth and unsettling throng, the terms referred to the uneducated mob-like populace. Xu's words represented not just the opinion of one upright scholar-official, but also the verdict of the political establishment. Lower-class smokers made opium smoking visible and disgraceful as a social and moral problem. They degraded opium smoking and irritated their upper-class counterparts. Scholars and officials condemned them. They would make them scapegoats of China's economic and social-moral problems. The participation of the lower classes altered the nature of smoking. This was the beginning of a political redefinition of opium consumption, and is well illustrated by the complaint of the Imperial Investigative Censor, Feng Zhanxun: 'The poison of opium is that when the people smoke it, they wasted themselves and ruined their businesses; and when the soldiers smoke it, they became tired and break the army's discipline.'[7] The 'people' did not know how to smoke and were turning smoking into a social epidemic. Was Feng suggesting that the upper and upper middle classes would never bring about such problems? Lower-class smokers were regarded and treated as evil-doers and were ultimately criminalised; they should never be allowed to smoke opium. Instead, what they should be and how they should behave can be seen from the memorials of the time. A key phrase here is *minfeng chunpu. Minfeng* means 'the custom', 'the practice' or 'the tradition' 'of the people'. *Chunpu* means 'pure, honest, simple and unsophisticated', the opposite being decadence and corruption of the body, mind and soul.

Yuan Wenxiang, also an Imperial Censor dispatched to Guizhou, memorialised the throne in April 1835: 'The customs of Guizhou have always been simple and unsophisticated. Recently it started to have opium smokers, opium cultivators and houses.'[8] Guizhou is an immediate neighbour of Yunnan and at the time it was evolving into a region of large-scale intensive domestic cultivation. The people of Guizhou, who were largely ethnic, had always been considered scheming and rebellious. Yet they ought to have been simple and unsophisticated when it came to opium smoking. The call for prohibition was becoming louder by 1837. Qi Ying, Governor-General of Fengtian, still used *minfeng chunpu* in April 1838. His memorial reads: 'Fengtian is the important birthplace of our dynasty. Its customs have always been simple and unsophisticated. There never has been, until now, such evil things as smoking opium, chanting scriptures and practising religion.'[9] Fengtian had access to opium earlier than other provinces. Many fine sons of distinguished imperial families were among the first to adopt it. The practice of copying each other's key phrase was not unusual. However, when all those in authority repeatedly used the same phrase, it was an indication of consensus. Men of letters and power did not run out of words to describe a social phenomenon they had never seen before; neither did they run out of ideas as to how to deal with it. 'Simple and unsophisticated' subjects were easier to rule. The participation of the lower classes in opium smoking challenged both authority and social control.

Minfeng chunpu demonstrates the defining power scholar-officials had over both moral principles and the common people. Their job was to restrain and lecture lower-class smokers. Daoguang responded to Qi Ying's memorial with a determined tone: 'The four criminals captured, all from Fengtian, either sold opium or wore a religious talisman. From this, we can see how this province has contracted such evil habits. This must be thoroughly investigated and suppressed.'[10] Daoguang had enjoyed opium two decades previously. But it had turned into an 'evil habit' that his Fengtianese subjects in particular and the lower classes in general had 'contracted'. The emperor and his scholar-officials asserted themselves as the interpreters and upholders of high moral principles because they had the power to redefine those principles and to apply them to the lower classes. Tens of thousands were arrested throughout the country because of the few puffs they enjoyed, while officials of all ranks smoked considerably within the security of their offices and homes.

The story of opium is similar to the story of vodka in Russia and that of tavern drinking in France. Tavern drinking in France was condemned by the 'three robes', that is, the clergy, the nobility and the liberal professions.

Listen to the essayist Louis-Sebastien Mercier: 'Disreputable cabarets, otherwise called taverns. You will not go there delicate reader, I will go for you. You will only see the place in description and that will spare you some disagreeable sensations. This is the receptacle of the dregs of the populace.'[11] Vodka and alcohol attracted the dregs of the Russian and French populace; opium attracted the dregs of the Chinese masses. The French 'robes' considered public drinking 'a major contribution to, and expression of' the degraded nature of the lower classes, and the tavern as 'a symbol of misery and debauchery'. The Chinese 'robes' saw opium in essentially the same way in the 1830s. The 'Living Water' played a vital role in the Russian economy and throughout society on the eve of the Russian Revolution; so did tavern drinking in France on the eve of the French Revolution. More so, I would argue, did opium smoking before the Chinese revolutions of the twentieth century. This raises questions about class formation, popular culture and the politicisation of demand. The story of opium is also similar to the case of qat in contemporary Somalia.[12] The chewing of the quasi-legal qat by the upwardly mobile urbanites of Somalia challenged state control. The Somalia government response was a ban in 1983. Despite the ban or perhaps because of it, qat chewing has flourished, not only in north-east African but also within Somali communities overseas. Vodka or tavern drinking, qat or opium, they all teach us that consumption has never been a matter of simple economics.

What was an economic matter, however, was the silver drain and its socio-economic consequences. The silver drain had begun in Jiaqing's reign. It increased in the 1820s with the growing consumption of *yanghuo* and opium. Michael Greenberg believed that the flow of silver was reversing its direction from about 1826. Hao Yen-p'ing gives a 'conservative estimate' at $74,700,000 between 1801 and 1826, and $133,700,000 between 1827 and 1849.[13] The lower classes certainly made the consequences of opium smoking social, but quite how much they were responsible for the silver drain is unclear. This was pointed out by an official of the time: 'Those who smoke opium must be from well-to-do families; the poor can't even feed themselves, how would they have money for opium?'[14] Those with silver were the Manchu aristocrats, high-ranking officials and rich scholars. It was more likely that the lower classes smoked ashes left by rich smokers mixed with tobacco or locally grown opium. However enormous the import in the 1830s, it could only have served the '5 per cent or so of the population'. However staggering the outflow, it could only have been drained by those who owned silver, not those who lived on copper cash. This is a point few historians have pointed out.

THE OPIUM WAR ALREADY LOST

No one can deny the moral degeneracy of the 1830s. An example is the Yao uprising and its suppression. The Yao were an ethnic minority who lived in the Nanling Mountain range that zigzagged Guangdong, Guangxi and Hunan provinces. When opium smoking was urbanised nation-wide, it was already widespread in the rural areas of the coastal provinces. It had penetrated these rural areas due to their natural advantage, namely, the opium trade along the coast and opium's long march to the interior, which cut through their territories. The rural/lower classes of the coastal regions took for granted what for urban middle classes in the interior regarded as still a luxury. In other words, the participation of the larger national urban population in the 1830s coincided with the thorough penetration down to the lower classes and throughout all rural areas of the coastal provinces. This speaks to phases of consumption – different consumers, different phases. The Nanling mountain range was a chain of valleys and mountain peaks incised with treacherous roads and rapids. The Yao people spoke their own dialect. They had resisted Chinese rule throughout their history. Although their resistance was not a military threat, it had to be suppressed. Thousands of soldiers were sent to Lianzhou in northern Guangdong. Xi En, then Minister of the Imperial Household, was swiftly appointed as the new Governor-General to help crush the rebellion. Urgent memorials, rather than news of victory, reached the throne. Xi En wrote of the soldiers: 'Although there are more than ten thousand of them, seven out of ten are Guangdong natives. They are cowardly and not used to marching in the mountains. Plus most coastal soldiers are opium smokers.'[15]

Seven out of ten soldiers were opium users. This was to say, 7,000 out of 10,000 soldiers were invalids. The result was not just devastating, it heralded defeat. Feng Zhanxun blamed the soldiers: 'Many Cantonese and Fujianese soldiers smoked opium, there are even more among the officers. They are cowards and they have spoiled our operation. They are really despicable.'[16] Feng also reported that opium smoking was common among the soldiers in Yunnan, Guizhou, Sichuan and Zhejiang provinces. Xi En and Feng put the blame on the soldiers rather than the officers, some of whom were their own colleagues. Soldiers may be illiterate and numerous, but they mattered because they helped to safeguard the empire. Yet the problem ran deeper than the mere fact that they had become addicted to opium: addicts were unlikely to be sent into combat because they no longer wanted to fight. The problem was one of morale. Legends of Manchu banners sweeping through

China on their horses were but history. The years of conquering peripheral principalities were long gone, as well. The demoralisation of the military machine, which had begun with commanders like Mukedengbu, was now almost complete. War was history and gallantry was memory. Opium had demilitarised the fighting machine, as soldiers found the best way to escape boredom and combat responsibilities. Given seven thousand soldiers out of ten thousand were invalids, any battle would have been lost. Here, however, it was not only the battle against the Yao people that was lost but also the first Opium War itself, which would be lost since it would take place in these self-same provinces. Huang Yue explains China's forthcoming defeat at British hands well:

> Lusty friends gather two or three,
> Lie down face to face like an old couple.
> A bowl of light sits in the middle,
> It flames in both darkness and dawn.
> A naughty boy lights it for you,
> It matters not how much you inhale.
> Small talk knows neither winter nor spring.
> Day and night, one forgets cold and hunger.[17]

Huang Yue's poem celebrates the quintessence of opium smoking. It is certainly natural for friends to gather and to indulge in what they all enjoy. This custom is not necessarily Chinese. For underpaid risk-taking soldiers, this was the best way to forget 'cold and hunger'. Huang was among a handful of high-ranking officials invited to the Jiaqing emperor's birthday party in 1819, where he was promoted to Minister of Rites and was given an exquisite snuff bottle. As men of letters and power like him continued to enjoy and philosophise opium, they themselves redefined it and prohibited its use among the lower classes. 'Lusty friends' reminds us of the art of sex, whereas 'naughty boy' evokes sodomy and pederasty. Young boys had a unique role in this business, one circumstance of which has been discussed by Frank Proschan and depicted in Marc de Smedt's *Chinese Erotism*.[18]

John K. Fairbank was correct in emphasising that 'the origin of the drug traffic lay first of all in the Chinese demand for opium'.[19] But opium smoking would not have spread like wildfire without the infamous smuggling. China would not have seen the coming of the opium-smoking consumer trend in the 1830s without the end of the East India Company's exclusive trading rights in China in 1834. It would have taken a much longer time to arrive. Opium might well have followed tobacco's footsteps, as

Table 1 *Opium shipments to China, 1830–1839 (chests)*

Season	Bengal	Malwa	Turkey	Total
1830/31	5,672	12,856	1,428	19,956
1831/32	6,815	9,333	402	16,550
1832/33	7,598	14,007	380	21,985
1833/34	7,808	11,715	963	20,486
1834/35	10,207	11,678		21,885
1835/36	14,851	15,351		30,202
1836/37	12,606	21,427	243	34,276
1837/38	19,600	14,773		34,373
1838/39	18,212	21,988		40,200

Source: Michael Greenberg, *British Trade and the Opening of China, 1800–1842* (Cambridge: Cambridge University Press, 1951), appendix 1.

domestic cultivation might well have satisfied increasing consumption. Michael Greenberg was the first of a handful of outstanding historians who have scrutinised the Jardine Matheson archive and have provided evidence of the magnitude of opium smuggling that was taking place in the crucial years before the war (see table 1).

Hao Yen-p'ing believed that it was 'probably the world's largest commerce of the time in any single commodity' and that it yielded 'one-seventh of the total revenue of British India'.[20] The smuggled opium satisfied many on the one hand, but caused problems on the other. A series of works painted by the artist Sunqua, who was active in Canton in the 1830s, shows this well. The *Chinese Repository* printed a literary explanation in 1837. It stated that the pictures represented 'the rapid career of the opium-smoker, from health and affluence to decrepitude and beggary'; 'in fact, they are a counterpart to Hogarth's famous "Rake's Progress"'.[21]

Admonitory Pictures

The son of a gentleman of fortune, his father dying while he was yet but a youth, comes into possession of the whole family estate. The young man having no inclination for either business or books, gives himself up to smoking opium and profligacy. In a little time his whole patrimony is squandered, and he becomes entirely dependent upon the labour of his wife and child for his daily food. Their poverty and misery are extreme.

No. 1. This picture represents the young man at home, richly attired, in perfect health and vigour of youth. An elegant foreign clock stands on a marble table behind him. On his right, is a chest of treasure, gold and silver; and on the left, close by his side, is his personal servant, and, at a little distance, a man whom he keeps constantly in his employ, preparing the drug for use from the crude article, purchased and brought to the house.

No. 2. In this, he is reclining on a superb sofa, with a pipe in his mouth, surrounded by courtesans, two of whom are young, in the character of musicians. His money now goes without any regard to its amount.

No. 3. After not a very long period of indulgence, his appetite for the drug is insatiable, and his countenance sallow and haggard. Emaciated, shoulders high, teeth naked, face black, dozing from morning to night, he becomes utterly inactive. In this state he sits moping, on a very ordinary couch, with his pipe and other apparatus for smoking, lying by his side. At this moment his wives – or a wife and a concubine – come in; the first, finding the chest emptied of its treasure, stands frowning with astonishment, while the second gazes with wonder at what she sees spread upon the couch.

No. 4. His lands and his houses are now all gone; his couch exchanged for some rough boards, and a ragged mattress; his shoes are off his feet; and his face half awry, as he sits bending forward, breathing with great difficulty. His wife and child stand before him, poverty stricken, suffering with hunger; the one in anger, having dashed on the floor all his apparatus for smoking, while the little son, unconscious of any harm, is clapping his hands and laughing at the sport! But he heeds not, either the one or the other.

No. 5. His poverty and distress are now extreme, though his appetite grows stronger than ever – he is as a dead man. In this plight, he scrapes together a few copper cash, and hurries away to one of the smoking-houses, to buy a little of the scrapings from the pipe of another smoker, to allay his insatiable cravings.

No. 6. Here his character is fixed – a sot. Seated on a bamboo chair, he is continually swallowing the faeces of the drug, so foul that tea is required to wash them down his throat. His wife and child are seated near him, with skins of silk stretched on bamboo reels, from which they are winding it off into balls; thus earning a mere pittance for his and their own support, and dragging out from day to day a miserable existence.

Fortune is reduced to ruin and a healthy human being turned into a sot. And the above writing was only the first episode, because his wife, children and family would have to continue to eke out a wretched existence, whether he lived or not. The addictive and destructive nature of opium is fully exposed here. The writing roused consciences in China and England and generated a moral debate.

The debate in England over the opium trade was battled out between the church leaders and the business community. William S. Fry believed that 'nothing can be more injurious to the British character'. Robert Philip

considered it 'the crisis of Christianity', while an anonymous church minister called it England's 'national sin'.[22] John Abel Smith and Alexander
Graham led the campaign in Parliament for government intervention.
Graham was indignant about the confiscation and destruction of British-
owned opium and emphasised 'the right, obligation and interest of the
government of Great Britain to request redress from the government of
China'.[23] Samuel Warren even predicted victory: 'The bloated vain-glory
and grandiloquence of the Chinese would probably collapse at the very
first prick of a British bayonet; their flimsy armaments fly like chaff before
the wind at the sight of one single British man-of-war.'[24] In China, debates
took place between prohibitionists and legalisation advocates. Prohibitionists emphasised moral decline, while legalisation advocates stressed that
legalisation would stop the silver drain. Who would prevail depended on
who could win over the emperor. Huang Jueci, the prohibitionist leader,
knew who smoked opium and why: 'In the first instance, the use of opium
was confined to the pampered sons of fortune, with whom it became an idle
luxury.'[25] He pointed his finger at the upper classes: 'its use had extended
upwards to the officers and belted gentry, and downwards to the labourer
and the tradesman, to the traveller, and even to women, monks, nuns,
and priests'. Huang's daring and patriotic words helped to win over the
Daoguang emperor and to put opium on the course of prohibition.

Legalisation advocates also knew who smoked opium and why. Xu Naiji,
its outspoken leader, wrote: 'It will be found on examination that smokers
of opium are idle, lazy vagrants, having no useful purpose before them,
and are unworthy of regard, or even of contempt.'[26] Xu had harsh words
for those 'who have overstepped the threshold of age' and 'do not attain
to the long life of other men'. And he saw something else in lower-class
consumption: 'new births are daily increasing the population of the empire;
and there is no cause to apprehend a diminution therein: while, on the
other hand, we cannot adopt too great, or too early, precautions against the
annual waste which is taking place of the resources, the very substance of
China'. Xu's thoughts, in the words of the *Chinese Repository*, 'approached so
nearly to the Malthusian principle of population, that it is for the general
good for a closely peopled country to have its numbers thinned by any
means whatever'.[27] This was not the first time a scholar-official was blunt
in his remarks about the lower classes and over-population, but it was
certainly the first time anyone had seen a remedy in opium. Legalisationists
and prohibitionists differed in their perspectives and approaches. But they
painted a more complete picture of who smoked opium and why on the
eve of the Opium War.

Other contemporaries, both native and foreign, also observed and assessed the spread of opium in the late 1830s. C. Toogood Downing, an English medical man in Canton, saw that 'the class of people who consume opium in China are those of the male sex, chiefly between twenty and fifty-five years old, and of all ranks in society . . . It affects soldiers very much, rendering them weak and decrepit.'[28] John Ouchterlony took part in all the operations of the first Opium War and remembered that 'the people of all the southern portion of the empire were known to be all more or less addicted to the use of the drug'.[29] The assessment of Jiang Xiangnan, a well-known scholar, came probably closest to the reality. Jiang believed that opium smokers constituted 10 to 20 per cent of the officials in the central government, 20 to 30 per cent of those in local government, 50 to 60 per cent of private secretaries – and the proportion increased as the list moved down, to attendants as well as to underlings of the officials.[30] Provincial scholar-officials and their hangers-on made up the largest army of smokers. These men were the breadwinners of their families and the backbone of the country. Gong Zizhen (1792–1841), a deep thinker and patriot, lamented before he died in 1841:

Since the end of Qianlong, officials, gentlemen and ordinary people, they are all in a sorry plight. Five or six out of every ten, gentlemen behave unlike gentlemen, farmers unlike farmers, artisans unlike artisans, merchants unlike merchants. Some are addicted to opium smoking; some learn evil religion; some kill while others die of cold and hunger. Yet they still do not want to learn the skills of weaving an inch of silk or cultivating a grain of rice to help themselves and others. Qianlong's sixty-year peace and prosperity is followed by a time when people become used to extreme decadence and to habits of squandering. This is especially true in the capital. From there to the four corners of the empire, the rich become poor and the poor become beggars. The leaders of the four peoples degrade themselves; the situation in the provinces is so precarious that they cannot survive from month to month, let alone a year.[31]

Gong's life coincided with opium's thorough penetration of officialdom and with its spread into the interior and throughout the lower classes. His heartfelt words spelt out a fundamental problem. He lamented that the Chinese people did not cultivate productive skills, but instead indulged in decadent lives. They had forgotten about fundamental values. Chinese moral philosophy emphasises hard work and frugality, but the Chinese people had created one of the most decadent cultures in the world.

The epidemic that was opium swept across China in the 1830s. It was to plague the extended royal family. Prince of the First Degree, Yi Mai,

Prince of the Sixth Degree, Fu Xi, and Prince of the Seventh Degree, Mian Shun were found to have been smoking opium with prostitutes for years. Daoguang deprived them of their titles and banished them.[32] As he was dealing with this family crisis, the prohibition versus legalisation debate intensified. Morality weighed heavier than silver, and the prohibitionists prevailed. Mainland historians have argued that Daoguang's own personal knowledge of addiction was what helped him make up his mind. The victory reinforces the conviction that a moral-philosophy-supported officialdom would not have tolerated so liberal an idea as legalisation. Nevertheless, the fact that legalisation commanded an audience shows how pragmatic, if not liberal, some Chinese officials could be. Daoguang declared war on opium; he did not know that the first Opium War had already been lost. Indeed, he did not know how the British saw his naval power: 'the marine of this vast empire presents a state of things unparalleled among even the most savage states of islands that we know of'.[33] The Opium War, a pivotal episode for scholars of China, has been superbly studied and written by generations of historians in the West. Meanwhile, the *Opium War* movie has educated millions of Chinese youth, like me. I can still recall the images of big-nosed and deep-eyed evil British smugglers, soldiers and officers. A new version was released on the eve of the handover of Hong Kong, in 1997. Patriotic education via the Opium Wars continues.

DISCOURSE AND POLITICISATION

The first Opium War ended in August 1842, but the political redefinition would turn into a longer-running political discourse that helped to define the struggle for a new China in the late nineteenth and early twentieth centuries. Missionaries, who poured into China to save the opium-ridden Chinese, were prominent in the crusade against opium. They imagined what opium would do to its smokers and believed that everyone who smoked opium was an addict. This could not have been more obvious than with Osmond Tiffany:

The victim inhales his allotted quantity and his senses swim around him, he feels of subtle nature, he floats from earth as if on pinions.

He would leave his humble station, his honest toil, his comfortable home; he would be great. He runs with the ease the paths of distinction; he distances rivals; wealth and power wait upon him, the mighty take him by the hand. His dress is sumptuous, his fare costly, his home a palace, and he revels in the pleasures he has read of and believed to be a fiction.

Music sounds through his lofty halls, sages assemble to do him honour, women of the brightest beauty throng around him, he is no longer poor, lowly and despised, but a demigod.

The feast is spread, the sparkling cup filled to the brim with hot wine, and he rises to welcome one whom he has left far behind in the path of glory, to tender to him triumphant courtesy.

And as he advances a step, he reels and staggers wildly, and competitors, guests, minstrels, magnificence, all fade from his vision, and the grey, cold reality of dawn breaks upon his heated brain, and he knows that all was naught, and that he is the same nameless creature that he has ever been. A cold shudder agitates his frame, weak and worthless he seeks the air, but finds no relief.

He cannot turn his thoughts to his calling, he is unfit for exertion, his days pass in sloth and in bitter remorse. And when night comes in gloom, he seeks again the sorceress into whose power he has sunk and whose finger mocks while it beckons him on.[34]

This American missionary turned illusion into reality. How could he have been so detailed if he had never touched opium himself? Even if he did as he confessed, 'as a matter of curiosity', how would he know what exactly was in the mind of the smoker when he was deluded? Many like Tiffany would look exclusively for and take only this kind of 'admonitory picture' as they travelled and worked in China. They misrepresented the realities of opium consumption by focusing on the worst scenarios and the poorest fraction of the populace. However, their work would inspire crusaders, politicians and would mislead historians.

The fact was that many, both rich and poor, enjoyed opium without becoming addicted. But for the missionaries opium was the 'devil's food', as alcohol and tobacco were labelled by the good Calvinists in the Dutch golden age. Many devoted themselves to saving the Chinese people. E. H. Parker was one, Mr Curnow of the China Inland Mission another. Curnow told the Royal Commission: 'China is being whirled to its ruin by a means more subtle and ferocious than any hitherto recorded in the annals or ruins of ancient Empires.'[35] And he concluded: 'Nothing but the Spirit of the Almighty can stay the plague. I do not believe China is able to save herself.' Yet God did not stop the private English man, mostly Christians, from smuggling. Would He save the ungodly Chinese people? Opium would entitle China 'the sick man of Asia'. Like foot-binding, gambling and polygamy, it became an obvious badge of China's sickness. S. W. Williams labelled opium an 'article of destruction'.[36] This was what Dr Griffith John of the London Missionary Society told the Royal Commission: 'Opium is not only robbing the Chinese of millions in money year by year, but is actually destroying them as a people.'[37]

Opium certainly destroyed many people, men and women, rich and poor, but not the Chinese as a people. So how can we reconcile the words of the 'three robes', be they Chinese or western? What are at issue here are two important aspects of consumption, the first of which is the stage of awareness. Opium had been consumed as a luxury since the mid-Ming. When increasing availability made lower-class consumption possible, their smoking made the fatal consequences of opium visible. This led to a political redefinition of consumption; it also made some recognise and others accept the lethal character of opium. This stage of awareness is unique to potentially destructive commodities such as opium. The message of destruction would sink in with wars and prohibition. The second aspect is the phase of consumption. Taste-making and trendsetting is one phase; another is political redefinition. Scholars and officials enjoyed opium long before the lower classes could lay their hands on it. The elite made opium smoking fashionable, while the lower classes made its consequences undesirable. Scholars and officials might have grown out of their initial fascination with opium when the lower classes began to embrace it. The result is clear. Some condemned lower-class smokers, some assumed a moral responsibility, while others continued to smoke in private and supported prohibition in public. They did not understand that while they philosophised opium, the lower classes, coolie labourers for example, depended on it for a living. Even if the latter realised its danger, they had no choice when daily survival was their priority. This phase of consumption is common to the gradual downgrading of luxury commodities.

As more people resigned themselves to opium in the late nineteenth and early twentieth centuries, the 'three robes' stepped up their action. 'The sick man of Asia' raised consumption to the level of national survival. Gong Zizhen had denounced opium as one reason for China's decline, and many agreed with him. Liang Qichao was one. He considered opium smoking and foot-binding, among others, to be China's obstacles to progress and modernity: 'with any one of these, a body would be ruined, a family broken and a country extinct'.[38] Foot-binding had been practised in China since ancient times; it broke a woman's body, but it did not break families and China did not vanish. Liang was patriotic and enthusiastic for a new China, he saw China's problem as lying in these Chinese cultural practices. It was these practices that made her the easy target for foreign powers. His heartfelt words inspired many, and they would continue to politicise the consumption of opium. Sun Zhongshan went even further. He stated that opium 'has destroyed the whole country and the country cannot survive without its extermination'.[39] Despite the propensity of the problem and the urgent need for change, Sun overstressed the situation to drive his message home. Opium had destroyed many individuals, but not the whole of China. Sun inspired generations of patriots. Indeed, 'extinction of the country and the Chinese race' became a common phrase in the political writings of the time.

Opium helped to conceive and to define the struggle for a new China; it was 'the arc of modern Chinese state-making'.[40] R. Bin Wong believes that opium is 'related to three different aspects of modern Chinese state-making'. First, to the decline of the late imperial state and the subsequent construction of a replacement. Secondly, to China's relationship to foreign countries. And thirdly, to the political economy. Opium was the arch of state-making, the key in diplomacy and the source of revenue that would finance the process. It was not only a cash crop, but also a political crop. Mao Zedong's words were to the point: 'The current war against Japan can be traced to the Opium War. It represented the Chinese people's continued struggle against the imperialists.'[41] In order to save China and the Chinese people from extinction, the imperialists and the evils they brought had to be driven out. Mao Zedong was right about the imperialists, both the British and the Japanese, and his words galvanised the struggle for a new China. But opium smoking had been introduced by the Chinese themselves. Communist state-making via opium would deepen in the 1950s, as opium was successfully eradicated. But the opium discourse would surface again, for example during the handover of Hong Kong in 1997. The politicisation of opium, from Confucian scholar-officials to missionaries and on to Communists will continue. Political regimes and patriots can always dig up the old case of opium. No other commodity has ever led such a social, or rather political, life.

CHAPTER 7

Outward and downward 'liquidation'

This chapter discusses the proliferation of domestic cultivation, smuggling and domestic consumption from the end of the first Opium War, in 1842, up to the end of the second Opium War, in 1860.[1] The interwar years were an important period in the social life of opium, because this time saw the 'extensification' of smoking. Opium had undergone a process of 'intensification' when men of letters invented symbols and values for opium. This process gathered momentum in the late eighteenth century and during the early days of Daoguang. The interwar years would see opium's 'extensification', when increased domestic cultivation and smuggling transformed opium into 'something ordinary'. This is a most crucial phase of consumption. Hao Yen-p'ing summarises the post-war economy: 'The enormous outflow of silver that resulted from the opium trade dealt a heavy blow to China's economy as evidenced by falling prices and the recession during the second quarter of the nineteenth century.'[2] Despite this drain, opium smoking exploded. This raises questions over the quick replacement of silver and over exactly why consumption boomed during economic contraction. Not only did foreign opium continue to pour into the country, but also Chinese opium began to compete with it. Both helped to regenerate the economy, and smoking penetrated thoroughly down to the peasantry. The Opium War seemed to have boosted the popularity of opium and brought about a sense of resignation.

DOMESTIC CULTIVATION

The cash-cropping market town economy had once helped to spread and naturalise tobacco. Now it would help opium. The domestic cultivation of opium began as early as the 1800s. By 1830 it was causing concern to the smuggling community. On 15 October 1830, James Holman visited an English factory in Canton. It was an eventful day because 'a very fair example of opium from the western part of China was brought for examination

today to the houses of Messers. Jardine and Matheson'.[3] This illustrates
how well aware the British were of Chinese competition. But the British
needed not have worried. Chinese opium, thanks to the popularity of
yanghuo, would never surpass Indian, Turkish and Persian brands. Increasing domestic cultivation ultimately alarmed officials. Also in 1830, those
in Zhejiang and Fujian began to report the cultivation and sale of locally
produced opium. Ruan Yuan, Governor-General of Yunnan-Guizhou, and
Yilibu, Governor of Yunnan, memorialised Daoguang in June 1830: 'The
people who live on the border with the barbarians (Burma, Laos and Vietnam), due to the warm weather, have always cultivated the poppy. They
collected the liquids and boiled it into *furong* and then sold it as opium.'[4]
Bao Shichen tells us that Yunnan had begun to make its own opium paste
in 1806, and by the 1810s this industry was on the increase. Indeed, it was
certainly late for Yunnan's high-ranking officials to find out and report
it in 1830.

Li Hongbing, Governor-General of Guangdong-Guangxi, reported in
August that he had discovered opium in the Chaozhou area, where the
Hakka people were concentrated.[5] E'shan, Governor-General of Sichuan,
confirmed in November that he had found opium in western Sichuan,
close to the barbarians (of Burma and Tibet).[6] Sichuan had been a home to
Chinese opium from the Tang dynasty. Some Sichuan farmers had begun
to make their own paste and syrup in the 1810s, as Liang Shaoren tells us.
Yet it took twenty more years for Sichuan officials to find out. Domestic
cultivation flourished in the south-west overland border and in the south-
east maritime region. One is reminded of the entry route of the peanut,
the sweet potato, maize and tobacco. Yang Yuchun, Governor-General of
Shaanxi-Gansu, memorialised the throne in June 1831: 'Large chunks of
land is cultivated with opium, I am afraid they would harvest the juice and
make it into the opium mud.'[7] Shaanxi and Gansu were located at one end
of the Silk Road, on the route to Xiyu or central Asia, where the Ming court
sent eunuchs to procure opium in 1483. Opium as herbal medicine was first
introduced to China via the Silk Road. Zhang Jixin spent a large part of his
official career in the region during the reigns of Daoguang and Xianfeng,
and he wrote of the situation: 'The poppy flowers grew everywhere, in
May and June they blossomed like clouds. Women, old and young, used
bamboo knives and copper pails to wipe out the juice. Merchants from
Jiangsu and Zhejiang converged with big money.'[8]

The south-west and the north-west were becoming the sources of supply. Cultivation also flourished in the interior and along the upper east
coast in the early 1830s, as referenced by the memorials from Shandong,

Table 2 *Opium consumption in China,*
1810s–1880s (million Mexican dollars)

Decade	Imported	Domestic	Total
1810s	4.6		4.6
1820s	9.7		9.7
1830s	13.2		13.2
1840s	18		18
1850s	30	3	33
1860s	35	8	43
1870s	36	13	49
1880s	34	17	51

Source: Hao Yen-p'ing, *The Commercial Revo-*
lution in Nineteenth-Century China (Berkeley:
University of California Press, 1986), pp. 68–9.

Jiangxi, Jiangsu and Shanxi, which read essentially the same as those above.
Domestic cultivation gathered momentum on the eve of the second Opium
War, and the war only served to accelerate it. Wang Hongbin believed that
smokers increased to a number between 2 and 3 million after the first
war. Consumption on such a scale exceeded the supply provided by foreigners. Domestic cultivation, in other words, filled the gap and met the
demand. Hao Yen-p'ing has studied domestic cultivation. His work shows
that there was a big increase in imported opium in the 1850s (see table 2).
And domestic cultivation suddenly surged in the 1850s. Ultimately, it would
outgrow and replace imports in the late nineteenth and early twentieth
centuries.

Growing opium was a way of life for many before the war. It would
remain so. Peng Songyu, who was surprised at his colleagues' after-lunch
opium session when he first arrived in Yunnan, found out more about
opium: 'The Yunnanese depended on opium, if cultivation is forbidden,
they [smokers] would buy from the foreigners.'[9] Prohibition would damage
the livelihoods of the growers. Peng's job was to persuade the Yunnanese
to grow grains rather than opium. The result was that 'they complained
that I did not understand their situation'. Opium generated sure and good
money, and was and would remain the basic and in some cases the only
income for peasants. The Yunnanese saw the same fat profit in opium
as their Ming counterparts saw in tobacco. Cultivation at this time was
voluntary. It would become involuntary in the early twentieth century,
when warlords and political regimes tried to control and profit from its

taxation and traffic. No one was more familiar with the facts on the ground than the Inspector General of Imperial Maritime Customs, Robert Hart, and his team of devoted servants.

A Customs-wide survey in 1863 showed that only a few port cities used (small amounts of) native opium. This would soon change. The 1887 survey provided information on the places that cultivated opium, the cities and towns they served, prices, the taxes paid, numbers of smokers and how opium was consumed, that is, whether pure or mixed. The survey found that 'Native Opium is used at all the Treaty ports'; it was used 'almost exclusively' in Ichang and Wenchow, 'chiefly' in Newchwang, Tientsin and Chefoo, 'largely' in Hankow, and 'to a considerable extent' in Shanghai and Ningpo.[10] It stated that 'Szechwan produces the best quality of opium and a larger amount than any other provinces.' Other exporting provinces included Yunnan, Zhejiang, Henan and Manchuria. Opium from Sichuan and Yunnan was consumed locally, although it also reached southern Manchuria, Shangdong and all the Yangtze river valley provinces, namely Hunan, Hubei, Jiangxi, Anhui and Jiangsu. Zhejiang opium supplied the east coast, Shanghai and Hankow in particular, Fujian and even Taiwan. Henan opium was 'becoming very popular' and was 'considered as good as Patna'; it filled the markets in the central plains and southern Manchuria. Manchurian opium was quickly catching on as well; it was 'extensively cultivated throughout the province'. Manchurian opium supplied Shandong and Shaanxi.

Chinese opium from the south-west would soon make its way through Burma and other south-east Asian countries to end up as 'foreign opium' in Shanghai and other localities along the coast. Map 1 shows the overland trade routes between the opium-producing areas of Yunnan and the southern coast. T. G. Luson, assistant-in-charge of Canton Customs, reported the situation: 'The reason that so much mixed native and Malwa opium is sent to Kwangsi appears to be that it is there sold as Foreign Drug, and thus affords a larger profit to the dealer.'[11] 'Mixed native' was south-west China opium mixed with foreign brands. The situation was not limited to Guangxi, as native opium was also mixed with Malwa, Benares, Patna, Turkish and Persian brands. Chinese opium had come to China as 'foreign opium', and this demonstrates the popularity of foreign opium and the high prices it commanded. Chinese opium would mislead unsophisticated buyers and inexperienced smokers. Yunnan–Burma cross-border smuggling intensified. It became so systematic and profitable in the late nineteenth century that George J. Litton, a British diplomat stationed in Yunnan, recommended regulation:

In West Yunnan opium is practically the only export product which can be given in exchange for foreign goods. A great part of this opium finds its market in Canton, Shanghai and the East Coast of China, but under the Burma China Treaty, it is not permitted to take its natural route, i.e, across Burma and then via Rangoon and Singapore . . . Smuggling across into Burma is known to be rampant and there is some reason to hope that if a legitimate outlet for the West Yunnan opium crop across Burma were to be opened up, that the trade would get into the hands of large capitalists buying for the Canton market and that smuggling would decrease.[12]

Just as Jardine Matheson worried about Chinese competition in 1830, British civil servants were still preoccupied by the threat of the Chinese outmanoeuvring them in the late nineteenth century. Both British individual (smugglers) and national (diplomatic) interests seemed to be married with opium at this time. Yunnan and Sichuan would remain the centres of domestic cultivation and commerce in the late Qing and beyond.

UNPARALLELED SMUGGLING

Although it would take the second Opium War to legalise the import of opium, the Treaty of Nanjing, which did not mention the word opium, served to legitimise smuggling. The *Chinese Repository* noticed the situation in 1838: 'The Chinese coast from Macao to Chusan is now the constant cruising ground of twenty opium ships. The waters of Canton are converted into one grand rendezvous for more than thirty opium boats.'[13] Smuggling continued throughout the first Opium War and 'attained a magnitude that it had never before approached' in the interwar years.[14] The Revd W. M. Lowrie, an American missionary on his way to Amoy in August 1843, made this entry in his diary:

During the voyage from Hong Kong to Amoy, we passed in sight of three of the great opium depots along the coast. These three were Tong-shan, How-tow-san, and Namoa. At these three places, the opium dealers in Canton and Macao have ships constantly stationed to keep supplies of opium, and to them the smaller vessels, or opium clippers, as they are called, resort for cargoes which they carry to different parts of the coast, and dispose of always for silver. The number of vessels employed in this traffic is very great. A single mercantile house in Canton employs about fifty vessels, ships, barks, schooners and brigs, while another house has thirty or more. It is impossible to find a vessel going up the coast which does not carry opium.[15]

Opium smuggling was an integral part of the coastal landscape in the post-war years. Robert Fortune of the London Horticultural Society travelled to China in August 1843. He also saw the 'opium stations' along the coast and wrote about the one in Namoa. Missionaries, travellers and British civil servants are the best witnesses to smuggling, because they all had to ride on opium-freighting ships to reach their destinations. Henry Charles Sirr, the British Vice-Consul in Hong Kong from 1843, wrote about the smuggling between Macao, Canton and Shanghai, as did the Revd Johnson and S. W. Williams. The Revd Dr Smith, later Bishop of Hong Kong, visited Zhoushan (Chusan) in 1845. This was the harbour that greeted him: 'the fumes of opium, which at all times are wafted on the breeze and infect the whole atmosphere around, together with the numerous native smuggling craft which beset the sides of the opium-vessels, are some indication of the extent of this brand of traffic.'[16] Smith saw the magnitude of opium on his way to Shanghai: 'our own vessel, though not engaged in the opium traffic, carried 750 chests of opium as a part of her freight, which were discharged on board of one of the receiving ships stationed at Woosung (the port of Shanghai)'.[17] A non-engagement vessel that carried 750 chests – we can only imagine the size of the cargoes of those who were engaged in trafficking – in Smith lingered on the vessel to witness a transaction and detailed the process in his memoirs:

We went on board this ship and saw the process of preparing the inspissated juice of the opium for test, previous to purchase. On opening the chests, and clearing away a number of dry poppy leaves, an oblong dry case, of a brown colour, was taken out, weighing four or five pounds. In the boxes made up by the East India Company, greater care is taken. The balls are more round, and are placed in partitions, each box containing forty, and being, moreover, carefully cased in hides. The bargain is soon struck with the Chinese broker, who incurs the risk of purchasing for the more opulent Chinese opium merchants at Shanghai and in the neighbourhood. A piece of opium is taken as a sample from three separate balls, and prepared in three separate pots for smoking, to test its freedom from adulteration. This process took nearly half an hour, during which the opium was mixed with water, and often simmering and straining, was kept boiling till, by evaporation, it was reduced to a thick consistency, like treacle. Each box is sold for nearly £200; and we saw about 1500 taels of *Sycee* silver in large lumps of the shape of a shoe, weighted out and paid into the iron chest of the ship. Shroffs, opium dealers, interpreters, and native accountants, were closely standing together on different parts of the deck which were a busy and painfully animated appearance.

This is a most meticulous description of an opium transaction, a scene few were privileged to witness. New and raw to China, the Revd Smith was fascinated with opium. John Francis Davis, Governor of Hong Kong, knew the situation better: 'in 1845, the growth of smuggling of every description, in connection with that of opium, reached such a height at Whampoa, within the Canton River, as to interfere seriously with the rights of the fair traders'.[18] In fact, the Hong Kong government 'drew large revenue from opium' between 1845 and 1941, as Christopher Munn has pointed out.[19] Westminster never denounced the opium trade in practice. Instead, its tacit endorsement sanctioned smuggling before the first Opium War, and the war itself only gave heart to the smugglers. The *Chinese Repository* also watched the growth in smuggling. It estimated that imports would total 48,000 chests in 1845, which at $700 each would make a return of $33,600,000; they would increase and jump to 60,000 chests in 1847 with a profit of $42,000,000.[20] Britain and its colonial regime in Hong Kong were indeed the first 'opium regimes'.

Jardine Matheson spearheaded smuggling in the post-war years, as it had done previously. Hao Yen-p'ing has studied this smuggling under the treaty system. Jardine opened its Shanghai Office in 1843. To lay one's hands on Shanghai was to control central and northern China. As Jardine's operation was 'institutionalised by the mid-1850s',[21] half of post-1849 total imports went through Shanghai. What made smuggling so successful was not just the protection of the Treaty of Nanjing but also 'progress, the deity of the nineteenth century'.[22] The clipper was 'dethroned' by the steamer, and 'the most active opium ship in Chinese waters was built in New York and was flying the flag of the United States'. Russell & Company, America's Jardine Matheson, was a major player in post-war smuggling. Unlike previous pioneers from Scotland, who had taken out non-British papers in order to avoid the hassle of the East India Company, Paul S. Forbes, head of Russell & Company, was simply the American Consul in China. The style of the Americans was no-nonsense. Like the English, who had tried to cut into the China trade against Dutch competition in the eighteenth century, the Americans tried to cut into the opium trade against British competition in the nineteenth century. The interwar years saw a rise in American smuggling and also the technological contribution of America. In the second Opium War the United States would play a key role.

We must not forget, however, that Chinese merchants who worked for and dealt with the foreigners 'played a leading role' in the smuggling joint venture.[23] The Chinese language materials in the Jardine Matheson archive yields some information about their operations. These merchants were the bridges between China and the West, between the smugglers and the smokers. In the early twentieth century H. B. Morse carefully studied the increased shipment of opium from Calcutta and Bombay, that is, of Bengal and Malwa opium, between 1840 and 1860. Table 3 shows his findings.

Table 3 *Shipments from India, 1840–1860 (chests)*

Year	Bengal	Malwa	Total
1840	18,965	1,654	20,619
1841	17,858	16,773	34,631
1842	18,827	14,681	33,508
1843	18,362	24,337	42,699
1844	15,104	13,563	28,667
1845	18,350	20,660	39,010
1846	21,437	12,635	34,072
1847	21,648	18,602	40,250
1848	30,515	15,485	46,000
1849	36,566	16,509	53,075
1850	34,863	18,062	52,925
1851	33,561	22,000	55,561
1852	36,600	23,000	59,600
1853	39,463	27,111	66,574
1854	48,319	26,204	74,523
1855	53,321	25,033	78,354
1856	44,938	25,668	70,606
1857	42,441	29,944	72,385
1858	38,611	36,355	74,966
1859	34,685	41,137	75,822
1860	25,950	32,731	58,681

Source: Hosea B. Morse, *The International Relations of the Chinese Empire* (London: Longmans & Green, 1910), p. 556.

Opium poured into China under the protection of the Treaty of Nanjing. The five treaty ports, Canton, Xiamen [Amoy], Fuzhou, Ningpo and Shanghai, were not the only entry routes, however. The French missionary M. Huc travelled through the south-west region in the early 1850s. Opium was making its way from India, via Burma, to Yunnan and Sichuan, as he detailed:

Our palanquins proceeded between a double line of lancers on horsebacks, whom it appeared the governor of Khioung-tcheou had given us to protect us from rubbers. These rubbers were the smugglers of opium, and we were informed that for several years past they had come in great numbers to the province of Yun-nan, and even as far as Birmah, to fetch the opium sent to them from India. They came back with their contraband goods quite openly, but armed to the teeth, in order to be able to defy the mandarins who might oppose their passage.[24]

Indian opium came to Yunnan and Sichuan via Burma, just as Yunnan and Sichuan opium travelled to the south and east coast of China via Burma and other south-east Asian countries. Burma and Indochina had become the crossing point of opium. This was where the 'motley throng', the many diverse people of the Sino–south-east Asia border, lived and thrived.[25] It had seen the introduction of new world produce. It continued to be important, this time for the spread of opium.

Smuggling was not limited to the south-west overland border region. The north-west corridor was equally busy with the traffic. P. T. Etherton, Her Majesty's Consul-General in Chinese Turkistan, today's Xinjiang, knew the situation well:

A considerable amount of opium is grown in Afghanistan, whence it is imported into China through the Afghan province of Wakhan. As some of the local officials are interested in the trade, they do not display much activity in its suppression. In its passage to Chinese territory the opium traverses the Roof of the World, being convoyed by Kirghiz, hardy nomads whose lives are largely spent at an altitude higher than the summit of Mont Blanc. From the World it would pass across the plains of Turkistan and thence into China proper, and so to the East, a journey of several thousand miles, and may, as in the case of the Russian article, ultimately figure in a police court case in London.[26]

The geography of north-west China, like that of south-west China, offered the perfect milieu for smuggling. David Bello has studied smuggling carried out by Inner Asians and Qing ethnic subjects along the old Silk Road in the late Qing. The two western frontiers of China, central Asia and south-east Asia, were influential in opium's historical transformation. They would remain crucial in the twentieth century. In the south-west, opium thrived on the infamous Burma Road and in the Golden Triangle–Mekong River area. In the north-west, it resurfaced in the post-Mao era when Afghanistan opium once again made its way to China via the hands of ethnic Chinese and/or central Asians, as it had done for hundreds of years.

Opium was coming from all directions. John Francis Davis pushed for legalisation: 'Every endeavour was made by both Sir Henry Pottinger and myself, to persuade Keying to use his influence at Peking for legalising the trade, but entirely without success.'[27] The interwar years were a critical period. On the one hand, friction between China and Britain increased. On the other hand, tensions between the Chinese people and their Manchu overlord heightened. This contributed to the rapid breeding of secret societies and revolutionary parties. One result was the Taiping rebellion (1850–64), which broke out in the last year of Daoguang, and which was a dire beginning for his son, the Xianfeng emperor. The rebellion heralded the end of the Manchu mandate. But questions over the financing of the campaign were raised. Mountains of official communications concerning the suppression of Taiping point to one single issue – funding. Ye Mingchen, Governor-General of Guangdong and Guangxi, where the rebellion broke out, squeezed Hoppo, the government agency that oversaw foreign trade, and procured 2,169,183 taels of silver in 1852.[28] Ye set an example for his colleagues. Wu Tingpu, an Imperial Censor, got the point: 'All the items in and out of the customs and passages are taxed'; 'opium constitutes the largest volume, and yet we allow it to be smuggled and not legally taxed'.[29] He proposed to 'take ten out of a thousand', in other words, a 1 per cent tax on opium.

Scholar-officials seemed to have reconciled theory with practice. Prohibition was absolute in theory, but otherwise in practice. The Xianfeng emperor was no exception. Many mainland historians have suggested that he indulged in opium. The circumstances of his life do not challenge this assertion. In public and in theory he was a prohibitionist. He did not consent to taxation, yet turned a blind eye to the officials who used opium-generated funds. He set the example and the standard for the court and for officials. Many used opium-generated funds and also enjoyed opium personally, yet denounced smoking and supported prohibition in public. This is not puzzling. People held public office but led private lives, the two occupied different spheres and spoke different languages. By 1853 a new tax was created. This was the famous *lijin/likin*, a 1 per cent tax. In the beginning it was levied on staple goods, such as rice sold through shops – this was called the 'sitting *li*'. It was then levied on goods in transit, that is, when they travelled through the interior – this was called the 'walking *li*'. The two *lijin* helped to raise money for the campaign against the Taiping. The stage was set for the opium political economy to come.

EXPLOSION OF CONSUMPTION

In October 1856, as the Taiping rebellion raged and western powers pushed for the legalisation of opium, the 'Arrow incident' occurred. It led to the second Opium War, the so-called 'Arrow War', which would end with opium's legalisation. John Wong has written extensively on this subject. The second war featured new players – the French, the Americans and the Russians – in the theatre of opium and China. Increased domestic cultivation, large-scale smuggling and an official sense of resignation contributed to an explosion of smoking during the interwar years, the 'extensification' period. Dr Ball, a missionary doctor in Canton, observed: 'There are, besides, multitudes of smoking-shops, where the smokers went by day and by night to refresh themselves with the fumes of this exhilarating stupefying drug, to pass a merry hour, or to drown their sorrows and their cares in a profound stupor.'[30] Canton had been the old capital of opium, a new capital was taking shape to the east. The Revd Dr Smith spent 1844, 1845 and 1846 in China, collecting information on 'the moral and religious character and wants of the Chinese'.[31] He rode on opium ships, witnessed opium transactions and visited many smoking facilities in Amoy:

During my stay at Amoy, I made many inquiries respecting the prevalence and effect of opium smoking, and often visited, with a missionary friend, some of the shops in which opium was sold. The first opium house which we entered was situated close to the entrance to the *taou-tais* palace [regional government office]. Four or five rooms in different parts of a square court were occupied by men stretched out on a rude kind of couch, on which lay a head-pillow, with lamps, pipes and other apparatus for smoking opium. In one part of the principal room the proprietor stood, with delicate steel-yards, weighing out the prepared drug, which was of a dark, thick, semi-fluid consistency. A little company of opium smokers, who had come hither to indulge in the expensive fumes, or to feast their eyes on the sight of that which increasing poverty had placed beyond their reach, soon gathered around us and entered into conversation.[32]

But Amoy could not be compared with the newly opened port city of Shanghai – the new capital of opium commerce and consumption. Increased opium, be it foreign or Chinese, and the explosion of smoking were seen by many. A correspondent of the *Chinese Repository* watched the opium commerce in Shanghai:

The use of opium among the Chinese was never more rapidly increasing than now, and its evil effects never more evident. Eighty thousand chests, reports say, are coming to China this year [1850], one half of which it is supposed will reach this northern market [Shanghai]. In this city, both the traffic and the use of opium are in no way concealed. Whole chests are carried through the streets in broad day [light]. The legalisation of the traffic is talked of everywhere, not only by those who are engaged in the trade, but [by] the officers of government . . . But whether legalised or not, there seems no immediate prospect of arresting the evil, – an evil that is taking away the vital energies of the nation.[33]

Mao Xianglin, a local scholar, wrote of its consumption:

Ever since the disturbance of *guichou* [1853, the Taiping rebellion], the city's defence is tight and the gate is shut at sunset. The brothel business within the walls has declined. But recently, they've moved to the foreigner's place [British and International Settlement]; and they have been joined by the travelling prostitutes from Guandong. These women wear strange clothes; they have no hair-buns, no tight skirts, no bound feet, no high heels, no jewellery; but they can sing. We don't understand the words, but the songs are sexy enough to tell . . . There are also *huagu* [flower-drum] women, they sing sensual words to attract clients. Since opium is fashionable, *yan guan* [opium dens] stand one after another. The cunning ones use women to allure clients; these women walk around, they wear long skirts and heeled shoes.[34]

Opium chests passed through the streets in broad daylight and prostitutes congregated where opium was smoked. Shanghai was emerging as the centre of sex recreation, with the help of opium and the protection of foreign settlements. Like his predecessors in the late eighteenth and early nineteenth centuries, Mao was very familiar with the sex industry and its latest highlight. He certainly was not alone. This can also be gauged from the life of Wang Tao, who worked in Shanghai between 1849 and 1862. His diary tells us of his smoking excursions:

24 October 1858: Liang Nianzhai asked me to lunch and furnished wine as well. After the meal, we went to *Minxiang* for tea; Chunpu joined us as well. In the tea house we waited for Qiu Boshen, he never showed up. *Sanpailou* has small rooms for opium smoking. Nianzhai and I went and smoked three rounds; my bones and joints feel really relaxed.

25 October 1858: At lunchtime Feng Huasan came and told me that he was going to return to his native place by boat. At sunset, I went to Xiaoyi's home and saw Chen Zijin there. Chen was very modest; he is good at astronomy, mathematics and geometry, and a native of Jiangning [Nanjing]. When it got dark, Nianzhai came. We went to Wu's small room to smoke two pipes of opium. Facing each other, we talked and smoked; it was really special and wonderful.[35]

Wang Tao called the place where he smoked opium *xiao shi* or 'small room'. This points towards the opium den. Dedicated smoking facilities surfaced in the 1820s and mushroomed after the war, but they were not the same as the later opium den. Instead, they were shops, especially those that sold *yanghuo*, where one could buy the paste, smoke it quickly on site or take it away. Most people bought the paste and smoked it at their own convenience. One missionary commented: 'the poorer classes generally resort to these shops, but the wealthier orders do their smoking more privately.'[36] Dr Ball called the facilities in Canton 'smoking shops' and said there were 'multitudes' of them.[37] Henry Charles Sirr found numerous 'smoking houses' in Shanghai in the early 1840s.[38] The first opium facility the Revd Smith visited in Amoy in mid-1844 was 'four or five rooms in different parts of a square court', inside of which were 'a rude kind of couch' with 'a head-pillow'; here the proprietor stood 'weighing out the prepared drug'.[39] One of Thomas Allom's famous pictures depicts just this kind of setting. Smokers purchased the paste and smoked by themselves in cubicles or on couches. Space and service were limited; but it was cheap, quick and easy. Lord Jocelyn also saw this kind of shop in Singapore, where Chinese coolies converged at night: 'The rooms where they sit and smoke, are surrounded by wooden couches, with places for the head to rest upon, and generally a side-room is devoted to gambling.'[40]

'Shops' and 'houses' with smoking rooms would transform into *guan* or 'dens' as consumption became more specialised, consumers more sophisticated and as competition intensified. *Guan*, explains Susan Naquin, is a suffix for inns, restaurants, theatres, tea houses, wineshops, in a word, buildings that are open to all.[41] *Yan guan* or opium dens were public places that were open to smoking. Smokers would select their run opium, which was then prepared and heated up in front of them, just as some Chinese foods were prepared before the eyes of diners. Dens would provide not only room service, from food to refill, but also encourage other pursuits, such as gambling, music entertainment and sex recreation. Women would play a pivotal role in this new phase of consumption. Opium smoking accompanied by sex recreation would rewrite the history of prostitution. Wang Tao had easy walking distance access to at least two opium 'small rooms', and this gives us an idea of the number of smoking facilities available in Shanghai in the 1850s. Wang Tao supported prohibition, but he never resisted the temptation of opium. Moral conviction and immediate gratification were two different things. Such resignation was common. It would lead many more to the road of opium.

The smoking industry experienced an unprecedented boom during the interwar years. Opium smoking rooms and smoking houses spread to the remote villages and clustered agrarian communities on the outskirts of Shanghai. The 1878 (compiled) *Nanhui County Gazetteer* recorded:

During the past thirty or forty years, smokers were not just confined to the cities but have become almost as common in the remote countryside. To give an idea of a town's daily consumption of opium, the amount of money spent on it exceeds that spent on rice. In addition there are also the *huayan guan* [flower-smoke dens]. They say they are husband-and-wife dens; but in reality they seduce the sons of good families. They are a place for secret adultery. Though the government has investigated and tried to deal with them, they would never disappear.[42]

So-called 'flower-smoke dens' were places where opium and sex could be had cheap, quick and easy – they were places of cheap recreation for the lower classes. When intensified smuggling made consumption available to the aspiring middle classes in the big cities, increased domestic cultivation made smoking accessible to the rural majority. Chinese peasants joined in the smoking of opium. This signalled the complete 'liquidation' or 'extensification' of opium consumption. Opium had become 'something ordinary'. Indeed, the above excerpt is located in a chapter entitled 'Indigenous Customs'. Opium smoking had become an indigenous custom in the countryside of greater Shanghai. It had also become indigenous in Taigu: 'The poison of opium smoking began in the reign of Xianfeng [1850–61], it dragged on to the reign of Tongzhi [1862–74] and flourished in the time of Guangxu [1875–1908].'[43] 'The rich and big families were all addicted to it, it then went down to the middle classes; even the small ones in remote villages used opium as if it was a necessity like cloth, cotton, vegetables and grains; they could not be without it and they depend on it.' Taigu's native banker sons had introduced opium before the war, and smoking blossomed in the interwar years. Taigu smokers would fashion the famous 'Taigu lamp' to dazzle smokers and collectors alike.

Opium had filtered down to the peasantry. They had been the largest army of tobacco smokers in the late Ming; they would be the largest army of opium smokers in the late Qing. Some had already substituted opium for tobacco, while others smoked their home-grown opium. Via the peasantry opium would become cheap and widely available; peasants would help meet the demand of a whole nation. Opium smoking raged like a wildfire in cities and villages alike. Meantime, the court was preoccupied with foreigners, and local governments with the Taiping. *Bibin Zaji* or *Miscellaneous Notes on the Escape from the Soldiers* painted a picture of the once rich and abundant Jiangnan in 1860, when the second Opium War ended:

When I was small, I saw tea houses and wine stores but they were not many. In recent years and day by day wine stores have out-numbered rice stores, tea houses have surpassed wine stores, and the foreign smoke shops have further out-numbered wine stores. Remote towns and little villages, they may not have rice stores, yet I have never heard of any place where you cannot get the foreign smoke.[44]

Chen Xiqi was a native of the rich Haining county. His family, like thousands of others, had fled their home to escape the advancing Taiping. Chen jotted down what he saw and endured, as did Ke Wuchi and Duan Guangqing. Ke compared the smuggling of opium to that of salt, while Duan remembered a local commercial guild's squabble over smuggling. These memoirs testify to the prevalence of opium amidst the destruction. By 1860 opium shops outnumbered other establishments that were essential to the Chinese way of life. In other words, opium had become an essential part of Chinese life, it had entered the bloodstream of Chinese society. When wars were fought, opium led a quiet life. As John Francis Davis commented on the Chinese policy towards opium in 1852: 'it is well known that not a single measure has been taken by the emperor's government against opium since the war'.[45] The Qing's preoccupation was clearly not with opium but rather with foreigners like himself and with rebels like the Taiping. Britain, however, humiliated China in 1842 and again in 1860, largely because opium had depleted China and demoralised the people. The two Opium Wars helped to put opium smoking on the map of China. In the century that followed opium would continue to both poison and regenerate the Chinese people and Chinese society.

CHAPTER 8

'The volume of smoke and powder'

This chapter studies women and how opium affected their social life.[1] The future of the Qing dynasty looked bleak in 1861. When western powers coerced China into unequal treaties at the end of the second Opium War, three major rebellions raged. As if this wasn't enough, the Xianfeng emperor died in August and left the throne to his 6-year-old son. From 1861 to 1908 the Qing dynasty would see three more boy emperors and the Empress Dowager Cixi. Many have blamed Dowager Cixi for the downfall of imperial China, but in reality she helped the Qing survive another half-century. A parallel study of Queen Victoria and Dowager Cixi still awaits to be written. Their empires were different indeed, but both were strong and capable women. England seemed to thrive on female monarchs, yet the Chinese empress dowagers ruled 'from behind the curtain'.

Opium use had started with the 'court ladies' of the mid-Ming. It would thrive among ordinary women during the late Qing, at which time it galvanised the sex recreation industry, saw 'the explosion of common prostitution' and ushered in the golden age of smoking.[2] Opium created jobs for women. It also intensified their subjugation. Yet we must not generalise the circumstances under which women succumbed to opium, as this chapter will explain.

BOREDOM KILLER AND APHRODISIAC

The union of women and opium has a linguistic aspect. *Yan* originally meant smoke from burning, vapour from heating or natural mist. It came to mean tobacco when it was introduced. *Yan* can be conjugated. *Yan hua* or 'smoke and flower' means the spectacular beauty that fireworks display as well as the world of prostitution. *Yan hua* was the inspiration of *huayan guan*, 'flower-smoke studio' or opium sex den. There was also *yan fen* or 'smoke and powder' and *yan xia*, 'mists and clouds'. *Yan xia bi* used to denote one's love for natural beauty, it was now extended to opium addiction, as one longed for manmade 'mists and clouds'. Opium revolutionised sex recreation and enriched the Chinese language. The linguistic connotations are worth investigating, but linguistic anthropology is not my subject here. Women first began smoking with tobacco. They certainly enjoyed opium when it came along. Women of upper- and upper-middle-class families had time to spare and space to share. Many studied the classics, some taught their own children, while others found ways to escape their boredom with recreations such as chess-playing, tea-tasting, and now opium smoking. Exposure and access were clearly important issues. Affluent women had access to opium in at least, if not earlier than, the mid- eighteenth century, as Wang Kangnian remembered:

There lived, in the middle of Qianlong, a woman of a very wealthy family in Canton. She lost her husband at a young age and became a nun after. Her mother's family built a nunnery for her to live in. After ten years of melancholy meditation, she became paralysed; her legs were stiff and she could not stand up. Her mother's family took pity on her loneliness and pain; they tried many ways to make her happy. This was an old and important family, most relatives and friends were wealthy as well. They often gave her rare curios. One of the thirteen Hong merchants sent her a cane prized by westerners, a bottle of perfume, a lamp and a box of opium paste.[3]

Opium proved to be a boredom killer and a medicine for this sickly daughter of a wealthy family; the story goes on to tell how opium smoking helped to cure her. To be widowed at a young age and to be childless were dreadful curses for a Chinese woman. Years of praying could not relieve this woman's suffering and led to difficulties in standing up. She commanded sympathy and lived a better life than many. Opium became a new addition to her sheltered and ennui life.

A picture taken in the late Qing shows a Manchu man and woman engaged in smoking. The woman holds a water pipe in her left hand and an opium needle in her right hand, a sign that she helped the man smoke. Opium was often smoked in rotation and with tobacco. The woman smoked the water pipe when the man smoked opium, and when he needed a break or had finished, she most likely would step in and continue, as illustration 2 shows. Tea and other accessories contributed to a proper smoking session. Such recreation became routine among many upper- and upper-middle-class women; by the late nineteenth century, when domestic opium hit the market, it would became common for middle- and lower-middle-class women. Opium was within the reach of well-off women regardless of whether they were with their husbands, on their own or with other women. This demonstrates the financial autonomy and domestic power

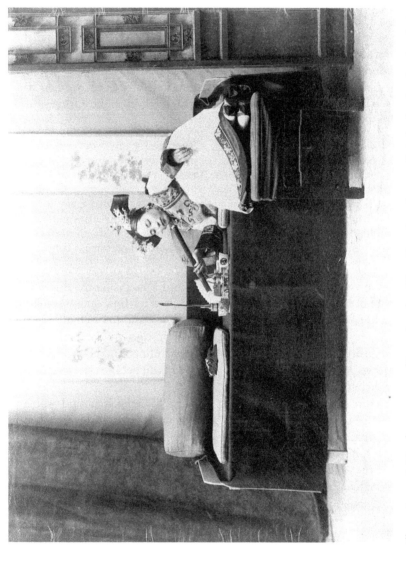

Illustration 2. A Manchu woman smoking opium, late Qing. Note the opium needle in her hand, a sign that she is a skilled smoker.

of Chinese women. Smoking was part of their ordinary lives and leisure pursuits by the late nineteenth century, as Mrs Archibald Little observed in Sichuan:

Except among the poorest of the poor, who do field-work or carry water, the women of China do little beyond suckling children and making shoes, except in the treaty ports, where now large numbers of them are employed in the factories late started. They smoke and gossip, give and go to dinner parties, and one of their great delights is to go on pilgrimages to distant shrines . . . Even when nuns invite ladies to come and enjoy themselves with them, it means drinking wine, smoking, and playing cards; and not uncommonly, in the west of China at all events, smoking includes opium-smoking. The ladies who are regular opium-smokers sit up late at night, and do not get up till five or six in the evening. They mostly have bad health, and generally say they have taken to opium-smoking because of it. Whatever effect opium may have upon men, the various ladies I have seen at ladies' dinners generally return from the opium-couch with their eyes very bright, their cheeks very red, and talking a great deal of nonsense very excitedly.[4]

The Sichuan women seemed to spend too much time partying, gossiping and smoking opium; of course, Mrs Little and her friends would have done just the same but with tea. As well as the upper and middle classes, courtesans and prostitutes also knew about opium. It was a part of their livelihood. Opium thrived on the Qinhuai River in Nanjing by, if not earlier than, the 1810s. The capital of Jiangnan decadence and the hub of the Chinese sex recreation industry had plenty of opium. Penghua Sheng or 'Flower-Holding Gentleman' detailed the social life of opium in this legendary neighbourhood:

Chen Xizi was the daughter of *Baoxia*, titled *Lanzhou*, Rank One, aged 20. She lived in the east end, her skin was lush and smooth. She socialised and entertained very skilfully and belonged to the gentleman *Lotus Six*. Within three years, he died of opium smoking. *Ji* [Chen Xizi] returned to her old business, but really it was not what she wanted to do. Another gentleman *Jiannan* was enchanted by her, spent gold to have her.[5]

Chen Xizi was a famous courtesan active in Nanjing in at least 1817, when *Qinhuai Huafanglu* was written. Rank One indicated that she was highly literate and exceptionally beautiful; she commanded a high price, affordable only to the lettered rich like Lotus Six, who had been smoking opium for three years. This reminds us of the 'several thousand *ji* of opium' amassed by Manchu commander, Mukedengbu when he was in Nanjing in the 1810s. To entertain Lotus Six, Xizi would have to, at least, lie down and alternate with him. Xizi might have been a smoker herself, or she may have smoked out of necessity. Although she was not addicted, she could have enjoyed opium. A picture taken in the late Qing shows two young men relaxing with a woman and opium (illustration 3). Sex recreation had always been an industry. Now the industry could not be without opium. Opium was as major an attraction as was a courtesan/prostitute's beauty and talent. It helped women entertain men of letters and sons of fortune; it also helped them to maintain their livelihood. Xu Huanyuan told stories of 'smoke and powder' in *Notes at the Hall of Grass in the South City* (the city being Hefei):

On the eve of the result [for the provincial examination], *Gongzi* was drunk and asleep. *Ji* sent someone to buy the list [successful candidates]. She paced back and forth, could not control her feet, sometimes murmuring to herself and at other times looking around nervously. Her servants, both old and young, laughed at her in private. Dawn was approaching, *Ji* secretly prepared the opium paste and waited for the news. Suddenly she heard hurried knocking, she opened the door immediately and the messengers were there, *Gongzi* had passed the exam. *Ji* rewarded [tipped] the messengers lavishly and began to think about getting money for the metropolitan [national] examination. *Gongzi* thanked her and stayed on with her.[6]

Ji was devoted to Gongzi and took care of him during the tense period of examination, even though he was not rich. She was rewarded, as he decided to stay with her after he passed the provincial examination. Beauty appreciated talent, or rather the talented captured the heart of the beautiful. This is the age-old tale of *caizi jiaren*, as we also see in Mao Xiang and his beloved Ji. But while Mao's Ji is skilled in tea-making, the above Ji is skilled in preparing opium. Times had changed. Yet this is not just about a union of beauty and talent. Highly literate and capable, many courtesans/prostitutes would marry and go on to lead respectable lives afterwards. Mao's Ji and the above Ji are good examples of female upward social mobility. Literary talent and sexual attraction are two means, opium another. Sex recreation is universal, but what distinguishes the Chinese institution is not only the literate woman but also her culinary abilities. Tea and now opium were essential in the encounter of talent and beauty. Fine dining accompanied by fine drinking and now fine smoking enriched their union. Opium smoking blossomed in the pursuit of verses, matured to the accompaniment of foods and flourished in the delight of sex.

LIVELIHOOD AND SOCIAL MOBILITY

Going to the brothel was costly, and maintaining a Ji was even more so. Opium could be enjoyed at a man's own convenience, without a woman.

Illustration 3. For many young men in the late Qing the best way to relax was opium smoking accompanied by women.

Many men had done so for years, without the companionship of women. Yet nothing could replace the ambience of the den or the pleasure of women. Smoking, inhaling and exhaling to be more precise, released a fog-like cloud that arose gently, lingered in different shapes and disappeared like a ghost. This was called *tunyun tuwu*, 'swallowing cloud and spewing fog'. Although many were captured by the 'cloud' and 'fog' that carried them away from the world of stresses and strains, many more were fascinated with the human 'cloud' or 'fog' that was sexual intercourse. *Yanyun xi* or 'drama of smoke-cloud' was an enigmatic phrase that denoted such an endeavour in central Hunan dialect, as Yang Enshou wrote of his own experience:

> At your first visit to *Taoyuan*, you are invited to play the drama of the smoke-cloud after tea. She, the beautiful, would lie down and languidly extend her luminous white wrist. Opium would be passed between her intertwining fingers and exhaled slowly as a cloud. Like the *sizhao* flower, one is never tired of looking at it through the mist. As for the smoking guns [pipes], luxurious ones come in jade and *daimao* [exquisite tortoiseshell], plain ones in square or mottled bamboo. Sometimes you would see black bamboo ones as big as a thumb inscribed with *Sandufu*; the characters were as tiny as ants but without any damage done to the bamboo and without any abbreviation of strokes. Ah, this truly is an object of lovesickness. Some *Gong zi* came to the province for the autumn examination, on the eve of the result, he gathered all the famous flowers [prostitutes] to celebrate.[7]

Opium smoking accompanied by sex recreation and poetry appreciation, what 'confusions of pleasure' indeed. Taoyuan was a town in northern Hunan where, legend had it, beautiful women came from; it also referred to dreamland. It might also be the name of the den, since Taoyuan would remind one of beautiful women and a world beyond ordinary reach. *Sandufu* was epic poetry written by the Jin dynasty scholar Zuo Si, a must-read among the learned. To appreciate *Sandufu* while smoking opium was indeed luxury redefined for the learned. Smoke cloud and human cloud echoed and gratified a man who knew how to put his experience into words. This was the essence of frequenting opium dens and brothels. Yang Enshou came from an influential provincial family in Changsha. Urban and well educated, he led a comfortable life regardless of whether he worked as a private secretary or as an official. Examination students bound for Changsha every year would not be without 'smoke' and 'powder'.

Yang's story illustrates the evolution of the opium den. It also illustrates the sophistication of pipe-making at the time. Like Prince Minning, Yang's generation of scholar-officials and urban rich were still fascinated with the pipe. Hunan was situated at the crossroads of opium importing and opium growing. What added to its geographical importance was the beauty and the abundance of its natural resources; the famed mottled bamboo, which was the raw material for the opium pipe and a profitable business for the Hunanese. The story also provides a vivid picture of a brothel's goings-on and the specialisation that was beginning to take place in the opium–sex industry. The business of opium smoking and sex recreation became increasingly sophisticated and competition more fierce. The process of heating up a tiny globule of opium paste until it bubbled, scooping it up with a needle, putting it into the bowl of the pipe and holding it at an angle over the lamp until it was evaporated turned into a craft and a means of livelihood for prostitutes and female servants alike. Yet setting up the opium smoke and ensuring that all was ready for smoking was only the beginning. Women were responsible for refilling both the bowl and the lamp, and for rotating or keeping the smoke evaporated when a client wanted a break. This was a delicate job. Temperature was critical, as the paste could not be overcooked or underheated. Either would make it impossible to scoop the paste up with the needle. Only 'intertwining fingers' could do all that was required with both grace and efficiency.

Zhou Sheng, another man of letters and leisure of the time, knew this well. He provided his first-hand observation in 'Yangzhou Dream':

Every day, she [*Yulin*] made herself up heavily and demanded one *liang* of silver [50 grams] when she saw a client. She led him to the inner room where a lamp and trays were already set up. Taking the Hunanese mottled bamboo pipe and lying down with a man she had never seen before, she shared the pillow with him on the other side of the lamp. She scooped paste and lighted the lamp. She lived on this business and had to tease her clients sometimes. Shy with her eyes, she was good at playful speech and seducing the young ones. When no one was around late in the evening, she would lie down and inhale face to face with him.[8]

Zhugao and *tiaogao*, that is heating and scooping opium paste, was a well-established profession by the 1860s, when Zhou Sheng lingered in Yangzhou. Located on the Grand Canal and the Yangtze River, and being the centre of the salt trade, Yangzhou was a capital in its own right. The city was famous for its women, who 'did a thriving trade' as domestic servants, wet-nurses and prostitutes.[9] Yangzhou prostitutes had their own guilds; they worked as far away as Beijing and Canton; the 'flower boat' prostitutes Shen Fu spent a night with in Canton in 1793 were from Yangzhou. Zhou Sheng encountered many and detailed their survival on such crafts scooping paste. The above 'she' was an orphan who had been sold a few times. She had started as a servant girl, but 'scooping paste' allowed her to undertake prostitution, should the situation arise or should she be willing. She made a living out of the craft, and also took advantage of the late evenings. Young boys were also employed in the 'scooping paste' business, as I mentioned in chapter 6. Not surprisingly, many of them would learn to smoke and would be abused at the same time. Wang Zhiping, a Communist official, was a shoe shop apprentice in Shanghai in the early 1930s, when he was thirteen. He spent his days boiling, filtering and preparing the opium paste for his boss.[10] He could not bear the abuse and left two years later. He was one of thousands.

Opium gave women a unique means of survival. Thousands used opium to make a living and thousands more supported their families, sometimes their father's and husband's smoking or addiction, by this means. Wang Tao was not just an experienced smoker, he was also an experienced *piao ke* or brothel-goer. He enjoyed opium and sex, and he loved discoursing with women:

Girl Hu, also called *Meizhu* or *Bao'er*, came from a lower family in Tinglin of County Song. Her father, *Futang,* worked for the county's policing service . . . At this time, *Ji* [Girl Hu] was only twelve. She liked to wear black clothes, people called her 'black peony'. She grew up, looked sweet and charming. She had graceful manners, could write verses, and was good at making herself up to look even more delicate and touching . . . A family surnamed Xu who lived in the neighbourhood had a son who was about twenty and not yet married . . . One day he saw the girl and said that she was a lotus flower floating on autumn waters . . .

Hu's father had the opium addiction, he needed one *liang* of gold every day and this could only be brought in by the girl . . . At this time, a new magistrate assumed office, he protected robbers and bandits, set them free and paid out no salaries. *Hu's* family became poor, the situation got so bad eventually that they were almost without food. They depended on the girl to lean against the door and smile at strangers passing by [prostitution]. She appeared to be selling opium but in fact she was attracting clients. Before long, she even went out and accompanied distinguished guests at dinner parties. This was real prostitution. Suddenly she became famous in the business.[11]

Filial piety was the foremost important virtue of a Chinese woman. Girl Hu's father took advantage of it. Some may agree that she was forced into this, as her family looked to her for salvation, while others may argue that this was indeed female upward social mobility, as she entertained men of higher classes. It is hard to determine the key motive, as it could be both, in this case and in many others. But what is quite clear is that women of poor families were just as responsible when it came to survival. Families often sold their girls or looked to them for a way out when difficulties cropped up. Poverty was the single most important motive behind prostitution, according to the interrogations of the Communist police in the early 1950s and the research of many. Some sold their girls, many as young as seven, for opium. This was noticed by many missionaries.

Travelling on the main road from the south towards T'ai-yuen Fu, I stayed at an inn a few miles from the city. During the evening and in the morning I heard children's voices. These I supposed were from the younger members of a family who were travelling. But while the mules were being harnessed, and the many carts were being packed previous to starting, I saw that eight little girls, ranging from seven to twelve years of age, were being placed in a cart. Enquiring about them from a fellow-traveller whose cart stood next to mine, he replied, 'These children have been bought cheaply in Ta-t'ong Fu [a city in the northern part of the province], by the man you see with them, who is going to sell them at T'ai-ku [a city about forty miles from T'ai-yuen Fu] for a high price. This has become very frequent lately, and is what your opium is doing.' By way of explanation he said the people in the north of the province being poorer, the opium habit reduced the victims to extremities more rapidly, and that selling their daughters was one resource to get money in order to procure the drug.[12]

Selling girls had been a common practice. Selling girls in order to smoke opium became common in the late Qing and Republican eras, when it extended to wives and concubines. As opium ruined many men, family responsibilities were pushed on to the shoulders of women, some even as young as seven years old. Feminised and institutionalised, opium further subjugated women by giving them a tool to make a living and to support their families. *Shen Bao* noted that there were more than 1,700 opium dens in Shanghai in 1872. This number quadrupled by 1928, when the French Concession alone had 8,000.[13] Lu Hanchao has shown that 171 brothels operated in the 'Alley of joint pleasure', a compound of 14,500 square feet with a main alleyway 15 feet wide by about 280 feet long.[14] Women selling quick sex with the help of a little opium now flourished in *huayan jian* or the 'flower-smoke studio' that both Christian Henriot and Gail Hershatter have detailed. This was mainstream sex recreation for lower-class men until the late 1940s. Given that China was already the world's most populous country at the turn of century, with a total population of around 500 million, it is perhaps not surprising that it also had the largest

population of prostitutes. Sidney D. Gamble compared the Chinese case
with others in 1919:

City	Number of inhabitants per recognised prostitute
Shanghai	137
Peking	258
Tokyo	277
Nagoya	314
Japan	392
Chicago	437
Paris	481
Berlin	582
London	906[15]

This was Christian Henriot's 'explosion of common prostitution'. Moreover, not only did China have the largest prostitute population, its prostitutes were getting younger, as Harriet Sergeant shows that they were 'no
more than twelve or thirteen' years of age.[16] Would there have been such
an 'explosion' if there was no opium available?

A TOOL AND A WEAPON

The experience of opium was double-edged for the women of China. On
the one hand it intensified their subjugation to men, family and society;
on the other, it enabled some to take not only their own but also their
family's life and destination into their own hands. Yu Yue knew this from
the experience of a friend:

Gentleman Gu of Wujiang went to Suzhou for the examination and he settled
down close to the *Jili qiao* [Bridge of Fortune]. A tea house called *Jinfeng lou*
[Pavilion of the Fine Peacock] sits next door. He had nothing to do after a meal
and went for tea there. It was a full house with only one table partially free in the
corner. An old woman and a young lady were there. Gu went to the table. The old
woman began to talk to Gu, after a while they found the conversation enjoyable.
The old woman said: 'It's boring here, come to my home if you are interested.
We'll have a nice meal.' Gu went along. When he got there, he was led upstairs;
the decoration there was quite fine. This was Daoguang's time, opium was already
popular. On the bed, the smoking sets were on display. She asked him to try. Gu
said that he was not used to it. The old woman said 'It's only occasional; it doesn't
hurt!' She asked the young lady to heat the smoke and serve the guest.

Gu got on the bed, the young lady took off his shoes and said: 'You can sit
or sleep, please feel at home. The old lady will be back shortly.' After a while, he
heard loud door knocking, the young lady got up and went downstairs to see what

was happening, Gu felt suspicious, he also went downstairs and hid behind a door. After she opened the door, some thirty men rushed in. They asked where the man is. She said 'He is upstairs.' The gang went upstairs, and Gu slipped out of the door. This was a custom of Suzhou, they always use women as allure. When a young man fell into the trap, they would rob him of all his possessions, sometimes forcing him to borrow up to thousands or even tens of thousands before they would let him go. This is called *xianren tiaoyun* [the celestial jumps to the cloud].[17]

Easy-going women and the appeal of opium proved to be the perfect catch for an examination candidate. The women seemed to have partnered, voluntarily or involuntarily, with local gangsters in order to squeeze out a living for themselves and/or their families. Women and opium became central to this kind of urban criminal activity. It happened so often that a timely phrase, *xianren tiaoyun*, was coined to enigmatically denote it: 'The celestial' is the god-sent victim, while 'cloud' indicates the set-up. Women had to support themselves when they were widowed or abandoned by their husbands and/or families. Some had children to bring up, while others were beyond that tender age. Like Yu Yue, many late Qing men of letters wrote about women who survived against many odds with the help of opium. Pan Lun'en's heroines not only managed to pay off the debts accumulated by their husbands, but also found friendship or companionship after they were abandoned by their husbands and/or families. Opium destroyed many men, the breadwinners of their families. It also gave power to many women, who rose to its challenges. Opium allows us to see the capacity and the complexity of Chinese women.

Women were praised when their menfolk passed exams or attained high offices. But a woman's ultimate goal was an entry in the local history books in the chapter entitled 'Virtuous and Heroic Women'. Many achieved this by remaining widowed for as long as six decades. In fact, the longer one remained a widow, the more virtuous one was admitted to be. The 'cult of widow fidelity' was common in history, and 'chaste widows' became the 'hallmark of the Qing's moral education program'.[18] Women who departed from such moral guidelines would encounter social prejudice of all kinds and punishments of every sort. Some were prepared to accept the consequences, and they found in opium a weapon of self-defence:

A certain family in Meizhou [Guangdong] had a son Zhang He. He was not good at anything but being intimate with a prostitute. He accumulated debts because although he visited her frequently, he brought very few presents. Her mother [foster mother or head of brothel] asked the prostitute to refuse him but she would not listen. While Zhang was drinking at her place one evening, her mother interrupted several times, asking her to do other things and ordering Zhang to go home. He became distressed and burst into tears. The prostitute was moved. She said: 'We love each other and cannot bear to part. You don't want to leave me but my mother has tried to break us up everyday. It is an impossible situation. It is better if we take drugs and die together, then we could be husband and wife in the *nine springs* [the nether world]. Would not that be better than being alive?' Zhang's mind went blank and he could not think of anything better. The prostitute took off her hairpin and gave it to Zhang, who exchanged it for money to buy wine and mixed it with opium. The two of them drank facing each other until they were drunk, they held each other in their arms and lay down. Her mother discovered it and she used the pouring method [by which medicine is poured down the throat] to save them, the prostitute was saved but her lover Zhang was not.[19]

In the above story, some may interpret opium-taking as the prostitute's scheme to get rid of Zhang, since he was poor. Yet one may agree that the prostitute was indeed in love with Zhang and so was not free to choose. Indeed, the story goes on to tell that she died a few months later. On yet another level, we must learn to read the word 'prostitute'. Some were certainly prostitutes of various ranks and occasions; however, others were just ordinary women or servants. Women could be easily branded as 'prostitute'. An independent life invited suspicion, prejudice and exclusion, as women must be virgins before they were married, and must remain widowed after their husbands died. The word 'prostitute' directs us to the issue of 'voice and text'; that is, we hear the 'author', we also hear 'representations of persons, events, and ideas that the author sets before us'.[20] We hear women from the voices of men. Men were free to enjoy opium and sex, and they judged women with their own moral yardstick. Many Chinese women were not free to choose however. Marriages were arranged. Many women were not free to live as they wished. Some dared to protest, but many had to use death to do so. Opium replaced the hanging rope, because it was less painful. Neither rebellion nor convention could save some women from such a fate. *One Hundred One Buddhist* tells the story:

In Jingkou [Jiangsu] there lived a good woman named Jiang, she was beautiful and virtuous, and married to the son of Chen who lived in the same neighbourhood. At the beginning, both Jiang and Chen belonged to families of equal means, but later the Chens declined and the Jiangs became richer. Jiang worked very hard to make ends meet; she was never proud and had no luxurious habits. Chen used to run a store that sold raw silk. To escape a local riot, he lived temporarily out of town and his store was destroyed.

Jiang sold her dowry, clothes and jewellery to keep the family going; she also went to borrow from her own mother who had no option but to help. Her father-in-law died, Jiang paid and arranged the funeral as well. Her husband had the habit of smoking, she tried to persuade him to stop but he would not listen. He planned to open a new store but needed cash. Jiang went again to her own mother who gave her several hundred gold with the intention that it would not go to her husband's smoking. The excuse was to open a new store, but it was really to support his addiction. Jiang thought it over and realised that she had no way out since she was married to him. She depended on her mother's family for every kind of relief, her brother and sister-in-law were unhappy about it. He was her husband; she should not fail him. Indeed, he had failed her. Was there any hope left in this life? She swallowed the opium paste and died.[21]

Jiang earned the ultimate label 'virtuous', but she paid for it with her death. She represents millions not only in the late Qing but also throughout Chinese history. Although she was born into a middle-class family, her socio-economic status changed with her marriage. She cannot be compared with her widowed and paralysed upper-class counterpart, who is showered with gifts including opium. She is unable to contemplate anything unconventional, like the two women who partner with criminals to trap Gentleman Gu. Raised with a set of moral principles which she does not dare to challenge, her options are limited. For her there is only one way of putting an end to it all, and she finds the means in opium.

Mao Zedong was famous for his remark that Chinese women had 'three big mountains', that is, family, society and the feudal system, on their back. The woman Jiang allows us to see these 'big mountains' in sharper focus. Female suicide by opium was so common that it filled the pages of many late Qing literary and historical works. Medical missionaries knew the phenomenon well, since they were often called on to save opium swallowers. William Lockhart worked in China for twenty-five years. He spoke about his rescue missions at the Royal Commission on Opium in 1893:

[Commission:] Speaking of suicides again, is it your impression that the use of opium in China provokes a tendency to suicide?

[Lockhart:] No, I think it is only when they get into very grave difficulties, into debt and circumstances of that kind, family discord, and so on, that they take opium. Women especially use opium as a means of suicide, sometimes after quarrelling with their mothers-in-law, because the females all live in one compound. Their mothers-in-law are sometimes very disagreeable, and to spite their mothers-in-law, and to place the death at their door, they will take opium. I have known that again and again, many I have been called to, and when I asked, 'What is the reason of this?' I have been told, 'Oh, she quarrelled with her mother-in-law.'[22]

That a quarrel with one's mother-in-law would lead to a suicide seems extraordinary. And yet it was ordinary for many women. Why did so many Chinese women kill themselves so readily? Easy access to opium certainly answers part of the question. But Lockhart's evidence points to another aspect – mothers-in-law. Many families were controlled by mothers or mothers-in-law, some dominating or jealous, others self-centred. These older women had themselves barely survived the crushing weight of the 'three big mountains'. They now began to pass the weight on to their younger counterparts. Was this tough love, or a vindication of decades of suffering? Older women often turned on their younger counterparts – be they concubines, daughters-in-law or servants. As Lockhart pointed out, 'mothers-in-law are sometimes very disagreeable'. There is a famous saying which goes: 'A thousand-year suffering daughter-in-law turns into an old and ugly mother-in-law.' The story of opium allows us to see this in action. Suicide by opium was so frequent and widespread among women that medicines were invented to save those who swallowed the substance. Pharmacies in Shanghai advertised the remedies in *Shen Bao*. Some would even deliver them late in the evenings, when the suicide attempts often occurred. *Shen Bao* ran frequent editorials counselling women not to commit suicide.[23]

Chinese women, like men of letters and the eunuchs, redefined the social life of opium. They constituted a large smoking population, and their motives for consumption varied dramatically. Opium was a luxury, an aphrodisiac, a livelihood and a 'pain-killer'. Some women used it to escape from boredom, some to make a living, some to make a protest, and others to protect themselves. Sex recreation was universal, but what distinguished the Chinese way was not simply literate women but more importantly opium. Youth and beauty made Girl Hu and her contemporaries successful. Their literary talents would be an asset, serving opium would become another. Opium smoking accompanied by sex recreation had been a cherished tradition among men of letters and the sons of fortune. Now it was extending to the lower classes with the help of ordinary 'intertwining fingers'. Men enjoyed opium and sex. They judged women by their own moral standards. Chinese women were oppressed, but many rose to the occasion with the help of opium. This shows both the capacity and the complexity of Chinese women.

CHAPTER 9

'The unofficial history of the poppy'

Opium improved sex. It also generated literature, both classical and vernacular.[1] This chapter explores the different kinds of literature that opium inspired. 'Language is of critical importance in cultural transmission', Evelyn Rawski writes.[2] Opium-generated literature will allow us to see this importance. Opium helped to electrify a leisure revolution; it was also involved in a cultural revolution, namely the modernisation of the Chinese language in the late nineteenth and early twentieth centuries. The late Qing was an outstanding period. At this time the Chinese language was simplified and vernacular literature flourished. Newspapers, magazines, popular fiction and local dialect drama became available, as governments, institutions and individuals embarked on a crusade to enlighten the poor. Scholars have made comprehensive studies of the literature of the late Qing, including Keith McMahon, whose recent book looks specifically at opium smoking in late Qing fiction. Whilst the enlightenment undoubtedly enlightened the poor, it also helped to further spread the gospel of opium. Men of letters found a new fountain of inspiration. Opium fared well in their hands, not only because it accompanied them in their lettered pursuits but also because it reinvented their talents and identities. Some sang praises to opium, some denounced it, some were anti-British, others were popular entertainers. The literature generated by opium can be placed in various different categories.

PRAISE AND CONDEMNATION

Early opium literature, that is, writings generated before the addictive and destructive nature of opium became widely known and accepted, was praise literature. Gao Shiqi sang of the seductive beauty of the poppy flower; Yu Jiao's friend bragged about the 'marvel of opium'; Prince Minning called opium the 'satisfier'; Huang Yue remembered opium among 'lusty friends'; and Zhao Guisheng dedicated 'Playful Verses to the Opium Smoke'. The

Yancao Lu or *Collections of Smoke and Grass* of 1820 consists of poems and prose inspired by tobacco, opium and smoking accessories. Generations of scholars and officials were fascinated with the opium pipe. Zhixi Jushi was one.

Song to the Opium Pipe

Hunanese bamboo and Yunnanese copper,
Skillful artisans turn it into artistic work,
One must be humble and calm to shape,
Straight forms into round gilded pipe.
Lying down on the mat and mists dawn,
Holding the beautiful as fragrance rises,
Wine and tea are old companions,
How wonderful they share the red light.[3]

'Hunanese bamboo' reminds us of Yang Enshou, who called the mottled bamboo pipe carved with the epic poem 'an object of lovesickness'. 'Copper' reminds us of Prince Minning, who knew that one must 'give it a copper head and tail'. The opium pipe was an object of inspiration and happiness. Whilst men of letters were at the pipe, 'swallowing cloud and spewing fog' and 'holding the beautiful as fragrance rises', they were also enjoying the literary or artistic inscription on the pipe's shaft. Wine, tea and opium all demonstrate the intimacy between Chinese cultures of consumption and the art of sex. And while the pipe was an object of literary affection, the lamp was another. Smoking, or inhaling to be more accurate, was accomplished via a pipe held over a lamp that burned oil. Xu Ziling, one of the three eccentric poets of Hefei, wrote about the opium lamp. Knowledge about both the addictive and the destructive nature of opium had been sinking in since the first Opium War. It sank in deeper during the late nineteenth century. Xu Ziling elaborated on the pleasures of the opium lamp, but he also emphasised its fatal consequences. Xu's generation of scholars and officials enjoyed opium, but they were more realistic about the consequences of smoking.

To the Smoking Lamp

Octagonal glass-wrought lamp bought with precious silver
Stands between them where they lie, hidden under the quilt,
eyes peering at opposite eyes.
The foreign efficacious paste in the small ivory box
is like the wings of a crow.
The taste and fragrance of *Lan She* [femininity]
pervades the room.
Young men of distinguished family clad in silk
love to chase *Qin Gong* [ravishing woman],

bed her and rise with her.
Sunrise and sunset come and go unobserved,
sun and moon wholly replaced by this lamp.
Love play and enchanting music go on and on,
did not you notice how that big house on the street
was torn down yesterday?
Tall columns, long-ridged roof sold off,
gold hairpins pawned and servants dismissed.
Poor wife pleading with passers-by at the roadside:
even a well-endowed fortune cannot last forever,
blown away by the wind, gone up in a puff of smoke.[4]

'Octagonal glass' and 'ivory box' indicate the profitability of the business; they also point to the sophistication of accessory-making at the time. *Ya pian*, literally 'crow slice', was opium's common name. Crows are inauspicious creatures in Chinese culture and mythology. The allure of *Lan She* and *Qin Gong* accompanied by the pleasure of opium drew men of letters and 'young men of distinguished family clad in silk' to dens and brothels. The opium lamp replaced sunshine and moonlight; it also helped to squander fortunes and ruined families. Years of prohibition following the first Opium War helped to educate some and to restrain others. But millions more would pick up the pipe, as opium became readily available in the late nineteenth century. Ephemeral delight was winning out over moral principle. A sense of moral resignation was all-pervasive. Wang Shangchen captured the sense of yearning well.

Song of Yearning

Hot Indian deserts exhale poisonous miasma,
roast worms to sandy gold;
Black crows tear flesh from the bones of corpses,
peck at the fat, dripping blood;
Blood red poppies spring up, for all this,
they make a paste of yearning.
Greenish smoke arises when paste is pounded to pieces,
it drains gold and money out of the country.
The vitality of a neighbourhood disappears daily;
the celestial mists become the sky of yearning.
Yearning and longing!
Yearning knows no morning!
May you never know that fatal taste of yearning,
regret comes too late when yearning is a reality.
Alas, how many queer young men there are in the world!
They would rather die of yearning.[5]

'Hot Indian desert' alludes to the merchants and sojourners who produced and brought opium to China. The metaphor of black crows tearing
flesh is to the point – opium would tear at one's flesh in the same way. Yet
death and destruction were not enough to prevent many, and especially
the 'vitality of a neighbourhood', from smoking. Wang compared their
yearning for opium to the longing of lovers. For some, the pipe was a lover
or 'object of lovesickness' they looked forward to and depended upon day
after day. At this point, Wang's poem raises two issues: youthful rebellion
and homosexuality. Although 'queer young men' is vague, it harks back
to 'city rascals', 'intemperate and reckless youngsters' and Yunxiang, the
18-year-old female impersonator. The Jiaqing emperor in 1813, a provincial
scholar-official in the 1830s and an eccentric poet in the late Qing all single
out the young adult male from among the urban classes, an indication that
they were noticeable consumers. When the message of opium coupled with
sex was loud and clear, it was the youth who were most likely to hear it.
Zhu Fengchun called opium a 'Buddha' and saw that 'many indulge in
such a Buddha'.[6] The opium 'Buddha' had saturated adults. It was also to
captivate adolescents.

Adolescents, the 'vitality of a neighbourhood' and the 'queer young men',
had much to rebel against in a society like that of China. The *fin de siècle* was
a time when new objects and ideas were picked up and tested to their limit.
Chinese adolescents could not be too direct, however, because the consequences were costly in a culture that did not encourage the expression of
individual feelings and ideas. Suppression, like oppression, led to many different reactions – resistance, rebellion, withdrawal, self-destruction. Opium
became an impromptu symbol of all this. Many young people had family
expectations to meet and future uncertainties to contemplate. Some might
have found out about opium from their parents, others might have been
persuaded by friends. The more opium was prohibited, the more it served
as a symbol of passive resistance or open rebellion. Opium was a form of
expression, similar to teenage slang. It was now part of an incomprehensible
youth culture. Like eunuchs and women, adolescents redefined the social
life of opium. The Chinese teenage rebellious spirit can be seen in the May
4th Movement, the Cultural Revolution and the democracy movement of
the late 1980s. Chinese youth deserves more studies.

Opium-inspired literature can be traced back to the seventeenth century. Patriotic, anti-British and prohibition opium literature, including
poetry, diary, fiction and drama, was collected in the Communist regime-
compiled *Yapian Zhanzheng Wenxueji* or *Literature of the Opium War*. Wei
Yuan's poem 'A Furong' laments the prevalence of opium smoking 'from

the imperial household to the bandit stronghold'. Lu Song's 'Jinyan Ge' or 'Song of Prohibition' denounces the barbarians who brought opium to China. Hua Changqing's celebrated classic sonnet, 'Jinyan Xin' or 'Ode of Prohibition', picturesquely tells of the harm opium has done to China and the Chinese people. Some of the pieces are devoted to battles fought and lives lost. Song Yiyan devotes a poem to each of the harbours lost during the first Opium War. Chen Kangchi dedicates a moving elegy to Chen Huachen, the naval commander of Canton who died in the fighting, while Yao Xie memorises the suffering of ordinary people after the Battle of Dinghai. These prohibition works emphasise the evil of the British. They also expose the destructive nature of opium. At the time they roused some, alerted others and helped to push prohibition closer to reality.

Sanyuanli was an important episode for the Chinese in the first Opium War. In May 1841 the villagers of Sanyuanli armed themselves in order to deter an advance of British troops attempting to capture Canton. Their strategy was unconventional and their weapons primitive, but nature favoured them. A sudden downpour of sub-tropical rain changed the dynamic of the confrontation. Flooded rice fields obliterated the footpaths, and this coupled with thunder and lightning and the problems of a foreign terrain all contributed to a wretched British retreat and a victorious Chinese pursuit. The English officers and their Bengali volunteers learned a lesson about indigenous resistance. And although Sanyuanli neither changed the course of the war nor prevented the capture of Canton, it signalled a turning point. On the one hand, Sanyuanli provided the resistance with new tactical ideas and rekindled the local fighting spirit. On the other hand, it aroused concern within the Chinese court, because armed villagers were potential rebels. Was there a hidden agenda to the gentry-led local resistance to the foreigners? Frederic Wakeman's *Strangers at the Gate* discusses the politics of patriotism, resistance and localism. The Cantonese did not think that their Manchu overlord cared to defend their territory. Instead, they took matters into their own hands, as this poem depicts:

> The sound from Sanyuanli thundered,
> thousands came and gathered at once,
> sense of injustice and anger brought out courage,
> villagers together could destroy the intruders.
>
> Every house and field must be protected,
> we had plenty of spirit without the drums,

even women joined like healthy young men,
ploughs and hoes in the hand were weapons.

Villages far and near, flags were multi-coloured,
brigades of ten-and-hundred advanced along the ditch,
the barbarians' faces went pale when they saw us,
black flags meant death, they could not escape.[7]

Sanyuanli is a household name in patriotic education today. The name evokes an image of British aggression. It also incites Chinese nationalism in particular and regionalism in reality. And it lives on alongside the discourse and politicisation of opium.

The enlightenment movement generated many vernacular works aimed at educating the common man to understand the harm of opium and to encourage him to quit smoking. Learning to read took time and effort, however, so some artists resorted to popular entertainment in urban public institutions. Writers and entertainers had been instrumental to the spread of opium; they remained so to the suppression of it. One popular entertainment was *shuo chang*, 'talk and sing' stories, which involved singing and talking accompanied by a small drum and other instruments, such as a *pipa*, a plucked string instrument with a fretted fingerboard. Many sung stories are colloquial and rhythmic, and are thus easy to understand and remember. The following enlightenment piece is a perfect example:

Five Geng Quitting Song

One *geng* one *dian* the moon rises,
so does the craving for smoking.
Alas, the craving starts.
Wring hands and muscles to light the lamp.
One pipe, joints become nimble.
Alas, joints become nimble.

Two *geng* two *dian* the moon is higher,
so does the craving for smoking.
Alas, the craving is hard to suppress.
Yawning and running nose do not stop.
One breath, gone half a *liang* of opium.
Alas, gone half a *liang* of opium.

Three *geng* three *dian* the moon sits in the middle,
so rests the pipe in the middle of the hand.

Alas, the pipe rests in the middle of the hand.
Big or small mud are all *lenglong*, no difference.
Soon, cabinets and chests are empty.
Alas, cabinets and chests are empty.

Four *geng* four *dian* the moon hangs on the wall,
so does the craving for *Tai* syrup.
Alas, the craving for *Tai* syrup starts.
No copper no money no negotiation, pawn clothes.
At the end, only the smoking gun was left.
Alas, only the smoking gun was left.

Five *geng* five *dian* the moon becomes yellow,
everything was spent on opium.
Alas, all was spent on opium.
Shoulders aloft and hairs long, like a devil.
Eating the dark smoke has no good end.
Alas, it has no good end.[8]

This is the story of an addict and his long evening with opium. It empha-sises destruction, cautioning some and schooling others, as many learned to moderate their smoking. It is hoped the message might sink in deeper with an animated storyteller/singer and with rhythmic words. But the piece cannot avoid mentioning the sunny side of consumption in the beginning. For the elderly who developed bone problems and arthritis, promises of nimble joints and an effective painkiller were hard to resist. Indeed, it was hard to define the boundary between treatment and recreation, as opium could be both for many, especially the elderly. Some of the vernacular lit-erature produced during the height of prohibition and the enlightenment in the 1910s was even more explicit. Writers, publishers and booksellers tried to surf the wave of opium. Writers penned works promoting, if not further popularising, opium. Although they aimed to give the people moral lessons, they also wrote at length on how to smoke as well as on the plea-sures of opium. They produced popular and entertaining reads. Not only that, they engaged their readers in a unique way. Similar to thrillers such as *James Bond* or even *Harry Potter*, the vernacular works of the turn of the century captivated people and fed into society's fascination with opium. Indeed, they are still mesmerising to read today. Here is an extract from *Furong Waishi* or *The Unofficial History of the Poppy*:

Cucai has just returned to his apartment, which he shared with *Wenlong*. He was about to knock but was afraid he would wake *Wenlong* up. So he decided to go in from the roof window. When he ascended the roof, he felt there were smoke and waves of fragrance everywhere. He stopped and looked around, it seemed as if he saw smoke rising from every house, there were even crows flying and dancing in the smoke cloud as if someone was directing them. He was fascinated and fixated on them; he saw a woman dressed like a warrior with a small commander flag in one hand and a silver gun in the other. She stood there and directed the throng of crows. Once *Cucai* had got a good glimpse of her, he knew that she was an evil spirit. With a sword in his hand and on tiptoe, he began to approach her. After twenty or thirty houses, he was closer and saw her more clearly. The female was very pretty, but full of evil spirit . . .

If he could get rid of this evil spirit without giving her a chance to resist, he would have wiped out an evil for the whole neighbourhood. He made up his mind and quickly jumped off the roof. He moved towards her from under the roof and saw her very clearly. Then he jumped onto the roof again, ran to the woman and suddenly brought his sword down onto her face. *Cucai* was really glad that he had hit her in the face and she was probably not prepared; so she must have been killed. But he did not know that his sword landed in a smoke cloud, there was nothing there. Because he used so much strength, he almost fell himself.[9]

The female evil spirit of course is opium and Cucai, a conscientious young urbanite who sets out to right the wrong. We see 'crows' again, this time 'flying and dancing in the smoke cloud as if someone was directing them'. This 'someone' alludes to the British, who had controlled the opium traffic. The 'silver gun' evokes the silver outflow that depleted China. These metaphors imply the evil forces at work and set the stage for prohibition. Cucai wants to 'wipe out an evil for the whole neighbourhood'. This is noble and is prohibition in theory. Cucai is not able to kill the evil spirit at his first attempt, however. Rather, in his continued efforts to apprehend her, as the story unfolds, he is himself, albeit unconsciously, conquered by her; he succumbs to opium smoking. The story goes on to detail Cucai's pursuit of the evil spirit into the mountains and into the unknown. It also features his initial attraction and gradual addiction to opium. It perpetuates the myth and pleasure of smoking. The evil spirit represents the beautiful, seductive but immoral opium, which lures innocent and good-natured souls. She was so mysterious and powerful that no one can track her down and capture her. In fact, those who try will in due course become enslaved by her. Do we have here another allegory to illustrate the captivating power of opium?

The story intensifies with Cucai's awakening and the realisation of his own enslavement. He miraculously escapes from opium addiction, and is determined to destroy the evil spirit. This seems to suggest that a strong will can help people quit smoking. Typical of heroic stories, Cucai pursues his goal with renewed vigour and captures the female evil spirit with the help of celestial beings. Does this suggest the hopelessness of prohibition? Another issue is why the anonymous writer designates female rather than male gender to opium. Could this be because of women's role in sex recreation? The author seems to have victimised women. Explicit portrayal and implicit ending, *The Unofficial History of the Poppy* was prohibitionist or enlightenment in theory but popular entertainment in practice. It was an offshoot of the vernacular movement, and was made possible by the immense popularity of opium. Another excellent read is *Yan Hua* or *Opium Talk*. Keith McMahon has expertly studied this piece of work. He considers it to be a counterpart of Thomas De Quincey's *Confessions of an Opium Eater*. Through his analysis of this and other works on opium in late Qing fiction, McMahon has exposed the circumstances under which some Chinese people succumbed to opium.

THE LITERARY LIFE OF OPIUM

The Unofficial History of Opium speaks to another aspect of the opium story, the naming of opium. Tang dynasty scholar-officials called opium *minang*. Su Shi called it *yingsu*, as did Gao Shiqi. *Yingsu* is more classic, since Su and Gao were leading literary figures of their times. *Huihui Yaofang*, the Islamic pharmacopoeia, dubbed it *a fu rong* or *a fei rong*, a phonetic translation of the Arab word *a fu yum*.[10] *A fu rong* was a popular name for opium. Editors of *Da Ming Huidian* labelled tribute opium *wu xiang* or 'black fragrance'. *Wu xiang* shows how the Ming court perceived or was introduced to opium; it also demonstrates the luxury status and feminine attribution of opium. Xu Boling explained that *hepurong*, a phonetic translation from overseas countries and central Asia, was *ya pian* or 'crow slice'. So did many medicinal works of the late Ming. These works also used *yingzisu*, *su mi*, *yingsu ke*, *su ke*, *yumi* and *yumi ke*. One story goes that the Tang dynasty general, Li Shimi was wounded, and a peasant nearby treated him with *minang* seeds. His pain disappeared and the wound healed within days. When he became emperor, *minang* was named *yu mi*, 'imperial rice', or *yu mi ke*, 'shell of imperial rice'.[11] The private English also contributed to the name game. Peter W. Fay has pointed out that the word *opium* disappears from the instructions of Jardine Matheson. If they absolutely had to specify the types and quantities, they clothed them in the nomenclature of the cotton textile trade, Patna becoming 'whites', Benares 'greys', and Malwa 'chintzes'.[12] This was copied by their compradors. Opium from Bengal (Patna and Benares) was called *gong ban* or 'official merchant', that from Bombay (Malwa) *bai pi* or 'white skin' and that from Persia *hong pi* or 'red skin'.[13] There were others, such as *hua hong* or 'flower red', *you hong* or 'oil red' and *ya niao hong* or 'duck urine red'. Ahee and Wu Binghuan, Jardine's compradors, dubbed opium *xingli* or 'baggage'. Students bound for the examination and Chinese sojourners would inherit this tradition. Opium balls were divided into *da tu* or 'big mud' and *xiao tu* or 'small mud'. Maurice Collis simply called it the 'Foreign mud'. As a *yanghuo* or 'foreign stuff', opium was first labelled *yang yan* or 'foreign smoke', and later *yang yao* or 'foreign drug'. Chinese-grown opium of the early nineteenth century was also coded. Liang Shaoren knew the names well. In Zhejiang it was called 'Tai *jiang*' or Tai syrup, in Fujian it was called 'Jian *jiang*' or Jian syrup, and in Sichuan it was called 'Shu *jiang*' or Shu syrup. The naming of opium flourished after 1860, in the golden age of consumption. Two of the most elaborate terms were *leng long gao* and *zi xia gao*.[14] *Leng* literally means cold, *long* means cage and *gao* means paste. Does 'cold cage paste' refer to the calming character and captivating nature of opium? *Zi* means purple and *xia* means sunshine. 'Purple sunshine' denotes the rising and lingering opium cloud; it points to the heavenly world where opium was said to elevate people.

Opium was so fashionable during the late nineteenth and early twentieth centuries that it was simply called *da yan*, 'big smoke'. Just as *da renwu* or 'big character' refers to larger-than-life figures, 'big smoke' illustrates the gravity of opium. Mao Xiang and his beloved Ji prepared and tasted *jiepien*, the most expensive luxury tea of the late Ming. Wang Tao would turn it around and call opium *pian jie*, the most expensive luxury smoke of the late Qing.[15] This leads on to the multitude of Chinese dialects and to their expressions for opium, a subject Inspector General Robert Hart and his team tried to decipher. Manchurian opium was called *dong tu*, southern Manchurian opium was *bendi tu* or 'indigenous mud', Ichang opium was *qiao tu*, Anhui opium was *xin tu*, Jiangsu opium was *xishan tu*, Zhejiang opium was *xiang jiang,* Tai *tu* or Tai *jiang*, Fuzhou opium was *tu jiang*, Guangdong opium was also *bendi tu* or 'indigenous mud' . . . and the list goes on.[16] Dialects are rich in culture and symbolism. The above examples expose the crude and original ways in which the Chinese people perceived and defined opium. We can only imagine what opium inspired amongst the hundreds of other Chinese dialects. The refining of opium paste was a specialised industry by the late nineteenth century. The guilds of Canton and Chaozhou were at the top of the business. Canton paste was known for its fragrance, while Chaozhou paste was known for its heating process. When the paste was about to bubble and one could see the foam, the shapes that formed were given elaborate names such as *liu jiao* or 'six corners' and *shizi yaotou* or 'lion shaking head'.[17] These legendary brands helped to galvanise consumer culture and society.

The wide range of opium vocabulary demonstrates the popularity of opium among the Chinese people. It also illustrates what Leo Ou-fan Lee and Andrew J. Nathan have called 'mass culture' in the late Qing and beyond. Prohibition and enlightenment targeted the ordinary people. And whilst literature was the monopoly of the leisure class, the literature of opium prohibition and enlightenment was helping to demolish this monopoly. Many who had never read before were now reading or listening to *shuo chang* in order to learn about the harms of opium. Opium stories such as *Furong Waishi* entertained both men and women, and both the learned and the illiterate. If a story had something to do with opium, it sold and sometimes very well. The following is from *Ye Yu* or *Wild Language*; it takes the reader for a wild ride in the world of opium.

A certain Banner General was stationed in Fujian. One of his domestic slaves was addicted to opium smoking. Warning and punishment did not stop him and he died of his addiction. The General examined his army and found that there were other addicts. He thought that he could reason them out of it and then push for prohibition . . . So he ordered the body of the dead slave to be opened up. The lung was dark black, he took it out and hung it under the roof so that he could observe its appearance. By noon the lung had enlarged to an unusual size. After a while many small worms crawled out from inside. The lung was like a film while the dark black colour were the worms. He called out the opium smokers to exhale opium smoke into the dead lung, the worms shrank back to the inside. The smokers continued for seven or eight mouthfuls, as a result the lung resumed to its former appearance. The reason for addiction is clearly demonstrated here. Gradually the smokers complied with prohibition.[18]

It is impossible to gauge the authenticity of this story, but the point is that it is entertaining. What we see here are stereotypes. The addict is the slave who can hardly afford opium, while the master who might have smoked it is his moral teacher. The opening of the dead slave's body and the exposure of his lung is both frightening and engaging. On the one hand, the story exposes the harms of smoking opium; yet, the front cover is eye-catching to bookstore and bookstall passers-by. Such prohibition and enlightenment literature reflected the Chinese fascination with opium, and further instilled opium into the psyche and fabric of Chinese society.

Much like public urban institutions, street-side bookstalls were powerful social gathering places. Here both children and parents met to read and share information. Bookstalls have remained popular until the present day. They normally stand on the corner of a street or in a shaded spot, and have little stools and observant owners. I myself remember many scenes from *lianhuan hua*, books that told stories in pictures, from the bookstalls of Hunan, where I grew up during the Cultural Revolution. *Lianhuan hua* have a long and rich history in China. Some were called *xiaoren shu*, 'little people's book' or 'children's book' and were aimed at children who were learning to read. Others were designed for the illiterate, to teach them about farming, law or history, or were commissioned by the leisure class to teach the ordinary people classics. These books were vivid, easy to understand and fun to flip through. They could be addictive. One of the most popular and enduring picture books produced in the late nineteenth century was the illustrious *Dianshizhai Huabao* or *Pictures from the Touch-Stone Studio*. It told in pictures the story of China and the Chinese people and of life in port cities such as Shanghai. It also told the story of opium in the late Qing.

The illustration entitled 'Intimate Friends in the Den' presents a den in Nanjing. The interior is decorated and clean, and smokers are at their pipes, chatting. One could make good friends while smoking. The picture is not altogether off-putting. It might even have encouraged more people to frequent dens in order to seek out birds of the same feather. The 'Smoking Dog' scene is hilarious. It depicts a dog inhaling from an opium pipe held by a richly attired woman while a well-dressed man looks on with amusement. The fine opium bed and tea sets indicate that this is a proper smoking session. 'An Apprentice Looking for Fun' (illustration 4) tells the story of a poor 18-year-old apprentice who steals 300 taels of foreign silver from his boss and is ready to spend it in an expensive brothel. A fashionable opium bed is set in the prostitute's room, and servants busy themselves getting things ready. One is reaching for the *pipa* hanging on the wall; she will perform and entertain the 'rich' client in style. This picture exposes the allure of opium smoking accompanied by sex recreation. It informs those who have never been to a brothel. 'Measuring the Volume of Swallowing' (illustration 5) focuses on an opium store where paste, pipes and accessories are sold. One of its latest innovations is a seven- or eight-foot-long pipe for potential customers to try for free. The pipe takes two people, in addition to the smoker, to hold, and the lamp is as large as a birdcage. The spectacle draws a large crowd.

Chinese men of letters were not the only literary talents who turned their ingenuity to opium. French men of letters were also enchanted by

Illustration 4. The allure of opium accompanied by the pleasure of women. In this late Qing illustration an apprentice is shown spending his stolen money in a brothel: a fine opium bed is ready and a prostitute will sing and/or entertain her 'rich' client in style.

opium in what Arnold de Liedekerke called 'la belle époque de l'opium' during the late nineteenth and early twentieth centuries.[19] Opium had long been available in western Europe, where it had its own aficionados in such famous figures as Samuel Taylor Coleridge and Thomas De Quincey. French opium literature sings the praises of opium the aphrodisiac. It also reiterates opium as the fountainhead of literary and artistic inspiration. Liedekerke believed that the French interest in opium had much to do with the decadent generation and *fin de siècle* pessimism and fatalism. Most French works were eulogies. Some were adorations, such as Jean Dorsenne's *La Noire idole* and Maurice Magre's *L'Opium, les belles de nuit.*[20] These works inspired exquisite illustrations and art works, such as Jean Boucheau's pictures for Claude Farrère's *Fumée d'opium* and the cover page of Delphi Fabrice's *Le lie fumeuse d'opium*, where opium and sex are depicted

Illustration 5. One opium shop innovation was a seven- or eight-foot-long pipe for customers to try for free. It took two people and the smoker to hold the pipe and the lamp was as large as a birdcage. The spectacle drew a crowd.

as quintessential partners.[21] Nice, for Guillaume Apollinaire, was a city 'ou l'amour et l'opium s'étaient donné rendez-vous':

> Pipes de nuit, pipes de jour
> Tout l'opium on chevelures
> Les cheveux bruns de mon amour
> Et ces lenteurs tandis qui dure
> L'éveil des monstres tour à tour.[22]

'Pipes de nuit, pipes de jour' reminds us of 'yearning knows no morning!' Men of letters, regardless of their nationality, venerated opium and spread the consciousness of consumption. Is there a relationship between creativity and opium? Many, like Akos Csernus, thought so: 'L'usage des drogues dans la creation artistique suppose un goût, une sensibilité du bizarre et de l'extraordinaire.'[23] Some, such as Edgar Allen Poe and Charles Baudelaire, tried to see whether opium provided a *méthode de travail* for poets. M. H. Abrams, Elizabeth Schneider, Alethea Hayter and Martin Cropper have all tried to analyse this. Hayter studied eight creative men who consumed opium – George Crabbe, John Keats, Edgar Allen Poe, Wilkie Collins, Thomas De Quincey, Francis Thompson, Samuel Taylor Coleridge and Charles Baudelaire. Her conclusion was simple: 'there is no clear pattern of opium's influence on creative writing'.[24] Nonetheless, European men of letters put opium in the dictionary of poetry, philosophy and more. There was a creative fascination with opium. Opium lived a lettered life, it became part of the literary heritage; it was writing a legacy of its own. Chinese-style opium dens appeared in Europe – in The Hague, Paris and London, for example – after 1850. The photographs of Gyula Halasz Brassai (1899–1984) reveal the secret opium dens of Paris in the 1930s. Jules Boissiere even built 'une fumerie tout au fond de ma maison chinoise, et chaque jour, de huit heures à minuit, des mandarins ou des lettres libres vinrent conserver avec moi'.[25] Europeans began to identify China with opium. Opium, in other words, was becoming synonymous with the Chinese people and with Chinese culture.

CHAPTER 10

Opiate of the people

This chapter studies the complete socialisation and naturalisation of opium smoking in the late nineteenth and early twentieth centuries. What happened to the Ming–Qing socio-economic transformation when western capitalist actors appeared on the China stage is a subject that has been at the heart of academic debates. Albert Feuerwerker believes that feudal autocracy had 'prevented the sprouts of capitalism in agriculture from developing into the dominant economic form', and that imperialism had aborted 'the promising capitalist sprouts in handicraft industry and commerce'.[1] Others, however, have taken the view that foreign trade and investment contributed to China's modernisation. Hao Yen-p'ing stresses that 'China's trade with the West during the nineteenth century gave impetus to a full-fledged mercantile capitalism that constituted a commercial revolution', while Gregory Blue has stated that 'the opium trade was instrumental in integrating China into the world market'.[2] It is true that western capitalism destroyed or weakened some industry and commerce, but it also helped to create and strengthen others. What must be understood is the intimacy and the friction between the treaty ports and the old cash-cropping market town economic structure, because both contributed to the complete socialisation and naturalisation of opium smoking. The commerce and consumption of opium flourished under this dual system, as foreign opium satisfied the rich and the urbanites while Chinese opium met the demand of the entire nation.

SMOKING POWER AND *YAO QIAN SHU*

The socialisation and naturalisation of opium was completed with the participation of the poorest members of society, such as coolie labourers. They now consumed a previously unaffordable luxury item on a regular basis, thanks to increased domestic cultivation that had made opium cheaper. What differentiated coolies from other smokers were their motives for consumption and the benefits they gained from it. For them, it was a luxury and a necessity, an energiser as well as anaesthesia. Coolies worked as agricultural seasonal hands, early industrial labourers, porters and physical labourers of various types, and depended on muscle power to make a living – shouldering loads, pulling, bending, pushing and so forth. These men were the steam engines and taxis of their age. They worked and lived like animals – they were truly the proletariats. Opium smoking relaxed the muscles and allowed a man to recuperate. It more importantly enabled a man to get along on a minimum intake of food. Many knew opium's addictive nature, but daily survival was the only priority. Regrettably, the much needed primary sources about them, such as their wages and life expectancy, are largely missing. James F. Warren's work on rickshaw coolies in Singapore not only provides a general picture of Chinese coolie life, however, it also shows the ways in which one could undertake such a study. For example, we can learn about them through the works of travellers and missionaries. These foreigners saw much of the country while being carried on the shoulders of coolies. For many travellers, the sedan chair was their first exposure to and most enduring memory of China. The Reverend A. Elwin worked in Zhejiang for twenty-three years. He talked about his personal experience with Chinese coolies at the Royal Commission on Opium in 1893.

I have started in the morning with the coolies and chair-bearers, we will say, and after travelling for about three hours I have noticed that the men began to get weak and were hardly able to move; and then I have been told, 'We must stop because the men wish to smoke opium.' Well, we would stop for perhaps an hour, while the men would go to an opium den; and they would come out of the opium den new men – the load that a man could hardly carry before he went into the opium den he was able to pick up and carry with the greatest ease. Of course, this only lasts for a time, as long as the opium effect lasts, and then, once more, he gradually gets weaker and weaker, until he can do nothing at all until he smokes once more. They are perfect slaves to the opium habit. That, as I have noticed, is the physical effect upon these people.[3]

After carrying a heavy load on one's back for three hours, anyone would have to take a break. Opium would loosen up one's muscles and recharge the body. It worked magic, since one returned a 'new man' and would continue 'with the greatest ease'. This was observed by the British adventurer Violet Cressy-Marcks. She saw that 'the men always worked harder after they had smoked, and obviously took a pipe before doing a strenuous job'.[4] It was also seen by Herbert Giles, who knew that 'after smoking their allowance, the occupant of the chair cannot fail to perceive the lightness and elasticity

Illustration 6. A den in Malinta Street, Manila, Philippines, where Qing working men smoked opium. Unlike the upper and middle classes, these men smoked opium on a crowded bed.

of their tread, as compared with the dull, tired gait of half an hour before'.[5] Giles saw that 'a great quantity is smoked by the well-paid chair-coolies, to enable them to perform the prodigies of endurance so often required of them', and that many men travelled at 'between five and six miles an hour'. Whilst men of letters philosophised opium and the sons of fortune squandered their fortunes on it, coolie labourers derived from it the physical and psychological strength to survive the day. Coolies consumed opium in a totally different fashion and in a totally different environment than their upper-class and middle-class counterparts, as illustration 6 shows. There are no 'intertwining fingers' or 'object of lovesickness' here; opium is smoked in a crowded room. George E. Morrison travelled, or rather, was 'carried' on a sedan chair, to be more precise, from Hankow to Burma via Sichuan and Yunnan. He knew how absolutely important opium was to his coolies.

On March 30th [1894] I reached Tak-wan-hsien, the day's stage having been seventy *li* [23 and one-third miles]. I was carried all the way by three chair-coolies in a heavy chair in steady rain that made the unpaved track as slippery as ice – and this over the dizzy heights of a mountain pathway of extraordinary irregularity. Never slipping, never making a mistake, the three coolies bore the chair with my thirteen stone, easily and without straining . . . Within an hour of their arrival all these three men were lying on their sides in the room opposite to mine, with their opium pipes and little wooden vials of opium before them, all three engaged in rolling and heating in their opium lamps treacly pellets of opium. Then they had their daily smoke of opium.[6]

Coolies were refreshed and energised by opium, but it also enslaved them. They were often unemployed, due to the seasonal and occasional nature of their work. Opium was both a luxury and a necessity when they worked. Little research has been done on the percentage of such labourers in the late Qing, and on what proportion of them were smokers or addicts and indeed how much they spent on opium. My impression is that most, if not all, used opium; certainly those who did not have families spent a large portion of their earnings on opium. Sidney Mintz has argued that the consumption of tea and sugar fitted in well with the tempo of working-class life, their having been introduced just as work schedules quickened, movements from rural to urban areas accelerated and the diets of workers looked 'both calorically and nutritively inadequate and monotonous'.[7] Tea with sugar boosted the morale of the English working class. Meanwhile, opium gave energy to the Chinese labouring poor. Sweetness and power – tea with sugar played a vital role in the Industrial Revolution. The same can be said of opium smoking during the build-up to the Chinese Revolution. Two further examples are vodka drinking in pre-revolutionary Russia and tavern drinking on the eve of the French Revolution. The Chinese working class helped to put opium in its indigenous context, as counterpart commodities had done in England, Russia and France. These commodities show a commonality of stimulus and also striking similarities in the making of the working class and rise of revolutions. We are once again reminded of the political redefinition of consumption. Coolie labourers were defining the social life of opium as men of letters, eunuchs and women had done before them. Their consumption marked the complete 'extensification' of opium.

Coolie labourers not only depended on opium to help them make a living, but many also learned to merchandise it. British Consul in Hankow, G. W. Caine reported in 1869 that the coolies who transported opium from Hong Kong to Hankow via Chang-sha-foo would 'on their return to the south, take back native opium'.[8] The Canton–Hunan–Hankow route was vital to the inland march and distribution of opium, as I discussed in chapter 4. Smugglers had used this route; so now did coolie labourers. Many bought opium in the up-river areas of the Yangtze, mostly Sichuan or Yunnan, where it was cheap, and carried it to down-river commercial centres, such as Hankow, where they could sell it at marked-up prices. Others would pick up western Chinese opium and carry it east to Shanghai or south to Hunan, Canton and even Hong Kong. Hankow, somewhat like Chicago, was the emporium of central China. It became the depot of opium. The nineteenth-century explorer Archibald R. Colquhoun travelled through Guangdong, Guangxi and Yunnan. He observed that 'The boatmen on this river [the West River, which connects the three provinces] make use of every opportunity to smuggle salt and opium into the interior, and when they have a mandarin of any position on board, it is said that they invariably try to introduce a good haul.'[9]

Official cargo boats were exempt from searches and taxation *en route*. So was the baggage of examination-bound students. Alexander Hosie, the British Acting Consul at Wuhu, rode with a few students in the late 1870s. He reported that the three candidates had 'a caravan of seventeen pack-animals laden with protected cases, which they unhesitatingly told me contained opium and marble from Ta-li'.[10] Hosie put his observation in context: 'It would be a consideration to many a Scotch student if, in going up to London to compete in the Civil Service Examinations, they were allowed to carry with them as baggage a few kegs of duty-free whiskey!' Here the monetary and fiscal functions of a lucrative commodity are revealed. Opium had been monetised and institutionalised since before the Opium Wars. Wu Binghuan, Jardine Matheson's comprador, travelled to north-west

Fujian. He could not procure the famous *Bohea* tea at an advantageous price 'because the *baggage* has not arrived yet'.[11] Opium was conveniently dubbed *baggage*. This term would remain in the business or rather the criminal vocabulary for quite some time. In order to secure a purchase, Wu 'immediately paid five chests of *baggage*'. Opium was in fact more desirable than money, as Wu informed his superior: '*Baoshun* [another firm]'s *baggage* has not arrived yet; if ours could get here earlier, that would be much better.'

The opium–money system had been institutionalised ever since the Opium Wars. Hao Yen-p'ing has studied this. A. G. Dallas, Jardine's Shanghai representative, reported that 'most of the other *Hongs* now I find are getting quite into the way of taking payment in opium and do not think of asking for cash'.[12] Opium money was so welcomed in the interior, in fact, that a Suzhou system came into being whereby Chinese merchants simply brought opium from Shanghai to the silk-producing regions of Suzhou as payment. Hao believes that 'because many Chinese opium and silk merchants belonged to the same professional guild or geographical association, this practice of mixing legal (silk) with illegal (opium) trade was carried on smoothly'.[13] M. A. Macleod, Jardine's Foochow representative, carried on an extensive up-country tea trade simply by advancing opium to the compradors: 'I had charged them with a full figure, considering the state of the market at the moment.'[14] Opium money was more standardised than the other moneys in circulation because its value was stable. Opium was indeed one of the 'new forms of money', as Hao Yen-p'ing puts it. The expansion of foreign trade and the economy in general 'called for the use of money more regularly and on a larger scale than ever before'. This was something the existing Chinese bi-metallic system of silver and copper coinage could not accommodate. Opium, like Mexican dollars and private notes, filled the gap.

Continued institutionalisation not only transformed grass-roots level economics but also politics. Jonathan Spence has summarised this: 'For at least the last fifty years of the nineteenth century, opium played an important role in the Chinese economy, in three major areas: it served as a substitute of money, it helped local officials meet taxation quotas, and it helped finance the self-strengthening program.'[15] The Imperial Maritime Customs aided in this. 'The opium work', as the great Inspector General of Customs, Robert Hart called it, was extremely important. Hart advised his protégé, H. B. Morse to have a special assistant dedicated to it, and suggested that the latter would 'be free to visit opium hulks, opium godowns and bonded warehouses whenever necessary'.[16] Hart and his team dutifully monitored the import of foreign opium, as table 4 shows.[17]

Table 4 *Total import in 1879 (piculs)*

Ports	Malwa	Patna	Benares	Persia
Newchwang	1,112.25	57.40	27.40	26.00
Tientsin	3,530.40	164.20	21.60	290.93
Chefoo	3,177.86	44.40	111.75	92.50
Ichang	10.00	1.20	–	–
Hankow	1,905.00	218.63	1.20	17.43
Kiukiang	1,474.89	8.40	–	169.93
Wuhu	2,324.50	2.40	–	54.00
Chinkiang	8,639.00	736.80	936.00	644.97
Shanghai	1,803.00	8,525.00	5,158.00	178.00
Ningpo	6,518.00	400.00	170.00	164.00
Wenchow	3.00	10.80	–	–
Foochow	1,452.60	1,715.61	231.60	625.50
Tamsui	–	25.20	1,398.00	513.90
Takow	19.74	38.40	1,480.44	1,229.14
Amoy	1.00	2,113.00	3,092.00	966.00
Swatow	4,763.87	3,510.53	1,320.99	–
Canton	14,700.00			
Kiungchow	242.61	730.99	–	–
Pakhoi	–	–	600.00	–
Total	51,677.72	18,302.96	14,548.98	4,972.30

Source: Inspector General of Customs, *China Imperial Maritime Customs* II, special series no. 4, *Opium.*

The Treaty of 1858, which was ratified in 1860, legalised the import of opium at treaty ports and stipulated that opium be taxed at 30 taels per picul, approximately 133 pounds sterling or about the weight of an opium chest. When in 1879 the import aggregate reached 89,501.96 piculs, it should have provided the imperial treasury with 2,685,058.80 taels revenue. Import duty hit opium when it landed at the treaty ports. Transit duties followed, once opium left the port cities and began to travel inside China. *Lijin* was a 1 per cent tax that was introduced during the campaign against the Taiping. The opium *lijin* could be twice the import duty. Assuming a rate of 60 taels *lijin* per picul, as Hart knew and suggested, the 1879 import should have given local governments a sum of 5,370,117.60 taels in transit duty. Foreign opium generated a total profit of 8,055,176.40 taels for central and local governments in 1880. This was an enormous amount of money, which could be both used and abused. Just as tea and vodka duties filled the treasuries of the British and Russian governments, opium was indispensable to the Qing regime. Opium-generated money helped to restore the dynasty and to modernise the military. Li Hongzhang used Jiangsu *lijin* to finance his Huai army, just as Zeng Guofan had used Guangdong *lijin* to finance his Xiang army. This set the stage for what Edward Slack has labelled the 'narco-economy' of the twentieth century. Stanley Spector studied the sources of the Huai army's income for 1885:

Hankow Customs	400,000 *liang* plus
Kiangnan Customs	400,000 *liang* plus
Liang-Chiang Treasury	100,000 *liang* plus
Shanghai Likin Bureau	40,000 *liang* plus
Kiangsu Opium Likin	100,000 *liang* plus
Liang-Huai Salt Bureau	700,000 *liang* plus
Szechwan (diverted)	200,000 *liang* plus[18]

Both the Huai army and the Xiang army were largely financed by opium-generated revenue. They would help to crush the Taiping, Nian and Muslin rebellions. The 1858 Treaty provisions stipulated that opium could only be sold by foreign importers at treaty ports and that it could only be transported to the interior by the Chinese. 'Customs' could levy import duties on firms such as Jardine Matheson when opium landed at the treaty ports.

Central and local governments both turned to the financial resources afforded by opium in their efforts to restore public order and to modernise the military. The period was the beginning of 'the decentralisation of military finance', as Hans Van de Ven has termed it.[19] Indemnities and modernisation would cost billions; an opium-based economic policy could not have come at a better time. Zeng Guofan and Li Hongzhang certainly were not alone. Liu Kunyi, Governor-General of Guangdong and Guangxi since 1875, used opium *lijin* to build gunboats for the coastal defence. So did Liu Mingquan, Governor of Taiwan and a commander during the Sino-French War in 1884, and Zhang Zhidong, the most eminent figure in the regime when the Empress Dowager died in 1908. Liu Kunyi not only listed the amount of *lijin* Zeng and Li used, but also encouraged others to do the same. Meantime, Zhang often complained that many local officials pocketed *lijin* for their own ends. Corruption was rampant, and with opium it only became easier. Opium helped Jardine Matheson build their commercial empire. It helped Zeng Guofan and Li Hongzhang restore the Qing dynasty. It also helped petty officials to make their fortunes. This would encourage gangsters, warlords, rebels, the Nationalists, the Japanese and the Communists. Opium had become a *yao qian shu*, a legendary tree that sheds coins when shaken.

THE 'McDONALDIZATION' OF OPIUM CONSUMPTION

Coolies or politicians, everyone depended on opium in order to survive. What happens when a commodity is needed so much? Like money and staple commodities such as salt, opium became individual, household and a national necessity. Charles de Contant had seen in the late eighteenth century that the Chinese passion for opium had become a necessity among the urban elite of southern China. A century later, smoking had permeated down to every single class and had become a necessity for all. The Peking Hospital tried to assess its prevalence in 1869:

Officials	40%
Field labourers [general]	4–6%
Field labourers [cultivation provinces]	40–60%
Merchants in Peking	20%
Mercantile community [treaty ports]	30%
Male attendants [of mandarin]	70–80%
Female attendants	30–40%
Soldiers	20–30%
Literary class	20–30%
Eunuchs of the palace	50%
Bannermen and reserve	30–40%
Male population [general]	30–40%
City population [general]	40–60%[20]

Dr Dudgeon, who helped compile the report, had more to say about the situation: 'In Peking, there are opium shops in almost every lane, and two or three in larger ones.'[21] He knew that the survey did not include everybody: 'The police at night beguile their long cold watches with the drug, and their offices on the streets, oftentimes without fires, or mats, and they themselves almost without clothes, are one of the most pitiable sights in the city.' In the opium importing or producing regions the situation was much worse. Acting Consul in Yichang (Sichuan), W. D. Spence examined south-west China in 1882. The percentages of addiction were as follows:

Labourers and small farmers	10%
Small shopkeepers	20%
Hawkers, soldiers	30%
Merchants	80%
Officials and their staffs	90%
Actors, prostitutes, vagrants, thieves	95%[22]

Scholar-officials, rich urbanites, Sons of the Pear Garden and women made up a large smoking army. The Maritime Customs was also interested in knowing how many smokers foreign opium supplied. Robert Hart ordered and participated in an 1879 Customs-wide survey. He concluded that the smoking population was 'one-third of one per cent of the population'.[23] Put this against a population of above 300,000,000 and less than 400,000,000 at the time, this was a smoking army of at least 1,000,000 strong. This figure was different from those offered by Xue Fucheng in 1891 and by Wang Hongbin in 1997. Xue argued that the smoking army was 4,000,000 strong, that is, one out of every one hundred with a population of 400,000,000.[24] Wang believed that smokers numbered between 2,000,000 and 3,000,000 in the late nineteenth century.[25] Such numbers would push demand beyond what the import could satisfy. Domestic opium, in other words, filled the gap. Many Chinese smoked home-grown opium, whether they were aware of it or not. The Revd Joseph S. Adams, a missionary in Zhejiang for thirteen years, reported in 1893:

> The opium that they have in part of China, the province of Cheh-kiang, is very largely grown in the Wen-chow district, which produces opium often disguised and sold as Indian opium. It is of such superior quality that the Chinese themselves sell it at the same price as the Malwa and the Bengal opium. The greater part of it came from the native cultivation, but that which is used by the higher classes, by the officials, or by wealthy merchants was almost invariably Indian opium. But I would like to say that when I first went to Kin-hwa I would ride for a whole day's journey and never see a poppy field, but now you can hardly go an hour's walk without seeing the poppies in cultivation during the season, so much has it increased during the past ten years in that province.[26]

Adam's evidence to the Royal Commission reminds us of the observation of Shi Hongbao, who saw that the Wenchow people had already begun to make their opium *gao* or 'paste' and *jiang* or 'syrup' in the 1810s. Adam's account helps to put the 1879 total import statistics into perspective. Wenchow's import aggregate was a mere 13.80 piculs. The region had become self-sufficient in opium.

Yunnanese peasants had complained to Peng Songyu, the official who tried to persuade them to grow grain instead of opium in the 1840s, that he did not understand their situation. By the late nineteenth century they had solved the problem. Major H. R. Davis travelled through Yunnan. 'Opium was in harmony with rice cultivation in Yunnan. When rice is harvested in October, opium is sowed for the winter.'[27] The Yunnanese had learned to take advantage of their local ecology and geography. They also made use of every inch of land, as Archibald Colquhoun noted: 'within the walled prefectural cities, and indeed under the very walls of the yamen or official court, we often found the poppy growing'.[28] Rotating rice and opium was perfect for the Yunnanese. It was also ideal for the Guangxi peasants: 'The poppy shoots out in January, and the harvest is gathered in May.'[29] Such rotation cropping was not limited to the south-west region. E. G. Kemp journeyed into Shanxi in May 1893 and saw that 'Shanxi is one of the worst provinces of all as regards opium-smoking, and the poppy is largely cultivated.'[30] Thomas Allen and William Sachtleben bicycled from Constantinople to Beijing via the Old Silk Road in 1894. 'Over the Gobi Desert and through the western gate of the Great Wall' they saw people 'splitting poppy-heads'; the chief of the Customs House was so hospitable he even gave them a 'lesson in opium smoking'.[31] Just as John Bell had seen 'great plantations of tobacco' outside the walls of Beijing in the 1710s, Mrs Sarah P. Congers, wife of the American minister, 'saw large fields of blooming poppies' on her way to the Imperial Tomb outside the capital in 1904.[32]

Times had changed, but the peasantry remained the same. From the south-east coast to the Old Silk Road, from the south-west borderlands to the capital, Chinese peasants now cultivated opium as they had previously done tobacco, when it was popular and profitable. Baron von Richthofen believed that Sichuan produced at least 60,000 piculs in 1872. Mr Bredon of the Hankow Customs estimated that it reached 150,000 piculs in 1878.[33] No one was more familiar with the decline of opium imports and the rise of domestic cultivation than the Maritime Customs. 'After a maximum import in 1879, however, foreign opium began to give ground to China's domestic production.'[34] In 1888 imported opium (Indian and Persian) totalled 82,612 piculs. By 1897 the total was less than 50,000 piculs. Lin Manhong of Academic Sinica asserted that China produced perhaps seven-eighths of the world total output of opium in 1906.[35] She also argued that increased demand since legalisation not only stimulated domestic cultivation but also served to integrate the underdeveloped economies of the north and west with the developed economies of the south and east. Sustained exchange between the core and the periphery helped to balance the overall economic development of China in the second half of the nineteenth century.

'MEASURING THE VOLUME OF SMOKING'

The people of China sank deeper into opium during the late Qing. The list of smokers is massive. Let me name a few. Grand Secretary Ju Hongji often had a big pipe in his hand and the Imperial Censor-in-Chief Lu Baozhong was an addict. The Governor of Jiangsu, Chen Qitai, chain-smoked, as did the Prefect Governor of Kaifeng in Honan, Wen Ti, and

Ji Chang, Manchu Provincial Surveillance Commissioner in Hunan. The boy genius Jiang Jianren sold his literary works for opium; the artist Ren Bonian did the same with his paintings. Scholar-officials and men of letters continued to lead the opium-smoking leisure revolution. Their champion was Liu Kunyi, Governor-General of Guangdong and Guangxi. His career depended on opium-generated funds, and he smoked opium as frequently as others ate rice:

Liu's capacity to smoke is unusual . . . Every morning, his servants would prepare about ten mouthfuls of opium paste, each mouthful was about one *qian*. Then they would wake him up. He would continuously suck about ten mouthfuls before he started to wash and eat breakfast, then he worked. He would not smoke until the evening. After dinner and desert he would smoke until the early hours of the morning. Although he smoked a lot, it did not affect his work. Among smokers, very few know how to be moderate like this.[36]

Liu's wake-up call was 10 *qian* or 1 tael. This is exaggerated, since one mouthful does not equal to 1 *qian* or mace. Nevertheless, Liu smoked for a few more hours after dinner and until the 'early hours of the morning'. He could easily consume two or three more taels, that is, 100 or 150 grams. This, even if mixed with domestic brands or tobacco, was a large amount for a person to consume daily. Yet Liu was outranked by his protégé, Su Zixi (Yuanchun), whom H. B. Morse worked with closely and called 'a man of good ideas who forgets to carry them out'.[37] Su, who was Military Commander of Guangxi from 1885 to 1903, smoked opium regardless of whether he was in his office, on the campaign trail or in the comfort of his own home. He was besotted with his lamp and was blessed with a steady supply:

Su's addiction was enormous, the smoking lamp he used was many times bigger and taller than those used by ordinary people, his daily smoking reached the unusual amount of four *liang*. He had two servant boys to assist him, one on each side. When he lay down on his Cantonese bed which was already furnished with five pipes, one boy would feed him these five pipes continuously while the other would stuff the emptied pipes. Therefore every time he lay down to smoke, he consumed ten pipes. After he had finished, he sat up and continued to smoke either water-pipe or cigar, sometimes accompanied by snuff. When the empty pipes were filled, he lay down again and smoked as he did before.[38]

Su's daily opium ration was the 'unusual amount of four *liang*', that is, 4 taels or 200 grams, in addition to a water pipe, cigar and snuff. The cases of Liu and Su raise an important question: what constitutes an addiction? Needless to say, this is difficult to answer given how different people are physically different from one another. Age, temperament and diet are all important, as are environmental factors such as climate. Brand mattered greatly where opium was concerned. Hart's devoted servants were probably the best judges. Ernest T. Holwill of the Kiukiang Customs put the time it took to become as addict at between 'six to twelve months'.[39] Jas Mackey of the Wenchow Customs, however, put it at 'six or seven' years.[40] Dr Kerr of the Medical Missionary Society's hospital in Canton noticed that 'the propensity becomes sooner and more deeply rooted in some systems than in others', and concluded that 'if a man smokes eight mace of opium per day, he will in any case at the end of ten years find it very difficult, if not impossible, to give up the habit'.[41] Francis W. White, Commissioner of Customs in Hankow, believed individual physiology and time and duration of smoking had much to do with tolerance, and hence that it was almost impossible to be definitive about addiction:

The time required to enslave a man in the habit of opium-smoking depends so greatly on the constitution of the person that it is almost impossible to fix any period, although, taking an average, the time given in the return is approximately correct. When the smoker is of a robust constitution, he will resist the effects of the drug, naturally, for a much longer time than he would were he weak and sickly, but great stress is laid by my informants on the regularity or irregularity observed in the daily hours for indulging in the habit. If the same time be observed, then a beginner will develop into an habitual smoker in about three or four months; but if, on the other hand, he smokes daily, but at uncertain hours, he may smoke for years, and then even be able to give up the habit without effort or inconvenience. It is to the strong and healthy that this remark applies, for when once a weakly person becomes a confirmed smoker, it seems next to impossible for him to give up the artificial stimulus that supplies him with life and energy, without a prostration very difficult to combat.[42]

Clearly timing was important. But much more so was the amount consumed. The Peking Hospital observed a hundred opium smokers and how much they consumed daily in 1869:

20 smoke 5 candareens per *diem*
20 smoke 1 mace per *diem*
20 smoke 2 mace per *diem*
30 smoke from 3 to 4 mace per *diem*
10 smoke 1 tael or upwards per *diem*[43]

In essence, 'the maximum quantity is 2 taels in 24 hours and the minimum 5 candareens to begin with'. The findings of the Peking Hospital came to serve as a benchmark. But the smokers and addicts they treated were northerners whose physiologies, diets and geographical environment (climate) were quite different from those of southerners. S. W. Williams studied opium addiction in the early 1880s. He stated that 'a novice is content with one or two whiffs, which produce vertigo, nausea, and headache, though practice enables him to gradually increase the quantity'.[44] Williams believed that 'a temperate smoker can seldom exceed a mace weight', which filled 'twelve pipes'; 'two mace weight taken daily is considered an immoderate dose'.[45] One mace filled between ten and twelve pipes. Wang Tao's diary shows that he smoked about once a week and indulged in two or three pipes each time, roughly one-third of a mace. This was an average intake for millions, who would not always have the time or the money to smoke everyday. These were the 'temperate' smokers. As for Liu Kunyi and Su Zixi, their daily ration reached 3 or 4 taels or about 150–200 grams. They were definitely addicts. Peter Lee has also studied addiction. He writes that for a novice, 'three to five pipes of opium smoked over a period of two to three hours' provides a very pleasant experience. For an occasional smoker who is not addicted, 'six to eight pipes is an adequate measure'. A habitual smoker 'who has already been smoking daily for at least three months may take twelve to fifteen pipes per day, divided into several sessions, without any ill effects'.[46]

The Maritime Customs studied consumption and addiction in the treaty port cities in the late 1880s (see table 5).[47] The figures in table 5 reveal a wealth of information. First of all, one mace filled different numbers of pipes – 22 pipes in Pakhoi, 20 pipes in Chinkiang, 16 pipes in Foochow, 10 pipes in Tamsui and Ningpo, 6 pipes in Shanghai and only 5 pipes in Newchwang. This says much about the size of the portion of opium paste heated up and used for each pipe. It seems that northerners (Newchwang) were more generous than southerners (Pakhoi). Secondly, the amount of native opium consumed by heavy smokers was 20 maces in Wuhu and Ningpo and 15 in Hankow. Southerners seemed to be more tolerant than northerners. This, however, does not mean that they were less likely to become addicted, given that their diets and climate were different. 'Twenty' maces are equivalent to approximately 2 taels. Although native opium was mild, the large amounts consumed might well match the potency of smaller amounts of a foreign brand. Thirdly, it can be said that the urban centres that had access to opium earlier had by the late 1880s become more moderate. Shanghai and Canton were exposed to opium much earlier than were inland cities such as Hankow and Wuhu. Consumers in the former cities might have grown out of their initial fascination with opium by the late Qing. They were blessed with a steady supply and might have taken for granted what their counterparts in the interior and the lower classes were

Table 5 *Daily toleration levels of opium smoking (in mace)*

Ports	Beginner	Average	Heavy	Pipes one-mace filled
Newchwang	1–1.5/2	3/4	10–15/10–15	5–8/5–8
Tientsin	3–5/6	1.2–2/3	3.6–6/7	10–14/10
Chefoo	1/1	3/3	10/10	10/10
Ichang	1/1.5	2–3/2	4/6	10/8
Hankow	2/2	4/4	15/15	3/3
Kiukiang	0.5/n.a	3–5/n.a	10–20/n.a	8–10/n.a
Wuhu	1.5–2/2	4–5/5	12–15/20	6–7/7
Chinkiang	1–2/1–2	3/3	5–6/5–6	20/20
Shanghai	2/2	5/5	10/10	6/6
Ningpo	1/1	3/3	7–25/10–20	10/10
Wenchow	0.6/0.6	3/3	8/8	7/7
Foochow	0.3/0.3	2/2	10/10	5–16/5–16
Tamsui	1.5/n.a	3/n.a	8/n.a	10/n.a
Takow	1/n.a	3–4/n.a	8–11/n.a	10–12/n.a
Amoy	0.5–2/0.5–2	2–5/2–5	8–12/8–12	5–20/5–20
Swatow	0.5–2/2–3	2–5/4–6	5–8/7–12	10–20/10–20
Canton	1/1	2/2	8/8	15/15
Kiungchow	0.6/n.a	2/n.a	4/n.a	20/n.a
Pakhoi	1/1	2–3/2–3	6–7/6–7	22/22

Source: Inspector General of Customs, *China Imperial Maritime Customs II*, special series no. 9, *Native Opium.*

still growing to appreciate. This harks back to the phases of consumption discussion.

Taste-making, political redefinition and 'extensification' are phases of consumption. So too is mass consumption. In the late nineteenth and early twentieth centuries opium had shifted its status from an upper-class luxury to a proletarian necessity. Mass consumption means economies of scale. The abundance of opium, the participation of coolie labourers and the fact that the urban middle classes took it for granted were all indications that opium was now widely available, and that consumption and addiction had become much more common. Five candareens was the minimum for the novice smoker. This did not cost too much. Two to six copper cash could purchase five candareen of prepared Malwa in Wenchow. In Chefoo it was four cash, and in Canton it varied from four to nine cash for three to five candareens of prepared foreign opium.[48] Four cash was the standard, according to the Maritime Customs and officials such as Xue Fucheng. Yunnan and Sichuan opium, when foreign opium disappeared, would also cost four cash. This demonstrates the popularity of western China opium, as other native opium would be as low as two cash. Cash are copper coins with a square hole cut in the centre through which they can be strung together. A string was normally ten cash. Although its value fluctuated depending on the locality and the time, it was the standard exchange for basic services, such as a rickshaw ride, a tip or a simple meal. Four cash made a round of luxury possible.

There were many 'humble establishments which devote themselves to supplying coolies and men of the lower orders generally, and whose rates are no doubt framed to suit the means of their customers'.[49] By now opium facilities targeted what George Ritzer calls the 'lowest common denominator'. Ritzer, in his study of present-day consumer society, identifies a 'McDonaldization' process in which corporations cater to the mass majority. This happened to opium in the late nineteenth century, as consumption catered to the lowest Chinese common denominator – the millions of coolies and poor peasants and the lower class in general. For the better off, 'A better style of divan, with superior furniture, would charge higher rates, and probably give a better quality of opium to the class of shopkeepers and merchants frequenting them.'[50] Many of these smokers would 'hand over to the proprietors of the establishments the dross or ashes left from smoking as payment for oil used'. Dross or ashes would be mixed with new opium to serve again. Mixing was profitable and a common practice. In Newchwang owners of dens made good profits by 'mixing sesamum cake and the ashes or residue of opium smoked by their customers with the pure article'. In Kiukiang the mixture was 'two-tenths of the Native' and 'eight-tenths of the Foreign'.[51]

Opium had become 'the opiate of the people'. 'Temperate' and 'habitual' smokers numbered millions. And millions more enjoyed smoking opium, including the Empress Dowager Cixi herself.

In old age and pale-faced, she [the Empress Dowager] was addicted to opium smoking, but she did not smoke too much. After work in the evening, she smoked recreationally. That was why she issued a prohibition edict saying that those who were over sixty who smoked should be excused. From herself, she pushed the drug onto others because people think opium is something for the recreation and entertainment of the elderly. Some say that even at such an old age, the Empress still had not forgotten the art of sex and she used opium to boost her performance. This is something I dare not to state with certainty.[52]

The moderate consumption of the Old Buddha, as the Empress was reverently addressed, was known to her inner circle. Der Ling, her lady-in-waiting from 1903 to 1905, wrote about the opium smoking of Li Lianying; Cixi was sensitive to the odour and knew when exactly to lecture her head eunuch. Katharine A. Carl, who painted Cixi's portrait, also noticed this sensibility: 'Her Majesty has unusually acute olfactories, especially for opium. This, it seems, can be detected by its odour, which hangs around the clothes, and, like the odour of the rose, one "can break the vase, it lingers there still"'.[53] But the most comprehensive account of the Empress comes from the private diary of her household comptroller, Ching Shan, which is now deposited at the British Library.

It may be added, in conclusion, as a sign of the times, that the Empress Dowager's sleeping compartment, prepared under the direction of Sheng Hsuan-huai, was furnished with a European bed. *Per contra*, it contained also materials for opium smoking, of luxurious yet workmanlike appearance.

Opium, like other luxuries, she took in strict moderation, but greatly enjoyed her pipe after the business of the day was done. It was her practice then to rest for an hour, smoking at intervals, a *siesta* which the Court knew better than to disturb. She fully realised the evils wrought by abuse of the insidious drug, and approved of the laws, introduced by the initiative of T'ang Shao-yi and other high officials, for its abolition. But her fellow-feeling for those who, like herself, could use it in moderation, and her experience of its soothing and stimulating effect on the mind, led her to insist that the Abolition Decree [22 November 1906] should not deprive persons over sixty years of age of their accustomed solace. She was, in fact, willing to decree prohibition for the masses, but lenient to herself and to those who had sufficiently proved their capacity to follow the path of the happy mean.[54]

Prohibition was absolute in theory and in public, but otherwise in practice and in private for the Old Buddha. What was really at stake here was not so much that the Empress Dowager smoked opium, but rather filial piety, the single most important virtue of the Chinese people. Though a Manchu, Cixi knew this Chinese virtue well and adopted it to suit herself. Indeed, by her actions she had justified both herself and also the millions who were old (around 60 years of age) by Chinese standards. For the Chinese, old age makes a sage, and not only can the elderly do whatever they prefer, no one can raise the slightest doubt against them – indeed, the younger generation must encourage them to demonstrate their filial piety. Filial piety helped opium to lead a secure and comfortable social life among the elderly. This certainly explains the massive consumption among the elderly population in the late Qing and beyond. The 'sages' contributed to the increased demand for opium. They helped to make the golden age of smoking. Opium had served and satisfied many, now it pampered the elderly. A combination of filial piety and opium helped the

Empress Dowager keep at bay her enemy, the reform-minded Guangxu emperor who also allegedly turned to opium for salvation. Opium had entered the bloodstream of Chinese culture and society when it appeared side by side with rice stores and tea houses after the second Opium War. Like filial piety, it was now in the bloodstream. The moral resignation to opium would only deepen in the twentieth century, when opium would be further politicised.

CHAPTER II

The road to St Louis

This chapter is devoted to the cult and culture of opium consumption in the late Qing and Republican eras. The reign of the Empress Dowager Cixi, from 1861 to 1908, was a time of great contrast. China slipped further into a semi-colonial era of foreign domination and internal disintegration, yet it also underwent restoration and modernisation. The story of opium at this time has parallels with the above. Whilst it continued to humiliate and sicken China, it also helped to crush rebellions and finance 'self-strengthening'. Wars and legalisation brought out a sense of moral resignation and ushered in a golden age of opium smoking. Opium was so chic and à la mode that not only individuals but also households identified themselves with it. Indeed, opium identified China on the international stage, as the 1904 St Louis Exposition showed. This example will be discussed later in the chapter.

By the turn of the century opium had become a refined material and a popular culture, a well-established social institution. Humiliation by the West did not diminish the smoking power of Chinese consumers. Instead, they turned opium smoking into a most sophisticated culture of consumption, one which helped regenerate the Chinese economy, Chinese culture and Chinese society. Humiliation and regeneration, like disintegration, restoration and even revolution, lived side by side. This was the paradox of opium and of China itself at the time.

THE MATERIAL LIFE OF OPIUM

'The Chinese did not discover opium, but they refined its recreational use into an art and craft of unparalleled sophistication', asserts Peter Lee.[1] This is no exaggeration. Take the exquisiteness of smoking sets and accessories as an example. Ordinary smokers perfected the art and craft of opium. Emily Hahn's observation below is authentic and meticulous:

Heh-ven had lain down on his left side, alongside the tray and facing it. He lit the lamp. One of his friends, a plump little man named Hua-ching, lay on his right side on the other side of the tray, facing Heh-ven, each with head and shoulder propped on the pillows. Heh-ven never stopped conversing, but his hands were busy and his eyes were fixed on what he was doing – knitting, I thought at first, wondering why nobody had ever mentioned that this craft was practised by Chinese men. Then I saw that what I had taken for yarn between the two needles he manipulated was actually a kind of gummy stuff, dark and thick. As he rotated the needle ends about each other, the stuff behaved like taffy in the act of setting; it changed color, too, slowly evolving from its earlier dark brown to tan. At a certain moment, just as it seemed about to stiffen, he wrapped the whole wad around one needle end and picked up a pottery object about as big around as a teacup. It looked rather like a cup, except that it was closed across the top, with a rimmed hole in the middle of this fixed lid. Heh-ven plunged the wadded needle into this hole, withdrew it, leaving the wad sticking up from the hole, and modelled the rapidly hardening stuff so that it sat on the cup like a tiny volcano. He then picked up a piece of polished bamboo that had a large hole near one end, edged with a band of chased silver. Into this he fixed the cup, put the opposite end of the bamboo into his mouth, held the cup with the tiny cone suspended above the lamp flame, and inhaled deeply.[2]

Heh-ven's 'knitting' reminds us of 'intertwining fingers'. Well-educated and worldly, he invited his colleagues home after a dinner in town and entertained them with opium smoking. An ordinary smoker among millions, his performance shows how ordinary people like him had perfected the art and craft of 'heating and scooping paste' by the early twentieth century. Peter Lee explains: 'The quality of the smoking mixture depends primarily on the experience and skill of the person who prepares it, rather than on the quality of the raw opium from which it is refined.'[3] In other words, mediocre opium could be transformed into an excellent smoking blend if the preparer knew the art of mixing and heating. Reputable opium shops, dens and sophisticated households refined raw opium themselves. Raw opium would be soaked overnight, boiled and filtered several times. The filtered fluid would be stored in a sealed jar for days, weeks or even months. This allowed 'the super fine sediment which escapes the filters to slowly settle to the bottom of the jar, where it collects in a dense, finely grained layer of gritty sludge'.[4] Not only the quality but also the quantity of opium produced was decided by this process. James Acheson, Maritime Customs's third assistant in Canton, knew that 'the quantity of prepared opium yielded by a given weight of unprepared drug depends very much upon the experience and skill of the operator'.[5]

Scooping up the prepared paste with a tiny spoon or needle and inserting it into the bowl, which Prince Minning called the 'eye' and Hahn called 'a pottery object about as big around as a teacup' was a delicate and demanding procedure. The bowl, or rather the hole in the middle to be more precise, must be heated in order to receive the cooked paste. Temperature matters greatly. Underheated holes will harden the paste and cause it to glue up the aperture while overheated holes melt the paste into a syrup. Both make it impossible for the paste to evaporate. Equally important is the angle at which the pipe is tilted over the lamp for continued heating and evaporation after the paste has been inserted. Many smokers would hold the bowl between their fingers over the lamp in order to ensure the right angle and temperature for initial inhaling. Needless to say, the opium bowl itself generated much artistic innovation. Ceramic bowls were very popular. So were bowls of unusual shape. The American collector Wolf K has amassed some of the rarest and finest bowls. Among his collection are one shaped like the poppy bud and another with a Buddhist theme. The collection also includes a bowl with incised trigram symbols from the classic *Yi Jing*, 'The Book of Change', and quite a few examples in classic 'blue-and-white-ware'. Some of the most extraordinary are two bowls in the form of a lady's three inch 'golden lily' (see illustration 7). The inscriptions typically found on opium bowls include: 'Swallowing clouds and spewing fog', 'Always the right time', 'Fragrant fumes of the immortals', 'To celebrate an auspicious day', 'Spring flowers and autumn moon' and 'The fragrance wafts for a thousand miles'.

Chinese artisans, like men of letters and women, also defined the social life of opium since the accessories they fashioned reveal, in Daniel Roche's language, 'a body of knowledge' and 'a surplus of meanings'. The sometimes elaborate, sometimes simple but meaningful opium sets and accessories are more than everyday objects. Such sophistication testifies to the fact that the Chinese had turned opium smoking into a refined consumer and material culture in the late Qing and beyond. The Chinese inscribed their ideas and ideals into the opium sets; they had reinvented the experience of smoking. Daniel Roche takes clothing as an example. 'Clothing speaks of many things at once, either in itself or through some detail. It has a function of communication because it is through clothing that everyone's relation to the community passes.' The story of opium is one of socio-cultural communication and differentiation. Opium smokers communicated through smoking, and they differentiated themselves through opium utensils. Roche stresses that we should pay attention 'to the whole as well as the parts, the signs which indicate minorities, the colours that can characterise social functions and

Illustration 7. Top: opium bowl with Buddhist theme from the Peter Lee and Wolf K collection. The two bowls in the form of a lady's three-inch 'golden lily' (below) are particularly extraordinary.

membership of different groups, the cut, the material, and the types of jewellery'. This observation can be extended to the other opium-smoking accessories.

The bowl sits on a smoking gun or pipe. Like the snuff bottle, the opium pipe is a genre all of its own. It has fascinated generations of smokers, from Prince Minning to Yang Enshou, who called his Hunan mottled bamboo pipe carved with the epic poem *Sandufu*, 'an object of lovesickness'. Yet nothing compares with a pipe carved with themes of loving-making that is

Illustration 8. Peter Lee's collection 'Breakfast in Bed' includes a lacquered opium tray
with a gold-plated lamp, black-lacquered pipe with silver and ivory fittings, skewers,
jar, dross box, cooking pan and cleaning tools. His pipe collection includes five pipes
with tips of jade and ivory.

shown in Lo Duca's work. The 'drama of smoke-cloud' on the pipe would
turn into real-life drama here. Authentic opium pipes are rare today. Among
Peter Lee's collection are five bamboo pipes, one of which is a Hunan mottled bamboo. Lee writes: 'a well seasoned bamboo pipe greatly enhances
the pleasure of smoking not only by improving the flavour of the smoke
but also by increasing its potency'.[6] His five pipes, which are displayed
on a rack, all have tips of jade and ivory (see illustration 8). Sophisticated
pipes were often made of expensive materials, silver for example, and paired
off with elaborate designs. Wealthy smokers adorned their pipes with precious gemstones (see illustration 9). Yang Enshou saw that 'luxurious ones
came in jade and *daimao*', an exquisite tortoiseshell found in south and
south-east Asia. Whilst some smokers were certainly addicted to opium,
others were addicted to their 'object of lovesickness'.

Illustration 9. Two pipe saddles of wrought silver. Wealthy smokers often adorned their pipes with precious gemstones.

The opium pipe was endowed with all the virtues of a collectible: utility, size, durability, artistry and history. The same was true of the opium lamp, nicknamed the 'magic lamp'. Three lamps were particularly popular: the Taigu lamp, the Jiaozhou lamp and the Canton lamp. Artistic and easy to carry, Taigu and Jiaozhou lamps were superbly designed. They were superior to other lamps because oil did not spill, even if the lamp was knocked over, as the top could be securely tightened. Although the Taigunese had not invented smoking, they had fashioned a lamp that dazzled smokers and collectors. The Canton lamp was remarkable because it was made of glass.

We can see one being used in Xu Ziling: 'octagonal glass-wrought lamp bought with precious silver'. Glass lamps were very fashionable, as one could see the oil level inside them at a glance. The lamps were useful for other things too. Zhou Sheng, who wrote about opium-serving Yangzhou women, marvelled: 'As to the smoking sets, they are really refined and exquisite. The lamp is especially simple and easy to handle. I put one in my four-poster bed for reading in the mid-summer night.'⁷ A Chinese four-poster bed is a world of its own. Many studied, smoked and relaxed there with the convenience of a single lamp that provided for both reading, smoking and sex recreation. Lee and Wolf K's collection includes a gold-plated lamp with a bell-shaped oil well, a lamp with an oil container shaped like a poppy pod and another shaped like a birdcage (see illustration 10).

Other accessories included trays, boxes, jars, needles, skewers, pans, pillows and beds. Lee and Wolf K have collected some of the best opium sets and accessories. 'Breakfast in bed' includes a lacquered opium tray with a gold-plated lamp, a black-lacquered pipe with silver and ivory fittings, skewers, jar, dross box, cooking pan and cleaning tools (see illustration 8). The rich and powerful, Liu Kunyi for example, started their day with opium in bed. Wolf K's container collection includes an enamelled silver opium box depicting the Chinese zodiac separated by a motif of characters, each one of which means 'long life', and an exquisitely detailed gold-plated wrought-silver opium box in 'inro' shape. Paul Unschuld's *Medicine in China* shows an opium box decorated on both the front and the back with love-making scenes. The 'art of sex' lived on. Lee comments on these objects that they were 'designed to please the eye with their beauty and delight the mind with their aesthetic form, as well as to provide practical utility in the hands of those who used them'.⁸ The Opium Museum in Chiang Rai (Thailand) has also assembled opium sets and accessories. Opium had created a consumer culture around smoking, and at the same time a lucrative commerce in sets and accessories. These objects reveal opium's 'materiality'.

Innovation was not limited to the decorative domain. As prohibition and enlightenment intensified, opium fans and opium shoes appeared. Fan stems made of bamboo or ivory were filled with opium, while shoemakers sold shoes with opium-filled soles and boots with small pockets that hid opium. The shoes continued to be made in the twentieth century. I have found several pictures, in the Singapore National Archive, of shoes whose soles and heels were filled with opium. The 1918 edition of the *Extended Shanghai County Gazetteer* reported: 'At the time when opium was at the height of its popularity, opium beds and sets competed with each other in exquisiteness and beauty. When friends and family gathered

Illustration 10. Gold-plated lamp with bell-shaped oil well and lamps with the oil containers shaped like a poppy pod and a birdcage, from Lee and Wolf K's collection.

and entertained, opium was considered something that must be served. It was also used when receiving guests.'[9] By the early twentieth century opium had entered stardom and was leading a rich life among the Chinese people.

CULTURE OF CONSUMPTION

Opium was used when receiving guests and entertaining friends and family. Li Zhaotang, an Anhui scholar, wrote: 'When I was small, the customs of our county were still simple and unsophisticated . . . As for the dishes of Chinese New Year guest entertainment, many would serve ten dishes, mostly vegetable dishes, no sea foods. Later, it got to two or three sea dishes; and then they added desserts, and now small side dishes and even opium smoking.'[10] Opium was a natural and welcome addition to the Chinese dinner table and Chinese entertainment. It had joined the most basic human ritual, and the one most favoured by the Chinese. Opium achieved such a status not entirely because of its gradual popularisation among all classes of people, but more importantly because it belonged to the wider cultures of Chinese consumption – namely, food, tea, herbs and utensils. Opium smoking was a fusion of these cultures. Like food, the cooking of opium paste was an art and craft. Like tea, smoking was social and recreational. Like utensils and snuff bottles, opium sets and accessories were functional as well as artistic. Like herbs and tea, opium was both a medicine and a preventative. It is imperative to understand the intimacy between tea-drinking, opium smoking and the cultures of Chinese consumption, because eating, be it fine dining or the humble meal, was the foremost ritual of a Chinese day.

A common Chinese greeting is 'Have you eaten?', and what greets a guest at a home is tea. The Chinese were preoccupied with food and drink, and this preoccupation extended to opium. People spent time eating, drinking and by the early twentieth century also smoking, because that was how they lived and socialised. Dinners and parties accompanied or followed by opium smoking had been a part of the elite/urban culture since the mid to late eighteenth century. By the twentieth century the practice had entered popular, consumer culture. The *Collection of Old Shanghai's Historical Sources* gives an example of the standard items used for dinner entertainments such as weddings in 1873:

Meat, 5 to 140 *wen* / every 100 *jin*
Winter bamboo shoot, 13 *wen* / every *liang*
Shao wine, 40 to 44 / every *jin*
. . .
Longjin tea, 84 *wen* / every *liang*
Charcoal, 84 *wen* / every basket
Dried *lizhi*, 1.6 *fen* / every *jin*
. . .
Opium, silver 1.8 *fen* / every *liang*
. . .
Theatre box, 8 *jiao* / every guest.[11]

A comprehensive list would be far longer. Opium was the most expensive item because it was paid for in silver money while other items were paid for with paper or copper money. A Chinese celebration could not be without a sumptuous meal accompanied by entertainment, and a meal now would not be complete without opium. Opium became part of legitimate socio-cultural events. It's consumption was fully sanctioned. Smoking fitted in well with the long-lasting Chinese banquet accompanied by live performance. Roche has argued that in our efforts to understand the history of consumption, we must analyse 'the structuring of needs', 'the texture of our ordinary life', that is, 'the real weight of everyday life' or the 'history of what seems to have no history: material life and biological behaviour, history of food, history of the consumption of food'.[12] Food is a basic human need. A sumptuous meal accompanied by opium smoking and live performance can be a need for some and completely unnecessary for others. A need can be natural; it can also be artificially generated. Opium is an example of both, as the boundary is often blurred between necessity and luxury. It was expensive and fashionable. Serving it signalled the socio-economic status of the party-giver. It was social, recreational and medicinal, and was not necessarily detrimental to party-goers. Putting smoking in such socio-cultural context helps us to see who smoked opium, when and why.

By the early twentieth century opium smoking had become a part of a larger culture, a sister culture, and was a culture all of its own. Dr George Dods spent eighteen years in southern China and observed the social life of opium. 'It is the accompaniment to a spree in China. When a man gives a dinner to his friends they always finish up with a pipe of opium.'[13] Just as westerners drunk alcohol during and after dinner, so the Chinese smoked opium. *Chacun a son goût*, as the French saying goes. Chinese people are hospitable by nature. Food is the way in which they communicate and exchange with each other, as do many other peoples. Alexander Michie talked about his forty-year experience in Hong Kong, Shanghai and Tianjin before the Royal Commission:

For example, you can hardly go to a Chinese dinner without having the opium pipe there; and when the guests have sat a long time at the table, and eaten a great deal, and drunk a good deal, one will retire to the divan where the opium pipe is and have a whiff of opium, and by-and-by when he has finished he rejoins the other guests; another one will go, and so on, just as you take a cigarette after dinner, or a glass of wine. That is the common practice.[14]

Dinner entertainment accompanied by drinking and smoking was a 'common practice' in southern and eastern China. It was even more so in western China, as Mrs Archibald Little remembered: 'at a good many dinner parties the opium-couch is prepared with all its accessories'.[15] One was expected to act hospitably regardless of one's means, especially if the guest was a foreigner from afar. Sichuan, where Mrs Little travelled, had plenty of opium, and offering something indigenous probably meant more to the hosts than to the guests. A few centuries back, the Bengalis, Javanese and Siamese had offered their best indigenous produce to the Ming empire, as would the late Qing Sichuanese, who became famous for their opium. Such events have historical significance and deserve independent studies. With them we see the similarities of human nature and the commonalities between cultures of consumption and identity. Opium smoking galvanised Chinese consumer society in the late Qing–early Republican era. Nowhere was this more evident than in Beijing. The strong wind of opium continued to blow from the north, where Manchu nobles, high-ranking officials, the literati-artistic elite, diplomats, missionaries and China helpers mingled. Isaac T. Headland recounted his family's experience in the capital: 'The common name for opium among the Chinese is *yang yan* – foreign smoke, and my wife says: when calling at Chinese homes, I have frequently been offered the opium-pipe, and when I refused it the ladies express surprise, saying that they were under the impression that all foreigners used it.'[16] People of different regions and different dialects followed the custom in the same fashion. This reinforces the standardising power of elite culture and the role of the '5 per cent or so of the population'. Opium smoking, which by now was embedded in the daily ritual of eating and dining, had become a 'texture' and 'real weight' of ordinary life.

Many were addicted to smoking. However, they were not addicts in the standard sense. Herbert Giles gave his opinion: 'The Chinese people are naturally sober, peaceful, and industrious; they fly from intoxicating, quarrelsome *samshu*, to the more congenial opium-pipe, which soothes the weary brain, induces sleep, and invigorates the tired body.'[17] He concluded: 'We believe firmly that a moderate use of the drug is attended with no dangerous results; and that moderation in all kinds of eating, drinking and smoking is just as common a virtue in China as in England or anywhere else.' T. W. Duff, a merchant in China for thirty years, gave his opinion to the Royal Commission: 'under the circumstances of their living, food, climate, and habitations, opium to them has no deleterious effects, indeed quite the contrary, for it is a positive need and they could not do without it'.[18] Opium smoking thrived in tropical south-east Asia. It also prospered with the industrious and introverted Chinese. George Dodds dealt with Chinese merchants who often excused themselves in the midst of a negotiation for a pipe before they 'completed a bargain with our English merchants for tea or silk'.[19] A moment of recollection might help them see things more clearly.

CONSUMPTION AND IDENTITY

Opium was a 'must' when it came to friends and family, according to the experience of many, both Chinese and foreign. It had become a protocol that dictated social contact and exchange. Food is what binds friends, family and colleagues. The dinner table is where kinship is maintained, contact established and exchange takes place. Claude Levi-Strauss suggests that food is the key to the soul of a culture. Simon Schama believes that smoking and drinking were the customs 'by which the Dutch recognised their common identity'. The intimacy between food and identity are found, as Peter Scholliers has pointed out, in an increasing number of recent sociological, anthropological, ethnographical, geographical, philosophical and gender studies. Chinese food and the Chinese cultures of consumption identify the country, namely, its material life and biological behaviour. When opium landed on the dinner table, it further distinguished the uniqueness of the Chinese people and their culture. When individuals and households entertained friends and family with opium, they were conforming to the new convention. Opium had become a socio-cultural norm that commanded conformity. This demonstrates the conformitive nature of consumer culture in general and of the culture of opium in particular. Sociologists and psychologists have both studied this.

Conformity shame regulates many behaviours related to dress, language, food consumption, rituals, deportment, and so on. The regulation may sometimes be arbitrary, with little or no inherent survival value. However, they determine what is appropriate for the social self in a variety of roles, according to class, status, ethnic group, age, gender, profession, and so forth.[20]

Conformity can dictate consumer behaviour. Veblen states: 'unproductive consumption of goods is honourable, primarily as a mark of prowess and a perquisite of human dignity; secondarily it becomes substantially honourable in itself, especially the consumption of the more desirable things'.[21] Opium was so 'desirable' that it became a 'must' of entertainment. This kind of 'unproductive' consumption marked the prowess of an individual or household; it had become the 'perquisite' of dignity among friends, colleagues and neighbours. Veblen's contemporaries continue to study this aspect of consumer culture and society. Where economists have dwelt on the utility function of consumption, sociologists have emphasised its cultural and social values. The case of opium reinforces a simple conviction: consumption can be needs-based, but not all consumption is needs-based. Some goods and services, in other words, are signs and symbols. They are used to send messages, they have an identity value in addition to their use value. Paul du Gay provides this analysis:

> The consumption of goods and services is therefore important not so much for the intrinsic satisfaction it might generate but for the way in which it functions to mark social differences and acts as a communicator. Style, status and group identification are aspects of identity-value, where people choose to display commodities or engage in different spheres of consumption with a view to expressing their identity as certain sorts of persons.[22]

The identity value of opium could not have been more valid to the Sichuanese that Mr Archibald Little knew: 'Numbers of young men, and not a few women, who do not need it are led to use the drug because it is, as they say, "*t'i mien*" to do so. The opium couch is inviting, and they are everywhere invited to sit and lie on it.'[23] The phrase 'ti mian' is unique to the Chinese language, but the notion itself is common to all consumer societies. It roughly means 'polite and fashionable'. Its undertone is face-saving or, to use contemporary jargon, politically correct. 'Ti mian' illustrates the sophistication of Chinese consumer culture. It also points to the simple fact that choice was not always needs-based when it came to opium. This was and would continue to be the case for millions. 'Ti mian' is conspicuously used and it thrives in a conformist society such as that of China. Indeed it is the very essence of the 'external sanctions for good moral behaviour' that I discussed in chapter 4. It also relates to what Richard Wilson called 'group orientedness' or 'sociocentricism'. Wilson's analysis of moral behaviour in Chinese society can help us to understand the social significance of opium smoking.

> High degrees of group orientedness in Chinese society appear to be related to particular forms of social sanctions that are utilized by those in dominant positions. The primary sanctions are those that arouse the ubiquitous fear of abandonment. Freud has noted how individuals are tied to group leaders and to other group members and how anxiety can be aroused by the possibility of a cessation of these emotional bonds. The anxieties associated with these bonds can be manipulated in shame socialization, which involves training in comparing one's own behaviour with the ideals manifested by models and perfecting one's behaviour in a process of comparison and competition with other members of one's group.[24]

Fear of social ostracisation has long dictated human behaviour, and not just in China. 'Ti mian' was one of the many socio-cultural circumstances under which people succumbed to opium in the late Qing–early Republican era. When the rich and the powerful smoked it, it was fashionable and desirable. When one's friends, colleagues and neighbours smoked it, it involved 'ti mian'. One needed to be 'ti mian' even if one had to stretch one's means to do so. 'Ti mian', like filial piety, is highly representative of Chinese culture. With opium, it had become a means to social identity. Mr Curnow of the China Inland Mission knew this well. 'Nearly every house keeps it as a common requisite. A most horrible development of the evil is the constancy with which the opium pipe is offered you in the homes of the people as a matter of courtesy.'[25] This was only part of the problem. Curnow continued: 'Under the garb of a social "whiff", it is spreading and sapping the whole superstructure of society. No class is exempt.' Every class participated in opium smoking. Scrutinising the lives opium led among its various smokers helps us to see who smoked opium. Investigating the symbols and values smokers attached to smoking helps us to understand why they smoked.

Fuel, rice, oil, salt, soy sauce, vinegar and tea had been the essentials of a Chinese household. Now opium had become the eighth necessity. One had to make sure that one's household was furnished with it so that one could be 'ti mian' to friends, colleagues and guests. Here are some words of Wang Tao: 'In the afternoon, Sun Cigong came to visit; it was very simple and nice. At twilight, I went to visit Tengzhi with Cigong and Renshu . . . The small building Tengzhi lives in is shaped like a boat. It is really refined and elegant; the furniture is also unconventional. Tengzhi's relative the gentleman Wang prepared opium for us.'[26] Tengzhi offered opium regardless of whether Wang Tao and the others would smoke or not, because he wanted to be 'ti mian' to his friends. This was the same scenario with Heh-ven, Emily Hahn's colleague and opium teacher. Casual and random visits among friends were normal as illustration II shows. Tengzhi and Heh-ven had to make sure that their households had opium regardless of whether they themselves liked it or not. Opium was also money. It was safer to save opium rather than paper money in times of economic uncertainty. When one household offered opium, other households had to have it. Soon every household owned it. One did not compete with the Joneses; one only looked up to them. 'Human beings demonstrate strong tendencies to conform to group standards.'[27] 'Ti mian' was the most important group standard. It helped opium lead a secure and comfortable life among the conformitive Chinese.

Illustration 11. Joint smoking had become a means of hospitality to friends, colleagues, family and guests, where casual and random visits were normal in China.

Wang Tao kept up opium smoking and going to the brothel, as his diary shows:

In the morning, I went to *Jingyang* restaurant for a small drink [small meal] with Xiaoyi, Nianzha and Jipu, Jipu was the host this time. Delicacies and novel foods, it was a feast for a hungry pig. In the afternoon, Boshen came to visit, we went to walk in the horse-race field, Xiaoyi also joined us. Then we went to *Qinglo* [brothel] to visit the beautiful inmates. The hostess greeted us with opium. She was magnanimous. But none of the prostitutes was as pretty. It was as if we had

Illustration 12. Going out for a drink or a meal followed by opium smoking and sometimes by sex recreation was common among many urbanites in the late Qing.

gone to the country of *Luosa* [where ugly female demons came from]. After two rounds, we did not ask for any more.[28]

Going out for a meal followed by opium smoking and sex recreation had been common among the lettered, from Shen Fu in 1790s Canton to Wang Tao in late Qing Shanghai. A picture taken in the late Qing illustrates the scene (illustration 12). The women had to be literate and pretty, otherwise the opium might smoke different. Regardless of whether Wang Tao and his friends 'asked' or not, the hostess must entertain them with the most fashionable item. In fact, offering opium had nothing to do with 'asking'. They might have been there to survey the women. What mattered was whether the hostess was 'ti mian' or not. It was a matter of formality. Her brothel would drop from the list of not just Wang Tao but of many others if she was not 'ti mian'. Like an invisible hand, it regulated consumer behaviour and helped opium live harmoniously with the values of social contact and exchange. It is fascinating that Paul Cohen should justify Wang Tao's opium smoking: 'the personal psychological pressures under which Wang Tao lived may account, in some measures, for his intemperate drinking, his frequent debauches, and the fondness he eventually developed for opium.'[29] Wang Tao's personal psychological pressures were no more severe than those endured by prostitutes or coolies. Cohen has justified smoking for millions.

'Ti mian' is what Jean Baudrillard called 'the social logic of consumption', and what I call the Chinese law of consumption.[30] Baudrillard argued that consumption might be analysed from two basic angles:

1. As a process of signification and communication, based on a code into which consumption practices fit and from which they derive their meaning. Consumption here is a system of exchange, and the equivalent of a language.
2. As a process of classification and social differentiation in which sign/objects are ordered not now merely as significant differences in a code but as a status values in a hierarchy.[31]

'Ti mian' was and still is a common phrase in China. Tengzhi and Heh-ven spoke a coded 'language' when offering opium to friends and colleagues. They communicated through opium. They also derived meaning from being 'ti mian'. They were happy and proud that they could offer the most fashionable item. Opium helped them to communicate. It also generated satisfaction and significance. Serving opium singled out Tengzhi and Heh-ven, as we see from the fond memories of Wang Tao and Emily Hahn. There was a demand for social differentiation, and opium served as a means to that end. It was important to maintain one's social status. Maintenance might come at no cost, but it would be a worthy cause even if it was costly.

THE GLOBALISATION OF OPIUM SMOKING

Chris Bayly has recently coined the phrase 'the culture integers of consumption'.[32] Chinese food is a 'culture integer', and so was opium. Foreigners had begun to identify the Chinese with opium ever since the late eighteenth century. Some visited dens to see for themselves, some wrote about opium in detail, some learned to smoke it, while others sent or

Illustration 13. Late Qing postcard depicting the perfect middle-class smoking scene.
These genteel urbanites look civil, relaxed and happy.

brought souvenirs of it home. Foreigners helped to open the international
chapter on opium. One such souvenir is the Chinese postcard. During the
late Qing–early Republic era thousands were printed. One postcard, captioned 'The Chinese Eat Smoke', depicts a perfect middle-class smoking
scene (illustration 13). Genteel urbanites are socialising over a smoking session. Surrounded by good furniture, they look civil, relaxed and happy. The
postcard is postmarked 'Shanghai, 15 January 1904'. Another, captioned 'A
Smoking Subject of the Qing Dynasty', depicts a poor opium smoker. He
is alone on a bed with a simple set beside him; he is thin and haggard-
looking. This postcard was posted from Jiujiang of Jiangxi province on
22 March 1906. A third postcard, made from the photograph that appears
at the start of this book, is titled 'Opium Smoking Husband and Wife'. It
is postmarked 'Beijing, 6 February 1906'.

The Orient was regarded as exotic by the West, and opium made it even
more so. Postcards transmitted the image of China to a wider audience
who would never go to the country. They also stereotyped the Chinese
people and Chinese culture. But postcards were just the tip of the iceberg
when it came to opium–China publicity material. Chinese writers and
publishers used opium-containing headlines and opium stories to attract
readers. So did their foreign counterparts. Barbara Hodgson has studied

some of the well-known works. The lead article of the July 1907 issue of the French journal *Le Petit Parisien* featured 'Une fumerie d'opium en France'. Three French men are depicted at the pipes while two Chinese servants deliver tea and man the evaporating paste. Arnold de Liedekerke included many celebrated French literary and artistic works inspired by opium and the Orient in *La Belle époque de l'opium*. Drugs consumption was becoming a significant social problem in the United States in the early decades of the twentieth century. The June 1914 issue of the *American Magazine* contained a picture by N. C. Wyeth entitled 'A Modern Opium Eater'. Wyeth depicted two men smoking opium on a sofa with a dragon drawing on the wall behind. The men may be Caucasian or Asian, but one of them has on a Chinese robe. Wyeth had never been to China, he had only visited a den in Philadelphia's Chinatown.

The front cover of the April 1943 issue of *Short Stories* advertised Walter C. Brown's Chinatown adventure novelette *Blood Red Cash of Kublai Khan*. The advert featured two dark-faced and ugly-teethed Chinese men looking at the seal of Kublai Khan – the story was already told. There were also stereo-view cards and posters. Dodgson also examined American stereo-view cards that showed the seduction of white women by Chinese smokers. A famous poster was *Queen of Chinatown* by Joseph Jarrow, which showed a den in Chinatown where young Caucasian women were lured into smoking. Two white men are also shown, one of whom is dropping into the lower level of the den pushed by a Chinese, while the other enters through a secret window, also aided by a Chinese. The message could not have been clearer. American drug users allegedly numbered 1,500,000 in 1923.[33] Many Americans, namely journalists and professionals, pointed their fingers at the Chinese. H. H. Kane was frank: 'young men who had no work to do, were to be found smoking together in the back rooms of laundries in the low, pestilential dens of Chinatown, reeking with filth and overrun with vermin'.[34] For many, the Chinese were vice-ridden, and they had spread vice to America. Was Dr Kane or Chinatown itself to blame for this kind of 'racial profiling' to use today's jargon?

Many Americans and indeed the outside world in general were introduced to China via the works of Pearl Buck. Many of her works, *The Good Earth* for example, contain stories of opium. This novel tells the story of the rise of a landlord family. The landlord allows his poor relatives to indulge in opium so that they will soon die and will not be a drag on his fortune. Buck's China experience was real, and her fiction should be regarded as factually accurate. Fiction allowed novelists to depict opium smoking in detail. Even more so did the movies. Motion pictures are powerful experiences because the images shown are intense and captivating. *The Letter*, starring Bette Davis and Herbert Marshall, tells the complicated story of Sino-Caucasian inter-racial sexual relations and sexual intrigue set in the even more intriguing south-east Asia. In this film the close-up shots of rooms in the Chinese house always featured opium sets and smoking. More explicit were the spectacular scenes of smoking and addiction in *The Dividend* (1916). There were other films too, such as *Drifting* (1923) starring the famous Anna May Wong, *The Man Who Came Back* (1930) and *Charlie Chan in Shanghai* (1935). Opium–China postcards, magazine covers, posters, fiction writing and films spread the image of opium and China. The exotic Orient and its opium spiced up literary and artistic works; they perpetuated the image of the opium-ridden Chinese people. These works stereotyped the Chinese people. They also related a reality known to many.

The Chinese themselves contributed to this kind of racial profiling through their continued consumption. As Chinese labourers sojourned and settled in North America and Europe, foreign newspapers began to write about them. An article in *Harper's Weekly* on 7 March 1874 investigated Chinese opium smoking, while an editorial of the *New York Times* on 6 July 1875 read 'Chinese customs. Their life and education. The craving for opium and its effects'. There were many such articles and editorials, from San Francisco to Paris. Coolies in China needed opium to function, as did their counterparts away from home. For the Chinese abroad life was a matter of survival, as they lived in strange lands and worked at brutal jobs. Opium massaged their suffering bodies and reminded them of home. The lower-class Chinese largely represented China to the outside world. They were the 'Chinamen'. Opium was the 'China effect'. As Keith McMahon puts it: 'China was the opium addict, sottish, sedate, antediluvian, loose-robed, reclining, euphoric.'[35] McMahon continues: 'China was a mystery that had to be solved, a closed country that had to be opened, a heathen place that had to be Christianised, a backward place that had to be modernised, a country of liars who had to be outwitted or else taught the value of truth.'

Just as Chinese merchants and labourers of south-east Asia had introduced opium smoking and carried opium to the mainland during the Ming and Qing, their counterparts in the late Qing exported opium smoking to North America and Europe. The culture transmission had continued. Opium had been and was being used in many parts of the world. But it was the Chinese way of opium consumption that became synonymous with China itself, as North Americans and Europeans learned to smoke in the Chinese fashion. This was not only because it was the Chinese who had perfected the art and craft of smoking, but also because the Chinese were the agents of transmission from south-east Asia to their native China and beyond. Jack Goody suggests that spaghetti is an early example of the globalisation of food (see his *Food and Love*, 1998). Surely tobacco, sugar, tea, the peanut, the sweet potato, maize and opium should be added to the list. Goody has argued that the Chinese cuisine was globalised. Should this include opium smoking? To turn Goody's argument around, the globalisation of Chinese food also saw the sinicisation of foreign foods in China. Smoking and opium are perfect examples. Globalisation and indigenisation are two sides of the same coin. But it takes the 'genealogical method of anthropological inquiry' to see this. The globalisation and indigenisation of commodities and consumption demands more study.

Foreigners stereotyped China. China itself contributed to this type of racial stereotyping, however. This could not have been more plain than at the Louisiana Purchase Exposition held in St Louis in 1904, which was dubbed 'the coronation of civilisation'.[36]

The Items China Sent to the St Louis Exposition
The Chinese government's gallery at the St Louis Fair was despicably vulgar. It openly displayed the shame of our country with the items. I list the worst:

A dozen opium-smoking pipes,
Several opium-smoking lamps,
An official with an opium-smoking face,
Several daggers,
Some pictures of murderous-looking people,
A miniature magistrate,
A set of instruments of torture,
A cangue,
Foot-bound women in Shanghai, Beijing, Guangdong and Ningbo costumes,
Several hundred small wooden figures of such people as beggars,
    opium-addicts, criminals, coolies, concubines, prostitutes, etc . . .

The government spent millions. But the items they sent were such repulsive, vulgar, and immoral things that represented undesirable habits and superstition. They were not appropriate for an international fair, they caused us humiliation. I detest those officials who were responsible; they have no conscience![37]

The anonymous writer is accurate about opium in the Chinese exhibition, which even included raw and prepared opium, poppy-cutting knives and scissors, and opium boxes made of precious materials. The Empress Dowager commissioned her portrait for the exhibition and Prince Pu Lun led the Chinese delegation. The officials who chose to send opium and smoking sets were not to blame. They only selected what they thought best represented the Chinese heritage at the time. From aphrodisiac to popular culture, the Chinese people had continued to define opium. Such was the capacity of their consumer culture, economy and society. But many would agree with the anonymous writer that this was indeed 'the shame' of their country. Opium impoverished China and allowed the West to humiliate the Chinese people. It was China's downfall. Capacity and downfall, this was the paradox not just of opium but also of China. Like tea and replacing tea, opium identified China on the international stage. Opium would continue to collect values richer than itself and symbols beyond the comprehension of smokers themselves. As I will show in the next chapter, the Republican era was another epoch during which the transformation of opium would intensify.

CHAPTER 12

'Shanghai vice'

This chapter studies the consumption of opium in the Nationalist period, 1911–49. It also looks at the post-Mao era, when modern opium derivatives found their way back to China. China was plunged into turmoil after 1911. For opium, this was a period when what was vital to know was not so much who smoked opium but rather who controlled the trade. According to a survey conducted in 1935 some 3,730,399 people out of a total population of 479,084,651 consumed opium or its modern equivalents.[1] Where late Qing politicians had used opium-generated revenues to keep the empire together, their twentieth-century counterparts used it to partition the country. This was the period of the 'opium regimes'. Whoever controlled opium, controlled China. 'Despite much continuity, China from 1800 to 1949 underwent tremendous changes.' Yet despite the changes, 'China's cultural differentness strongly persisted even though it was diminishing.'[2] This can be seen from the social life of opium. What is more, Shanghai vice continued to be Chinese vice right up to the 1990s. Historians of China have studied both its changes and continuity in the twentieth century, but my specific interest here lies in how opium survived and thrived in the midst of quickened disintegration and transition.

'L'AGE D'OR DE LA BOURGEOISIE CHINOISE'

The Republican era witnessed an increasing sophistication and indigenisation of opium smoking. Alexander des Forges was correct when he put opium in the context of leisure and urban economies of consumption. Not only tea houses and restaurants provided opium smoking, tourist destinations and public parks were also equipped with facilities for smoking, in case one fancied a whiff when on a stroll along the river or while relaxing in the park. Even *shuchang* or 'book theatres', where people listened to story-telling, offered opium smoking. In Shanghai, according to local scholar Chi Zhizheng, opium smoking was a must-do:

Every bed has a big mirror, when the electric light is on in the evening, the mirrors shine and lights glitter, they reflect each other. It is as if you are in a glass-made palace full of treasures, they dazzle your eyes and touch your senses. Some dens are restaurants, *Zuileju* on the main street is one. Some dens are tea houses, *Yicenlou*, *Wucenlou* and *Qingliange* on the fourth street are among them. Some dens are *Shuchang*, they include *Huazhonghui*, *Lunjiaolou* and *Jieyilou*. In the night of wind and rain, one bed and two friends, you face each other and chat. It only costs 100 or so money, one could stay for a half a day. Isn't this the happiness of life? You don't have to be addicted to opium to enjoy this. This really is a must-do for those who visit Shanghai.[3]

Listening to story-telling and sipping tea accompanied by snacks had always been a popular pastime – it was not just a recreation, but also an education. *Shuchang*, like opera houses to the rich and bookstalls to children, were a powerful social institution where knowledge was transmitted to the large masses of the lesser literate population. When opium joined *shuchang*, this sanctioned smoking from a higher if not moral ground. Like tea, opium had become acceptable in a public institution of leisure and learning, another mechanism of culture transmission. *Shuchang* were still common in remote Sichuan and among the rural poor in the 1940s. Cecil Beaton, the British photographer, saw that 'In tea houses of bamboo-matting, the tea-drinkers smoke pipes three feet long, while they listen to the itinerant professional story-teller.'[4] Chi Zhizheng recommended opium smoking to 'those who visit Shanghai'. Among them was Somerset W. Maugham. The many descriptions of Chinese opium dens Maugham had read made his blood run cold. He made sure he visited one:

I was taken into an opium den by a smooth-spoken Eurasian . . . the narrow, winding stairway up which he led me prepared me sufficiently to receive the thrill I expected. I was introduced into a neat enough room, brightly lit, divided into cubicles the raised floor of which, covered with clean matting, formed a convenient couch. In one an elderly gentleman, with a grey head and very beautiful hands, was quietly reading a newspaper, with his long pipe by his side. In another two coolies were lying, with a pipe between them, which they alternately prepared and smoked. They were young men, of a hearty appearance and they smiled at me in a friendly way. One of them offered me a smoke. In a third four men squatted over a chess-board, and a little farther on a man was dandling a baby while the baby's mother, whom I took to be the landlord's wife, a plump, pleasant-faced woman, watched him with a broad smile on her lips. It is a cheerful spot, comfortable, home-like, and cosy. It reminded me somewhat of the little intimate beer-houses of Berlin where the tired working man could go in the evening and spend a peaceful hour. Fiction is stranger than fact.[5]

Gone were the dim lights, dazed eyes and haggard faces. Modern facilities and polite urban consumers replaced filthy dens and awry smokers. The scene seems to mock prohibition and enlightenment. The consumption of opium had modernised just as China itself was modernising. Both entrepreneurs and consumers were improving the service and consumption of opium in the twentieth century. The harmfulness of opium was obvious to all and accepted by many as was, the determination to moderate and improve its consumption. Smoking was being justified from a higher ground. It was mainstream, as is evidenced by the civil and clean smoking facilities. This testifies to the elasticity of the Chinese consumer economy, culture and society. It allows us to see the progress of opium's complete sinicisation. Foreigners appreciated the Chinese way of leisure. It certainly meant more to the Chinese. Hu Xianghan remembered the good old days in the *Small Gazetteer of Shanghai*:

The spectacle of opium dens in the old days was grander than tea houses, they were what people called the *biggies* in the International Settlement. They were lined up one after another; you couldn't really count them. At the beginning the *Mianyunge* in the French Settlement was the best; then they started to compete with each other. Later *Nanchenxin* was the best. It was spacious, grand, exquisite and sumptuously decorated. Big ones were like a couch bed and small ones were cubicles. Even those who are not addicted like to come and lie down. When evening descended and prostitutes converged, the whole place bustled with excitement. It was not strange that man and woman who never met before shared a bed facing each other. Secret lovers were found here. Businessmen as well as gentlemen frequented and hung around this kind of place.[6]

'L'âge d'or de la bourgeoisie Chinoise', Marie-Claire Bergère labelled the era. The spectacular scene of *Nanchenxin* is featured in the illustrious *Shenjiang Shengjintu*. Sophisticated Shanghainese replaced Ming–Qing scholars and officials as the new urban elite. This more diverse and professionally led class continued to spread the consciousness of consumption. Urban society was being changed and its social structure levelled out. And once again the role of public institutions was being highlighted. Businessmen and gentlemen gentrified public places of leisure, where they downloaded their stresses from work, escaped responsibilities at home and helped galvanise the sex industry. Meanwhile women, still 'prostitutes' in the eyes of a twentieth-century man of letters, found more avenues of upward social mobility. Shanghai was favoured by the bourgeoisie, both Chinese and foreign. It was a most charming city that provided everything, from Turkish baths to French, Russian and American prostitutes, from horse races and jazz bars to Chinese gambling salons, singsong houses and opium dens.

Shanghai was where the East and the West met. Some called it the 'Constantinople of the East', some the 'whore of Asia', some the 'city of Taipans' and others the 'Paris of the East'. Many foreigners made their careers, homes or fortunes in the famous Settlements. *Shili yangchang*, 'ten miles of foreign ground', were dotted with European-style offices. Besides old houses such as Jardine Matheson, there were newcomers – the Sassoons for example. These were the 'Shanghai gentlemen' or the 'greatest boosters of Shanghai'; they were also the 'spoilt children of empire'.

Shanghai was a paradise for the pleasure-seeker and the fortune hunter. But it was also a hell where poverty and vice lived side by side with wealth and God. Percy Finch, an American journalist who worked in Shanghai from the 1920s to the 1940s, summed up the social life of opium there:

Shanghai was the city of nepenthe. Wrapped in opium dreams, the coolie sloughed off the day's fatigue in some smoky hovel and the banker forgot business cares while he enjoyed ineffable self-satisfaction in his walled compound, with a deft servant to feed his filigree pipe . . . Shanghai was not only far and away the largest consumer of narcotics in the country, it was the reservoir for the stream of poison that slowed through China's veins. Incalculable quantities of mind- and body-wrecking poppy juice and its crystalline laboratory progeny, morphine and heroin, found their way into the city. Where hospital and scientific needs were reckoned in pounds, Shanghai dealt in tons – enough to supply any country, any half-dozen countries, or any continent.[7]

'Tons' was no exaggeration. Opium was 'la fortune de Shanghai' for the individual as well as for the Municipal Council, which profited from both licence fees and tax on sales.[8] Jardine Matheson might have made history. Twentieth-century Shanghai would produce the most sophisticated globally organised crime syndicate. Frederic Wakeman has studied opium's organised crime and the politics of policing, while Brian Martin has examined the rise of the Green Gang, which operated in the French Settlement, and their leader, Du Yuesheng, the 'opium king'.

Opium from India and Sichuan was unloaded and safely stored in the Settlement, where neither Chinese nor foreign laws applied. This required the agreement of and payment to the French consular and the police authorities. Not only did the French co-operate with the Green Gang, they also made some gangsters members of the French detective squad called the Chinese Uniform. Gang members also filled the ranks of the Chinese police and made up the regular spate of smokers, as 'pipes burned within the shadow of the central police station'.[9] Chinese underworld bosses were not in love with the French. They merely needed their extra-territoriality in order to escape the Chinese jurisdiction. The same conflict

and co-operation scenario was to be found in other Sino-foreign business partnerships. The French authority in Shanghai was indeed one of
the 'opium regimes'. Not only that, France also controlled part of the
supply route – L'indochine. Sichuan and Yunnan opium were smuggled
through Indochina to Shanghai and other parts of China. The governor
of L'indochine authorised the transport of Chinese opium via Tokin.[10]
French historians have studied 'la regie de l'opium en Cochinchine' and 'le
monopole au Tonkin et en Annam'.[11] The French profited from L'indochine
and the Settlement in Shanghai; they also enjoyed smoking, as Guy
Brossollet marvelled: 'quelques Français participent au trafic. Quelques
autres, en quete de bonheur artificiels, fument.'[12] The popularity of opium
among the French can be seen from *La Belle époque de l'opium* and the
photography of Gyula Halasz Brassai.

OPIUM'S MODERNISATION

Opium wrapped and gangster patrolled, Shanghai was a nation in micro-
cosm. China itself was in the hands of political gangsters – the warlords.
The issue of commodity control and regulation had become political. The
warlords found a sound solution in the cultivation, trafficking and taxation of opium. Donald Gillin wrote about Yen Xishan's 'opium monopoly',
James Sheridan about Feng Yuxiang's 'opium fines', Odoric Wou about Wu
Peifu's opium taxation and Diana Lary about the Kwangsi Clique's hand in
opium. Opium was vital to their survival and expansion. George B. Cressey,
an American geologist, travelled to twenty-eight provinces and saw how the
political economy of opium worked: 'In many provinces farmers have been
forced by the military authorities to raise opium for taxation purposes,
and in this way considerable areas of the best land have been removed
from food production.'[13] China had a shortage of arable land, but the 'best
land' went to grow opium. Richard Henry Tawney, a British geographer,
knew why so many cultivated opium: 'Since opium represented a more
lucrative source of revenue than other crops, peasants in many provinces
were encouraged or compelled to plant poppies.'[14] Peasants in the nineteenth century had responded to market demand and grew opium of their
free will. Their twentieth-century counterparts were either 'encouraged'
or 'compelled' to grow opium. When the wind of prohibition blew, some
fought against eradication in order to protect their livelihoods, while others
fought against excessive tax collecting.

   H. G. W. Woodhead, veteran journalist in China, saw the fundamental
problem: 'Militarism and opium are intimately related. It is the Chinese

Tuchun and his military parasites who have been mainly responsible for the recrudescence of poppy cultivation throughout the country.'[15] *Tuchun* were provincial military commanders. This reminds us of the great warlord Chang Tso-lin, a great opium smoker, and the famous *shuang qiang jun* or 'twin-pipe army'. Anhui provincial forces were known as the 'twin-pipe army' because soldiers carried both *yan qiang* or the 'opium pipe' and *bu qiang* or the 'rifle' on their backs.[16] Warlords needed opium, and so did 'rebels and revolutionaries'.[17] Edward Slack has studied the Nationalists' 'narco-economy', while Alan Baumler has shown that the Nationalists 'attempted, with considerable success, to profit both politically and eco-nomically from control of the opium trade and avoid the loss of legitimacy that came with involvement in the trade'.[18] The Nationalists were more sophisticated. On the one hand, they established the Shanghai Opium Suppression Bureau and the National Opium Suppression Committee headed by the paramount leader, Jiang Jieshi himself. On the other hand, the Bureau taxed opium shops and charged a licence fee to addicts while the Committee helped to protect the shipment of 'Jiang's opium'.[19]

China was 'sinned against and sinning'.[20] The 'narco-economy' turned opium into 'China's leading cash crop' and cities such as Peiling into the 'capital of opium', as a correspondent of the *East Magazine* reported in June 1935:

Peiling lies in the east of Chongqing and south of the Yangtze River. It is the famous capital of opium cultivation in Sichuan province. According to the statistics of the previous government, its annual production was more than 23,000 *dan* and the tax that government levied on it reached the incredible amount of 1,300,000 *yuan*. Local military expenditure depended on this tax, so did all kinds of local government expenditures. In Peiling every family grows opium. The price of opium was high in previous years; peasants had enough for other expenditures after they paid all the taxes.[21]

'Every family' was no exaggeration. John L. Buck, an American agricultural expert, knew that 'only by raising opium can farmers pay such a tax'.[22] Buck carried out a study of 16,786 farms in 168 localities and 38,256 farm families in 22 provinces from 1929 to 1933. Peasants sold only 15 per cent of the rice they cultivated but 74 per cent of the poppies they grew.[23] Domestic cultivation had died down before 1916 because of the ten-year plan and relentless prohibition, but it revived after 1916 and thrived until at least the late 1940s. Many missionaries, journalists, officials and also the League of Nations expressed their concerns. Famine was not the only outcome of the best land being used for opium production; the ultimate consequence was

Table 6 *Confiscated drugs
nationwide, 1935–1939*

Items	kg
Raw opium	318283.656
Cooked opium	6331.025
Smoked ashes	4696.935
Mixed material	7539.495
Fake mud	3026.370
Poppy seeds	3215.530
Poppy grains	120.000
Morphine	990.046
Heroin	1477.501
Cocaine	6.737
High heels	120.972
Narcotic pills	15808.865
Narcotic powder	844.64
Toxicant	1639.933
Raw toxic	2085.168
Others	3883.118
Total	370069,991

Source: Hongbin Wang, *Jindu Shijian*,
Changsha: Yuelu Shushe, 1997, p. 436.

rural unrest and revolution. Elizabeth Perry has studied Huaibei region: 'the greatest single cause of rural unrest in Huai-pei at this time were the opium tax'.[24] Local Communists were able to mobilise thousands of peasants for a two-month revolt against the unpopular opium tax.

The Nationalist regime used June the third, the day Commissioner Lin burnt foreign opium in Canton in 1839, to launch a six-year plan in 1935. This plan registered smokers and licensed their consumption; it allowed smokers a period in which to give up smoking. The programme appropriated the paste shops from which addicts bought opium and the dens where they smoked. For those who lived away, the programme would deliver to their doorsteps what was called *guan tu* or 'official mud'. Table 6 gives an idea of the kinds of drugs available on the street from 1935 to 1939.

The paucity of numbers here reflects the nature of prohibition and of government-compiled statistics. Smokable opium was predominant, but morphine, heroin and pills were catching on. Chinese consumers had become modern, and opium itself was modernising. The advent of science and technology made modern derivatives available to opium smokers and addicts alike. They had in fact surfaced in the late Qing. Morphine and similar extracts were called 'white powder'. They could be injected or mixed with other ingredients to smoke. *Shen Bao* ran advertisements for 'white powder' from the early 1870s which often read 'The foreign white powder that helps one quit smoking'. There were also 'white pearls' and 'red pearls', both made from heroin and smokable from a shorter pipe. These spread quickly, as George Morrison saw in Chongqing in 1894:

Morphia pills are sold in Chungking by the Chinese chemists to cure the opium habit. This profitable remedy was introduced by the foreign chemists of the coast ports and adopted by the Chinese. Its advantage is that it converts a desire for opium into a taste for morphia, a mode of treatment analogous to changing one's stimulant from colonial beer to methylated spirit. In 1893, 15,000 ounces of hydrochlorate of morphia were admitted into Shanghai alone.[25]

In their efforts to quit opium, many smokers sank deeper into addiction. Knowledge about the difference between opium and its derivatives was limited at the time, and many obviously took advantage of this. Here is a picture of Suzhou in 1902:

The smoker finds it cheaper and far more convenient to carry a morphine preparation in his pocket, and take an occasional dose, than to have to lie back and go through the slow process of smoking. It is also injected hypodermically. Ghouls, with dirty hypodermic syringes and morphine solutions made with any water are to be seen in the tea shops or restaurants in Soochow giving injections at the low rate of seven cash [one-fifth of a penny] each. As their victims pass before them each gets his allowance in succession without the needle being even wiped after the previous one.[26]

The book *Narcotic Culture: A History of Drugs in China* has dealt with this subject in detail. China itself did not possess the science and technology required to manufacture derivatives. Instead, the early industrialised countries would make them available to China. The Revd G. S. Muir, Honorary Secretary of the Edinburgh Committee for the Suppression of the Indo-Chinese Opium Traffic, reported: '2,000 chests of opium are made into morphine in Edinburgh and London annually, and this constitutes about half the world's supply [in 1910]'.[27] He also stated: 'A large proportion of this finds its way, directly or indirectly, to the East.' Muir and his fellow committee members were aware that 'the traffic in non-medical quantities is contraband so far as China is concerned'. Good Christians and anti-opium activists supported prohibition, but only in public and in theory. H. G. W. Woodhead tried to alarm the Chinese authorities. He pointed out that morphine imports through the Maritime Customs had increased 'from 120 ounces in 1909 to 26,092 ounces in 1914' and that 'there had been enormous imports of morphia annually into Hong Kong, where it was smuggled into the southern provinces'.[28] Even if the Chinese authority had heard him, however, a far greater menace than morphine was now confronting the country.

'As imperial Britain extricated itself from the nineteenth-century opium regime it had operated in China, imperial Japan began to assemble its own.'[29] John Jennings has studied Japanese drug trafficking in Asia. Japan established opium monopolies in Korea and Taiwan in 1895. As the first industrialised country in Asia, Japan also monopolised derivatives production. The newly published fifteen-volume *Riben Qinhua Zuizheng Dang'an Xinji* or (A New Archival Collection of Japanese Crimes in China) provides substantial evidence of Japanese war and drug crime in China. Japanese merchants opened opium dens in southern Manchuria as early as 1907, and they sold morphine as early as 1910. They established an opium monopoly in Manchukuo in 1932, as opium and narcotics poured into Tianjin. Motohiro Kobayashi has studied 'Tianjin opium' and drug operations by resident Japanese and Koreans in the 1920s and 1930s. Frank W. Price was there during that time:

> In the Japanese Concession at Tientsin last year [1936] I counted over forty tables on one street where opium-smoking and drug-taking paraphernalia were openly sold. I secured the names of 134 shops in the Japanese concession, under euphemistic names, where narcotics and injections were sold. The price was very cheap, often free, for the first injections, until the habit was formed. There were 800,000 drug addicts in the Tientsin area. Doped cigarettes were sold through the villages under Japanese influence. The Chinese protested in vain.[30]

Many foreigners, especially survivors of the 'Rape of Nanjing', witnessed Japanese war and drug crimes. George A. Fitch and Dr M. Searle Bates, members of the International Committee of the Nanking Safety Zone, risked their lives to help the Chinese. They witnessed Japanese atrocities, especially the establishment of opium dens and other drug-using facilities. 'That part of the Nanking Municipality which lies within and adjacent to the walls contains a population of about 480,000. It is served by 30 public stores and by 173 licensed smoking dens; 14 hotels are known to have licenses. There is a large illegal trade, which officials are continually trying to force into channels profitable to themselves. That is the extent of "suppression".'[31] Dr Bates estimated that fifty thousand persons, one-eighth of the total population, used heroin. The Japanese army reopened opium dens closed during prohibition; they released addicts from rehabilitation institutions sooner than the doctors could cure them; and they used narcotics as payments for labour and prostitution.[32] Historians have only just begun to examine Japanese war and narcotic crimes. Not only did Koreans collaborate with the Japanese. Timothy Brook has reminded us of the role of the Liang Hongzhi and Wang Jingwei puppet regimes. Opium was helping Japan to subdue China. A century of foreign humiliation and domination was destroying the country, and even the Chinese people themselves could see it. As Sun Zhongshan had predicted earlier, China would become 'extinct' if the Chinese people did not save it.

The threat posed by Japan, coupled with the opium problem, was a wake-up call. Within China there was a dramatic change of attitude towards imperialists in general and towards opium in particular. The whole nation was gripped by anti-Japanese feeling. The Nationalists and the Communists used this consensus to rally support and to strengthen their platforms. The time seemed to be perfect for renouncing opium. 'The sick man of Asia', sickened by opium, was now awakened by opium. It became a symbol of resistance during wartime, as Mark Eykholt has argued.[33] The struggle to free China from opium joined the struggle to free China from the imperialists. For Mao Zedong it was clear that the war against Japan could be traced to the Opium Wars; it represented the Chinese people's continued struggle against the imperialists. Although opium smoking was politically redefined, no one can deny that the opium trade and the unequal treaties represented the hegemonic forces of the imperialists. China fought to free itself from imperialists as epitomised by opium. Opium, seen through the designs and doings of the imperialists, was sentenced to political death at this historical juncture. Mao Zedong might be right about China's struggle against the imperialists being embedded in its struggle against opium; but the fact was that at this point in time the Chinese people were consuming home-grown, not imperialist, opium. Opium and its modern derivatives would return to China in the post-Mao era, when the imperialists were long gone. What would Mao have said? Opium had not yet died.

The determination to drive out the Japanese helped to unite the Chinese people. China, however, was geographically divided after 1937. The Japanese occupied Manchuria, east and central China, the Nationalists moved to the Sichuan and Yunnan while the Communists settled in Shaanxi and Gansu. The south-west and north-west were both steeped in opium. Chongqing was provincial, but it had everything needed to make it a capital. Winnogene

Harpold, for example, found things from London, New York and Hon-
olulu. D. F. Karaka enjoyed its Sing Sing Café and jazz bar. And Daniel
Nelson saw that 'the Chungking stores are stacked high with all kinds of
merchandise – fountain pens, watches, toys, shoes, toilet articles, bolts of
cloth, even luxuries. The restaurants and tea shops are filled with happy-
go-lucky civilians.'[34] More than anything else, Chongqing had plenty of
opium and its modern derivatives. The hospitable Sichuanese had used
opium to entertain guests, Mrs Archibald Little for example, in the late
nineteenth century. Han Suyin journeyed through south central China to
Chongqing in 1938. She saw many opium dens on the way, and she lodged
in village inns that served opium smoking. She arrived in Chongking in
time for the Chinese New Year in 1939.

Third Uncle made motions as if to depart, but all Third Grandfather's household
pressed us to *shua* a little longer. *Shua* is a Szechwan institution. Strolling in the
parks, ambling about the streets, flocking in crowds to temple fairs, going to theatres
and cinemas, sitting for hours in the tea shops, smoking tobacco, smoking opium
– all is *shua*. Visiting is *shua*. If you have sat for half a day, sipping tea, cracking
melon seeds, and eating peanut candy, until all you have to say has been said many
times over, yet you are entreated to *shua* awhile longer. If you have stayed three
months or more, you and all your family eating at your host's expense, he will
gravely protest that it has been a few days only and beg you to *shua* for a few days
more. *Shua* means to play, to linger, to idle, to neglect one's duty, to amuse oneself.
It expresses that Chinese philosophy of leisure which in Szechwan is carried to
the point of utter laziness. It is an attitude of mind remaining from the old days
of indolence, when for those who had plenty of money, and for sages and poets
to whom money was nothing, there was really nothing to do from morning to
evening but gaze at the bamboos reflected in the tranquil river, smoke the water
pipe, drink tea from covered teacups and wine from minute wine cups, and lie in
the shade exchanging gossip and composing balanced couplets with one's friends.[35]

Han's understanding of *shua* is correct. It was the Chinese style of leisure
'carried to the point of' complete laziness and idleness. *Shua* was not limited
to Sichuan. Born and raised in Hunan, I understand precisely the meaning
of *shua*. Like 'ti mian', opium lived comfortably with this Chinese socio-
cultural institution. *Shua* is yet another Chinese culture integer or law of
consumption. Opium smoking helped the Sichuanese to *shua* during the
Chinese New Year. It more importantly helped them to endure the long,
dark air-raid-filled nights during the Second World War, when only the
moon and the opium lamp shed any form of light. Like a beacon, opium
guided thousands to their destinations, as the French frigate captain R. de
Meurville recognised.

Le soir, le village dévient fantômetique. La lune, quand il y en à, est le seul luminaire: c'est le seul qui ne coute rien. Le passant s'en va, precede de porteurs de lanternes, s'il est riche; en tenant une d'une main prudente, s'il ne l'est pas – et une trique de l'autre. Des la nuit faite, la rue est morte. Les alveoles se referment, comme elles peuvent. Les seules lumières que l'on devine derrière les portes sont les discrets lumignons des lampes a opium, dont l'odeur caractèristique filtre, universelle. Les passants sont rares et se défilent craintivement le long des mûrs, car les attaques nocturnes song toujours dans le domaine des possibilités.[36]

The fragrance of opium and the flickering of the lamp guided wartime Chongqing residents, Chinese or foreign. Opium offered comfort and consolation in times of death and destruction. As the war intensified, some sank further into opium. It delivered them from everyday reality even if the experience was ephemeral. Many foreigners in China at the time enjoyed opium. Some depended on it, others made sure that they tasted it. Herbert O. Yardley, 'the father of cryptography in the United States', was one. A free agent hired by the Nationalists to break Japanese codes, Yardley endured hardship and frustration, but he did not forget there was opium:

To divert my thoughts from these depressing speculations, I asked Schwer if he had ever smoked opium. I had never done so, and it seemed improper to leave Chungking without having been in an opium den. Schwer professed to being an old hand and said it wasn't bad but that 'you sort of need a girl'.[37]

Opium was the single most important symbol of China, and experimenting with opium was a way of tasting the very essence of indigenous culture. Opium was available in many parts of the world, but it was the Chinese who perfected the art of smoking, as Schwer constantly reminded Yardley:

'Here you are', he said. 'It's simple. Hold the pipe bowl at an angle so that the flame touches the opium and suck on the pipe.'
I did as he said and took a few puffs.
'How'm I doing?'
'Just stretch out and keep at it. But it's no fun without a woman.'
. . .
'I told you opium was no good without a woman.'[38]

Schwer summarises the very essence of opium smoking. What matters is not only smoking in a Chinese den or with a few friends, but more importantly the ambience of smoking accompanied by Chinese women. From the 'court ladies' of the mid-Ming to the paste-scooping women of the late Qing and now of war-torn Chongqing, opium remained, amongst other things, an aphrodisiac.

'POPPY FLOWERS UNDER THE SUN'

No political regime of the twentieth century was free of opium, and certainly not the Communists. Whilst they undoubtedly should be credited for stamping out opium after 1949, one should take care to add them to the list of the 'opium regimes'. The Communists came across opium while on the Long March in 1934. Harrison Salisbury and John Service revisited the Long March route accompanied by General Qin Xinghan, a survivor and Director of the National Museum of Military History. Salisbury interviewed many survivors who recalled their encounter with opium:

Opium poppies were Yunnan's wealth. The Red Army confiscated enormous quantities of opium. It was the bread-and-butter of the countryside. The Red Army used it as money, trading it for supplies, or simply distributed it with a free hand to the peasants, comforting themselves with the thought that it was, after all, the product of peasant toil and sweat.[39]

Like the warlords and the Nationalists, the Red Army confiscated opium and made use of it accordingly. They needed money and supplies, and they certainly could use more support and sympathy. The army itself was made up of smokers and reformed smokers. The commander Zhu De was a reformed addict. In fact, as General Xiao Ke recalled, 'it was not possible to recruit unless the Army accepted opium addicts'.[40] The route of the Long March coincided with centres of opium production. 'Kweichow is famous for three things: hills, rain and opium', while the common saying in Yunnan was that 'out of ten men, eleven smoke opium'.[41] It was easy to defeat opium-soaked regions defended by opium-addicted soldiers. Their destination Yan'an, like Chongqing, was also deep opium country. The Shaanxi–Gansu region sits at the beginning of the Old Silk Road. It was a hub of domestic cultivation and central Asia–western China trade. A representative of the League of Nations saw opium crops in Yan'an in 1924: 'The poppy is grown within a few yards of that city's wall and that opium has been extensively and successfully grown in the district since the spring of 1918.'[42] So too did George Pereira and Edgar Snow. When Snow drove from Xi'an to Yan'an in the summer of 1936, he saw that 'opium poppies nodded their swollen heads, ready for harvest, along the newly completed motor road'.[43] Yan'an was certainly not free of opium before the Communists' arrival, and the Red Army was not about to destroy their best source of income. The Communist regime has maintained an opium-innocent face, but historians have now begun to question this position.

Chen Yongfa of Academic Sinica has pointed out that the Communist regime cultivated opium in Yan'an in order to survive the economic crisis of the 1930s and 1940s.[44] His claim makes sense. First, the Communist revolution was by nature guerrilla warfare. The Red Army was completely depleted when they reached Yan'an. They remained under-supplied and embargoed throughout their tenure there. Secondly, financing the Red Army and maintaining a central apparatus posed a huge problem, not to mention the problems of providing for the thousands of supporters who flooded in. Growing and selling opium to the Nationalists and the Japanese occupied areas would be a sound solution. Chen's evidence comes from the diary of Xie Juezai, one of the five intellectual patriarchs. His entry of 15 January 1945 tells of a meeting where he and other prominent leaders discussed the economic situation in Yan'an:

The same affair, those with humanist political view would say that they had no alternative. Mao [Zedong] once said that our party committed two mistakes. The first was that we took things from people without asking during the Long March, we won't survive without taking them; and the second was the cultivation of something; we couldn't get through the crisis without cultivating it. Those who lack humanist views considered this method advantageous; they even increased the domestic sale of this commodity.[45]

Chen argued that this 'something' that they had to 'cultivate' in order to survive was indeed opium. And he is most likely right. There is certainly a need to know more about the scale of opium production at this time and about the way in which it was sold. The Communists tried to make sure that their image was opium-clean. But there were Russians on the scene, members of the Executive Committee of the Communist International and other experts who lived and worked with their Chinese comrades. Peter Vladimirov kept a diary. His entry for 2 August 1942 reads:

Mao Tse-tung invited Yuzhin [Igor Vassilyevich] to his quarters: wanted to teach him how to play Mah-Jongg. During the game Yuzhin asked: 'Comrade Mao Tse-tung, how can it be that the peasants living in the Special Area used to be punished for the illegal traffic in opium, and now even troops and institutions headed by Communists openly engage in opium production?'

Mao Tse-tung vouchsafed no reply. The question was answered by Teng Fa [Security Chief]: 'The Special Area previously exported only salt and soda to the Kuomintang provinces. We fitted out caravans loaded with salt and brought back an undernourished purse. And only one! Now we send along an undernourished bag of opium and bring back a caravan loaded with money. The money is used for buying weapons from the Kuomintang, and with it we'll knock down the same Kuomintang!'[46]

Teng Fa justified the Red Army's cultivation and sale of opium to the enemy zones. The Communists' 'narco-economy' did not differ from that of the warlords or the Nationalists. The Communists were political beings endowed with basic instincts. Survival had turned them to whatever they could lay their hands on, as Vladimirov noted: 'Despite the blockade, the Special Area is carrying on a lively trade with the Kuomintang provinces and even with areas under Japanese occupation. From the Area come deliveries of salt, wool, and cattle, and, of late, opium in ever increasing amounts.' Vladimirov and Yuzhin were in Yan'an as *Tass* correspondents. Vladimirov was there from 1942 to 1945. He witnessed and jotted down many behind-the-scenes happenings. Trade with enemy zones went on throughout the war and even intensified towards the end, but the extent of the Communists' opium production and commerce may never come to light, as critical physical evidence may have been destroyed. The Communists knew that whoever controlled the peasants controlled China, and that whoever controlled opium could also control China. Their 'opium regime' deserves further study.

Thirty years of isolation and puritanical revolution helped the Communist regime to stamp out the three evils of opium, gambling and prostitution. They might have been successful inside China, but cultivation and consumption continued to thrive among the Chinese people of south-east Asia, especially in the Golden Triangle. Opium continued to enter China from and via this overland border region, and it continued to live among the Chinese people who lived there, as postcards show (see illustration 14). Chiang Rai, where the Golden Triangle stands, is a mecca for thousands of tourists and travellers every year. The Hall of Opium was under construction when I last visited, in 2002. Initiated by Princess Srinagarindra, late mother of the King of Thailand, the Hall is designed to teach the lessons of opium. It will undoubtedly attract more to the land of opium. The post-Mao era saw economic reform. It also saw the re-emergence of opium and its modern derivatives. 'The poppy flowers blossom again in the north and south' even as the police closed more than 700 underground dens in 1986 and destroyed 3,000,000 poppy shrubs in 1992.[47] Between 1991 and 1995 drug-related cases numbered 125,000 and criminals 189,000; the authorities confiscated 15.8 tons of heroin, 10.6 tons of opium, 3.4 tons of marijuana and 2.3 tons of frozen narcotics.[48]

The Communist regime has again been confronted with the concomitant problems of opium cultivation, trafficking and consumption. History is repeating itself. The 1999 British documentary *Shanghai Vice* explained:

Illustration 14. Thai postcards showing an opium field and an ethnic Chinese smoker in the Golden Triangle area. Opium cultivation and consumption continue among the Chinese in south-east Asia.

The buildings of Shanghai's waterfront echo with memories of the European past. For over seventy years the western powers ruled here in uneasy alliance with the Chinese underworld. Free trade and lax laws propelled an economy driven by opium and vice. Then under Mao, prostitution, gambling and opium addiction all but disappeared. Recently free trade and opportunities have returned to the city, vice has also returned fuelled not by opium but by its modern derivative heroin.

Opium's modern derivatives have come back to haunt China. Opium did not die a natural death during the Japanese war and in the thirty-year hibernation (1949–79). The Chinese people might have truly learned their lessons from history, but history alone does not make China clean of opium. What has saved China was the determination to drive out the imperialists who had humiliated and dominated the country since the Opium Wars. Today's Shanghai resembles yesterday's Shanghai. The underworld is growing. What complicates the case today is Muslim nationalism. Many of today's retailers are Chinese Muslims from the greater Xinjiang and Yunnan regions. They have networked with the suppliers of central and south-east Asia, and have also co-ordinated their activities with Muslim separatists who have intensified their campaign for independence in north-west China and Tibet.

Not only has opium come back to haunt China, but once again it has challenged the country's sovereignty. Thus far, the authorities have skilfully combined the war against opium's modern derivatives with the war against secession. China knows that the old imperialists are on its side in the crusade against drugs, and it also understands that its new platform is freedom and democracy. The events of September 11th have pushed China closer to the West in the common struggle against Islamic fundamentalism, but the war on terror has distanced the Chinese people. The social life of opium continues in the twenty-first century. A century of unequal treaties, 1842–1949, saw opium's institutionalisation in Chinese politics, economics, international relations and in Chinese culture and society. Never before had so many foreign players been involved in the making of Chinese history. Never before had opium lived so modern and political a social life. Opium has survived the destruction of two empires, the eras of the warlords and the Republicans and the ruthless campaign of the Communist regime. It seems true that 'What the Revolution in China wiped out, Reform brought back'.[49] The story of opium echoes the famous Chinese saying: 'Not even a prairie fire can destroy the grass; it grows again when the spring breeze blows.'

Conclusion

Opium has had 'a tenacious hold' on China over the past five hundred years, with the exception of the thirty-year hibernation (1949–79).[1] Since its epoch-making transformation, it has lived a social life unlike that of any other commodity. This book has set opium in its social and cultural contexts and has shown how the Chinese people developed a complex culture of consumption around its use. From the late fifteenth century up to the late twentieth century and indeed beyond, opium has been embedded in the changes that have taken place in China and also in its continuity. Mary Rankin, John K. Fairbank and Albert Feuerwerker believe that 'efforts to find a simple progression or a single key to the dynamics of all this change founder in the face of the size and geographical diversity of the country, differences of local social organisation, and unevenness of development in different spheres'.[2] This book calls such a statement into question. The social life of opium is a 'simple progression' and the 'key' that is opium allows us to understand many aspects of Chinese history from 1483 to 1999. No single paradigm, imperialism or China-centred, can single-handedly explain Chinese history; indeed, the story of opium reinforces this conviction. The introduction and naturalisation of opium smoking took both exogenous and endogenous forces. Chinese people of different classes, times and regions all contributed to the opium culture of consumption and to the institution that opium became. This book complements our common knowledge of opium and of modern China.

The art of alchemists, sex and court ladies opens our eyes to the court culture and medicinal science of the Ming. The studies of Robert Hans van Gulick and Joseph Needham have pointed to sophisticated sex practices. Opium sheds light on this subject. Opium's medicine-to-aphrodisiac transformation was its 'diversion'. We have seen how opium was diverted from its 'customary paths' and the 'irregular desires and novel demands'. The Ming court was behind this metamorphosis, which shaped the history of China for the next five hundred years. The importance of royal consumption is clearly underlined here. Although there were more 'diversions' on opium's road to St Louis, its aphrodisiac personality stayed with it; indeed, opium would enhance the art of sex and would galvanise the recreation industry. Opium came to China at an opportune moment, when the cultures of tobacco, snuff bottles, tea, cuisine, herbs and curios were laying down a solid foundation for its use. Opium exposed what I call China's political and genealogical intimacy with south and south-east Asia. China dictated the rules of exchange, as vassal states tried to please the country's elite with their best indigenous produce, such as opium. Historians of east and south-east Asia have laboured separately. The story of opium integrates their perspectives and points a way forward for this study. The ultimate significance of maritime trade is seen through its social and cultural consequences. Merchants and labourers to and from south-east Asia brought tobacco back to China. They also introduced opium. Yet their impact went beyond the shores where they sojourned. These men changed consumer behaviour and helped to shape history. A China-centred paradigm of study may flourish, but the story of opium has directed our attention to the dynamics at work when external and internal forces meet. Cross-language, cross-class and cross-continent mechanisms of culture transmission invite further systematic study.

Foreign smugglers only delivered opium to the Chinese coast. It needed the Chinese themselves to transport and distribute it to the vast interior. When the pipe passed from princes to eunuchs, Chinese smugglers carried opium to the four corners of the empire. These people had a unique role to play in the Ming–Qing economy, its culture and society. And they were instrumental in the quick spread of opium, because their guildhalls were the rendezvous for native scholars, officials, students and hangers-on. The inland march of opium complements the history of the opium trade itself. We see the dynamic of exogenous and endogenous forces in the making and coming of the opium consumer trend. Opium opens the discussion of *yanghuo*, a topic no historian has written about. The Chinese desire for foreign commodities and 'habits' has its origins in maritime trade and diplomacy. Although the Chinese called foreigners barbarians, they appreciated what the barbarians had to offer – tobacco, the peanut, fragrances, birds nests, singsongs and opium. This teaches us much about rhetoric and reality. Foreign 'stuff' was rare, expensive and a status symbol. It was an indicator of the sophistication of Ming–Qing elite culture and of urban society. Although domestic cultivation had started as early as 1805, opium did not repeat the quick naturalisation of tobacco because the Chinese craving for foreign stuff had partially kept the production of domestic opium in check. This is even more extraordinary in view of the fact that tobacco was completely new to China, whereas opium had been used as a herbal medicine since at least the Tang dynasty. A comprehensive study of *yanghuo* will help us to better understand the Ming–Qing–Republican economy, its culture and society.

Opium paints a detailed picture of the Chinese elite – the scholars, the officials and the moral guardians of the Chinese people. On the one hand, they read, philosophised and ruled; on the other, they gossiped, smoked and led sexually fulfilled lives. These men were the 'message-sending' and 'production-moulding' force of culture and consumption. Opium smoking was not 'a vice that the enlightened Chinese wishes to stamp out'; it was a tradition that they fashioned and indeed maintained for several centuries. Many wrote nostalgically about their own experiences of opium and sex. We must read more about them in their private capacities in order to comprehend how they shaped history. The elite converged in the cities and spread the gospel of opium as they dispersed to their home-towns or workplaces. They and their institutions were the agents and agencies of culture transmission. Opium enlightens us about social control. Mrs Archibald Little observed the social life of opium: 'With opium-dens all over the place, with exquisite opium-pipes and all the coquetries of opium-trays and other accessories in the houses of the rich, how is it that we all give warning to a servant when we hear that he has taken to opium? How is it that the treasure on a journey is never confided to a coolie who smokes?'[3] Like alcohol in the West, opium smoking challenged authority. When scholars and officials smoked, opium was cultured and a status symbol, but when the lower classes began to lie down, opium became degrading and ultimately criminal. What political redefinition achieved was obvious; it brought out a sense of resignation, as domestic cultivation, smuggling and consumption proliferated in the post-Opium War years and led to the rapid outward and downward 'liquidation' or 'extensification' of consumption.

Opium enriches our understanding of Chinese women. Women contributed to the making of the aphrodisiac myth. They also helped to write the legacy of opium. They had a special relationship with opium. On the one hand, opium victimised them and intensified their stratification. On the other, it gave them a tool of survival and upward mobility, as many helped feed themselves and their families with its help. This demonstrates the flexibility, capability and consequently the power of Chinese women. Opium highlights their role in the Chinese economy, and in Chinese culture and society. 'Language is of critical importance in cultural transmission.' Opium-generated literature was yet another mechanism or agent of culture transmission. David Johnson has discussed the gap between a diverse spoken language and a unified written language, and has emphasised that the first serves as a denominator of social differentiation while the second serves as a force for cultural integration.[4] The opium literature of the late Qing–Republican era helped to erase 'differentiation' and to fashion a unified code of smoking. This contributed to the golden age of opium and more importantly to the 'McDonaldization' of consumption. Sidney Mintz has positioned sugar in industrial Britain. Thomas Brennan has placed public drinking in pre-revolutionary Paris. David Christian has set vodka at the eve of revolutionary Russia. I have situated opium at the dawn of the Chinese revolution. All these commodities and the consumptions of them have undergone social change. All demonstate a similarity of stimulus and the same pattern of class formation.

Opium reveals what I call a Chinese law of consumption. It lived in harmony with Chinese social values and cultural practices. Indeed, smoking and serving opium came to involve one of the most important virtues of the Chinese people – 'ti mian'. This socio-cultural sanction dictated how people lived, socialised and, in the case of opium, how a product was consumed. 'Conspicuous consumption' had arrived, and opium exposed the 'conspicuous' nature of the Chinese consumer culture. The late Qing–Republican era saw the zenith of the opium material culture, as many came to perfect the art and craft of smoking. Opium earned China a new national identity and distinguished the Chinese people on the global stage. This drives home the conviction that consumption has an identity value. Indeed, we must now move away from a 'production-oriented explanation of society' in our efforts to comprehend consumer culture and social change. Opium educates us about phases of consumption. Opium smoking lived through five important phases: myth-making in the mid- and late Ming; taste-making in the early and mid-Qing; political redefinition in the late 1830s; 'extensification' in the interwar years; and 'McDonaldization' in the late Qing–Republican era. These phases allow us to see the journey of opium and the life histories of its consumption. Phases of consumption raise an important question about the ways in which we conduct our studies of consumption and social change. It is obvious that many historians have begun their studies of opium in the political redefinition phase and that they have stayed at this phase. We must look before and beyond this phase, however, even the framework of history as the 'genealogical method of anthropological inquiry' tells the story of opium.

Finally, this book puts the Communists in perspective. Opium-generated revenues helped to quell rebellions and to restore the Manchu regime.

Opium served the Qing reformers, the warlords, gangsters, rebels, the Nationalists, the Japanese and also the Communists. When opium became deeply entrenched in Chinese life, it also became inseparable from the political economy. Regardless of their moral pretensions, political regimes had to survive. Opium has outlived all the political regimes that it helped to shape and break, including that of the Communists. The Communists are indeed one of the 'opium regimes', despite their success in the thirty-year hibernation. Furthermore, it is important to understand the relationship between the Communists and opium, and not just because the Communist Revolution was conceived and materialised in the struggle against the imperialists who embodied the evils of the opium trade, the Opium Wars and the unequal treaties. Joseph Esherick argues this:

in all of these changes – political, economic, cultural, demographic, and environmental – the Chinese Revolution has played a crucial role in the transformative process. But in the end, these historical processes are larger than the revolution, and it will be necessary to subordinate the history of the revolution to these larger patterns of change. Only then can we escape the teleology of revolution and gain an understanding of China's past that provides a better key to understanding its present.[5]

Opium is one historical process that is larger than the revolution. It started centuries before the revolution, and it has survived it. It has been evolving along with Chinese international relations, Chinese culture, the Chinese economy, Chinese politics and Chinese society for the past five hundred years. Opium is a fruitful optic through which to look at China's capacity and complexity.

Notes

INTRODUCTION

1 Arjun Appadurai, 'Introduction: Commodities and the Politics of Value', in Appadurai (ed.), *Social Life of Things*, pp. 3–63; Kopytoff, 'Cultural Biography of Things', pp. 64–91.
2 Xu, *Yinjing Juan*, vol. X, pp. 14–15.
3 Roche, *History of Everyday Things*, p. 7.
4 Ibid., p. 194.
5 Ibid.
6 Ibid., p. 5.
7 Bourdieu, *Distinction*, introduction.
8 Ibid.
9 Atkins and Bowler, *Food in Society*, p. 7.
10 Baudrillard, *Consumer Society*, pp. 58–61 and 79.
11 Ibid, p. 78.
12 Lee Cassanelli, '*Qat*: Changes in the Production and Consumption of a Quasi-legal Commodity in Northeast Africa', and C. A. Bayly, 'The Origin of Swadeshi (Home Industry): Cloth and Indian Society, 1700–1930', in Appadurai (ed.), *Social Life of Things*, pp. 236–57 and 285–321.
13 Mary Douglas, 'A Distinctive Anthropological Perspective', in Douglas (ed.), *Constructive Drinking*, pp. 3–15.
14 Dwight Heath, 'A Decade of *Development* in the Anthropological Study of Alcohol Use: 1970–1980', in Douglas (ed.), *Constructive Drinking*, pp. 16–69.
15 Douglas, 'Distinctive Anthropological Perspective', p. 4.
16 Brennan, *Public Drinking and Popular Culture*, introduction.
17 Lupton, *Food, the Body and the Self*, introduction.
18 Ibid., p. 22.
19 Ritzer, *McDonaldization of Society*, introduction.
20 Atkins and Bowler, *Food in Society*, pp. 3–15.
21 Ibid.
22 Brennan, *Public Drinking and Popular Culture*, introduction.
23 Ibid.
24 Zhou, *QiZhen Yecheng*, vol. 1, preface.
25 Beasley and Pulleyblank (eds.), *Historians of China and Japan*, p. 5.

26 Evelyn S. Rawski, 'Concluding Perspectives', in Johnson, Nathan and Rawski (eds.), *Popular Culture in Late Imperial China*, pp. 399–417.

27 Holt, *Opium Wars in China*, p. 67.

28 Rawski, 'Research Themes in Ming-Qing Socioeconomic History', 84–111.

CHAPTER I   'THE ART OF ALCHEMISTS,
SEX AND COURT LADIES'

1 Xu, *Yinjing Juan*, pp. 14–15.

2 Yong Tao, 'Xigui Chu Xiegu', in Zhonghua (ed.), *Quan Tang Shi*, vol. DXVIII, p. 5923.

3 Su Shi, *Su Shi Shiji*, vol. XXV, p. 1347.

4 Needham, *Science and Civilisation in China*, vol. V, p. 198.

5 Huang, *1587, a Year of No Significance*.

6 Zhang (ed.), *Ming Shi*, vol. CXIII, pp. 3524–5.

7 Frederick W. Mote, 'The Ch'eng-hua and Hung-chih Reigns, 1465–1505', in Mote and Twitchett (eds.), *Cambridge History of China*, vol. VII, pp. 348 and 9–105.

8 Shen, *Wanli Yehuo Bian*, vol. II, p. 541.

9 Zhongyang (ed.), *Ming Xiaozong Shilu*, vol. II, pp. 9A–11A.

10 Zhang (ed.), *Ming Shi*, vol. CXIII, pp. 3524–5.

11 Gulick, *Erotic Colour Prints*, vol. I, p. 105.

12 Mote, 'Ch'eng-hua and Hung-chih Reigns', p. 365.

13 Wang, *Gubugu Lu*, p. 11.

14 Li and Shen (eds.), *Da Ming Huidian*, vol. CV, pp. 9B–11B, pp. 13A–15A and vol. CVI, pp. 5B–6B.

15 Yu, *Guisi Leigao*, vol. XIV, pp. 521–4.

16 Ibid.

17 Zhongyang (ed.), *Ming Shenzong Shilu*, vol. CCXII, pp. 3983–4.

18 Goodrich and Fang (eds.), *Dictionary of Ming Biography*, pp. 324–37.

19 Jin Lei, 'Rongcheng Xianhua', in Qi and Lin (eds.), *Yapian Zhanzheng*, vol. I, pp. 313–39.

20 Wang, *Jindu Shijian*, p. 15.

21 Li, *Bencao Gangmu*, vol. XXIII, p. 1495.

22 Gao, *Zunsheng Bajian*, vol. XVIII, pp. 55B–56A, vol. XVI, p. 19A and vol. XVII, p. 37B.

23 Zhang, *Jingyue Quanshu*, vol. LIX, pp. 1717–22.

24 Zhang, *Benjing Fengyuan*, vol. III, p. 857.

25 Wang, *Yifang Jijie*, vol. XVII, p. 248.

26 Smith, 'Gardens in Ch'i Piao-chia's Social World', 55–81.

27 Chen, *Bencao Mengquan*, vol. V, p. 5A.

28 Xu, *Gujin Yitong Daquan*, vol. XCVIII, p. 3A.

29 Ibid., vol. XCVII, pp. 26B and 30A–B.

30 Gu, *Bencao Huijian*, vol. VII, pp. 7B–8B.

31 Gao, *Beishu Baowenglu*, pp. 22A–B.

32 Fang, *Wuli Xiaoshi*, vol. IX, pp. 22A–B.
33 Arjun Appadurai, 'Introduction: Commodities and the Politics of Value', in Appadurai (ed.), *Social Life of Things*, pp. 3–63; Kopytoff, 'Cultural Biography of Things', pp. 64–91.

CHAPTER 2   AS THE EMPIRE CHANGED HANDS

 1 Timothy Brook, 'Communication and Commerce', in Twitchett and Mote (eds.), *Cambridge History of China*, vol. VII, pp. 579–707.
 2 Zhang, *Jingyue Quanshu*, vol. XLVIII, p. 44B.
 3 Zheng, 'Cong Guangxi Hepu Mingdai', 383–7 and 391.
 4 Ping-ti Ho, 'The Introduction of American Food Plants to China', in MacLeod and Rawski (eds.), *European Intruders*, pp. 283–94.
 5 Zeng, *Zeng Yuwang Riji*, p. 4.
 6 Ye, *Yueshi Bian*, vol. VII, p. 167.
 7 Lu Yao, 'Lu Shu', in Yuan (ed.), *Zhongguo Xiyan Shihua*, p. 40.
 8 Cong Chen, 'Yancao Pu', in Yuan (ed.), *Zhongguo Xiyan Shihua*, p. 87.
 9 Bell, *Journey from St Petersburg to Pekin*, p. 167.
10 Hentzner, *Travels in England*, pp. 29–30.
11 Mintz, *Sweetness and Power*, introduction.
12 Ibid., p. 93.
13 Veblen, *Theory of the Leisure Class*, pp. 68–101.
14 Bourdieu, *Distinction*, introduction.
15 Mintz, *Sweetness and Power*, pp. 183, 122, 151–2 and 173–4.
16 Wang, *Xiangzu Biji*, vol. III, p. 45.
17 Lee, 'Trade and Economy in Preindustrial East Asia, 2–26.
18 Wang, *Xiangzu Biji*, vol. VII, p. 131.
19 Xiang Mao, 'Yingmeiyan Yiyu', in Wang (ed.), *Shuo Ku*, pp. 6B–7A.
20 Levi-Strauss, *The Raw and the Cooked*, p. 336.
21 Lupton, *Food, the Body and the Self*, introduction.
22 Roche, *History of Everyday Things*, p. 7.
23 Linschoten, *Voyage to the East Indies*, pp. 157–8.
24 Tang, *Sanxian Zhengshu*, vol. II, p. 918.
25 Huai Yu, 'Banqiao Zaji', in Wang and Yu (eds.), *Yanshi Congchao*, p. 1A.
26 Ko, *Teachers of the Inner Chamber*, p. 152.

CHAPTER 3   'THE AGE OF CALICOES AND
TEA AND OPIUM'

 1 Blusse, 'No Boats to China', 51–76.
 2 C. A. Bayly, '"Archaic" and "Modern" Globalisation in the Eurasian and African Arena, *c.* 1750–1850', in Hopkins (ed.), *Globalisation in World History*, pp. 47–73.
 3 Greenlee (trans.), *Voyage of Pedro Alvares Cabral*, pp. 92 and 94, and Pires, *Suma Oriental of Tome Pires*, vol. II, p. 513.

4 Mundy, *Travels in Europe and Asia*, vol. II, pp. 247, 157 and 217.
5 Lockyer, *Account of the Trade in India*, pp. 60–1.
6 Stavorinus, *Voyages to the East-Indies*, vol. I, pp. 474–5.
7 Scott, *An Exact Discourse*, p. 173.
8 Anthony Reid, 'From Betel-Chewing to Tobacco Smoking in Indonesia', in MacLeod and Rawski (eds.), *European Intruders*, pp. 295–313.
9 Colenbrander (compiler), *Dagh-Register Gehouden int Casteel Batavia vant Passerende als over Geheel Nederlandts-India Anno 1636*, pp. 59, 61 and 64.
10 Zhang, *Dong Xi Yang Kao*, pp. 96–7.
11 Prakash, *Dutch East India Company and the Economy of Bengal*, pp. 145–57.
12 *Royal Commission on Opium*, vol. I, appendix II.
13 Reid, *Shape of Early Modern Southeast Asia*, pp. 241–3.
14 Lan, *Pingtai Jilue*, p. 50.
15 Huang, *Taihai Shicha Lu*, vol. II, p. 43.
16 Zhu, *Haidong Zhaji*, p. 29.
17 Gugong (ed.), *Gongzhongdang Yongzhengchao Zouzhe*, vol. XIII, pp. 750–2.
18 Yin and Zhang, *Aomen Zhilue*, p. 58B.
19 China supercargoes (ship's) diary, 1596–1840, British Library, East India Company Factory Records: China and Japan, 1996–1840, G/12/34, fos. 81–3 and G/12/35, fos. 1–2.
20 Nagtegaal, *Riding the Dutch Tiger*, pp. 143–7.
21 Stavorinus, *Voyages to the East-Indies*, vol. I, p. 295, Blusse, *Strange Company*, p. 31.
22 Trocki, *Opium, Empire*, p. 62.
23 Ibid., p. 48.
24 Greenberg, *British Trade and the Opening of China*, p. 18.
25 Canton diary, 18 March to 28 December 1782, British Library, East India Company Factory Records, China and Japan: 1596–1840, G/12/75, fo. 21; Canton consultation, 22 March 1782 to 2 January 1783, G/12/76, fos. 44–6, 46–8, 48–51, 51–3, 53–6, 56–8 and 58–62.
26 Huang, *Yuqiu Yaojie*, vol. VIII, p. 1098.
27 Zhao, *Bencao Gangmu Shiyi*, vol. V, p. 156.
28 Zhuquan Jushi, 'Xu Banqiao Zaji', in Wang and Yu, *Yanshi Congchao*, p. 2A.
29 Zhang, *Tao'an Mengyi*, vol. IV, p. 43.
30 Penghuasheng, 'Huafang Yutan', in Wang and Yu, *Yanshi Congchao*, p. 7B.
31 Ibid., p. 11A.
32 Shen, *Fusheng Liuji*, pp. 45–6.
33 Kopytoff, 'Cultural Biography of Things, pp. 64–91.
34 Yu, *Meng'an Zazhu*, vol. X, p. 372.
35 Dermigny (ed.), *Mémoires de Charles de Contant*, p. 205.
36 Staunton, *Authentic Account of an Embassy*, vol. II, p. 70.
37 Barrow, *Travels in China*, pp. 29 and 152–3.
38 Cranmer-Byng, *Embassy to China*, pp. 260–1.
39 Pomeranz, *Great Divergence*, p. . . .

40　Da Manzhoudiguo (ed.), *Da Qing Lichao Shilu: Gaozong*, vol. MCXLIII, p. 31.
41　Wakeman, *Fall of Imperial China*, p. 1.
42　Waley-Cohen, *Sextants of Beijing*, p. 4.
43　Brook, *Confusions of Pleasure*, p. 11.

CHAPTER 4　'A HOBBY AMONG THE HIGH AND
THE LOW IN OFFICIALDOM'

1　The quotation that forms the title of the chapter is taken from Lianfen Dai, 'Libianxuan Zhiyan', in Xiao (ed.), *Qingshuo Qizhong*, p. 57.
2　Aixinjueluo, *Yangzheng Shuwu Quanji Dingben*, vol. XVII, p. 22B.
3　Ibid., p. 23A.
4　Diyi Lishi (ed.), *Dang'an Shiliao*, vol. I, pp. 102–5.
5　Da Manzhoudiguo (ed.), *Da Qing Lichao Shilu: Renzong*, vol. CCLXX, p. 12.
6　Veblen, *Theory of the Leisure Class*, p. 68.
7　Ibid., p. 78.
8　Jonathan D. Spence, 'Opium Smoking in Ch'ing China', in Wakeman and Grant (eds.), *Conflict and Control in Late Imperial China*, pp. 143–73.
9　Barrow, *Travels in China*, pp. 231–2.
10　Dermigny (ed.), *Memoires de Charles de Contant*, p. 207.
11　*Royal Commission on Opium*, vol. I, p. 1388.
12　Ibid., vol. I, p. 1667.
13　Rush, 'Opium in Java', 549–60.
14　Deborah F. Greenwald and David W. Harder, 'Domains of Shame: Evolutionary, Cultural, and Psychotherapeutic Aspects', in Gilbert and Andrews (eds.), *Shame*, pp. 225–45.
15　Benedict, *The Chrysanthemum and the Sword*, pp. 156–7.
16　Zhang, *Qingdai Yeji*, vol. III, pp. 143–6.
17　Shi, *Min Zaji*, pp. 137–8.
18　Liang, *Liangban Qiuyu'an Suibi*, vol. IV, pp. 1A–B.
19　Bao, *Anwu Sizong*, vol. XXVI, p. 6A.
20　Zhu and Gu (eds.), *Yancao Lu*, p. 188.
21　Yue Huang, 'Yinpeng', in Qi and Lin (eds.), *Yapian Zhanzheng*, p. 317.
22　Diyi Lishi (ed.), *Dang'an Shiliao*, vol. I, pp. 13–15.
23　Sirr, *China and the Chinese*, vol. I, p. 138.
24　Ahee, undated, Cambridge University Library, Jardine Matheson Papers, large-sized Chinese language material.
25　Scarth, *Twelve Years in China*, pp. 72–3.
26　Zhou, *Siyitang Rizha*, pp. 251–2.
27　Peng (ed.), *Hengyang Xianzhi*, vol. XI, pp. 6A–B.
28　Milburn, *Oriental Commerce*, vol. II, pp. 219–20, 461–546.
29　Robert Taylor to Cruttenden MacKillop, 4 November 1818, Cambridge University Library, Jardine Matheson Papers, C1/1, fo. 10.
30　Morse, *Chronicles of the East India Company Trading to China*, vol. III, p. 259.
31　Abel, *Journey in the Interior of China*, pp. 214–15.

CHAPTER 5 TASTE-MAKING AND TRENDSETTING

1 'Journal of Occurrences', *Chinese Repository* II, 4 (1834), 574.
2 Greenberg, *British Trade and the Opening of China*, appendix 1.
3 Liang, *Tui'an Suibi*, vol. VII, pp. 371–2.
4 Waley-Cohen, *Sextants of Beijing*, p. 4.
5 Milburn, *Oriental Commerce*, vol. II, p. 479.
6 Linda C. Johnson, 'Shanghai: An Emerging Jiangnan Port, 1683–1840', in Johnson (ed.), *Cities of Jiangnan*, pp. 151–81.
7 Wu and Yao, *Shanghaixian Xuzhi*, vol. III, p. 6A.
8 Xu Cui, 'Ningtang Zhuzhici', in Lei (ed.), *Zhonghua Zhuzhici*, vol. I, p. 449.
9 Da Manzhoudiguo, *Da Qing Lichao Shilu: Xuanzong*, vol. XXIX, p. 24B.
10 Hu, *Dou Cun*, vol. III, p. 6B.
11 Zhangshen Yang, 'Jingchen Zalu', in Lidai (ed.), *Biji Xiaoshuo Daguan*, vol. II, pp. 1A–4A.
12 Anonymous (Que Ming), 'Yanjing Zaji', in Qu (ed.), *Beijing Lishi Fengtuo Congshu*, p. 119.
13 Zhao, *Yanpu Zaji*, vol. II, p. 37.
14 Naquin, *Peking*, p. 635.
15 Veblen, *Theory of the Leisure Class*, p. 70.
16 Ibid., p. 74.
17 Bourdieu, *Distinction*, 11.
18 Lupton, *Food, the Body and the Self*, pp. 94–5.
19 Bourdieu, *Distinction*, p. 13.
20 Mintz, *Sweetness and Power*, pp. 122, 151–2 and 173–4.
21 Peng, *Yuzhou Jitan*, vol. I, p. 63.
22 Xu, *Sanyi Bitan*, vol. II, pp. 48–9.
23 Guisheng Zhao, 'Xiti Yapian Yan', in Wang (ed.), *Tingyulou Suibi*, vol. VI, p. 341.
24 Yuanpu Ru, 'Buxi Yapian', in Wang (ed.), *Tingyulou Suibi*, vol. V, p. 328 and Songlin Li, 'Yapian Yan', in ibid., vol. VI, p. 346.
25 Pan, *Daoting Tushuo*, vol. II, pp. 30–2.
26 John R. Watt, 'The Yamen and Urban Administration', in Skinner (ed.), *City in Late Imperial China*, pp. 353–90.
27 Naquin and Rawski, *Chinese Society in the Eighteenth Century*, p. 56.
28 Ibid.
29 Da Manzhoudiguo, *Da Qing Lichao Shilu: Xuanzong*, vol. CLXXXIV, pp. 23A–B.
30 Ibid., vol. CXCII, pp. 5A–B.
31 Zhaotang Li, 'Luanhou Jisuoji', in Zhongguo (ed.), *Jindaishi Zilao*, vol. XXXIV, pp. 177–86.
32 Naquin, *Peking*, pp. 171–204 and 622–38.
33 Barbara E. Ward, 'Regional Operas and their Audiences: Evidence from Hong Kong', in Johnson, Nathan and Rawski (eds.), *Popular Culture in Late Imperial China*, pp. 161–87.

34 Qian, *Luyuan Conghua*, p. 26.
35 Cheng, *Cheng Silang Yiji*, vol. IV, p. 2A.
36 'Nest of Opium Smokers', *Chinese Repository*, IV, 7 (1835), 342.
37 Holman, *Voyage Round the World*, vol. IV, pp. 83–4.
38 Arjun Appadurai, 'Introduction: Commodities and the Politics of Value', in Appadurai (ed.), *Social Life of Things*, pp. 3–63.

CHAPTER 6   THE POLITICAL REDEFINITION OF
OPIUM CONSUMPTION

1 'Journal of Occurrences', *Chinese Repository*, II, 12 (1834), 574.
2 Greenberg, *British Trade and the Opening of China*, p. 191.
3 James Matheson to B. C. Wilcocks, 8 March 1837, Cambridge University Library, Jardine Matheson Archive, C5/2, fo. 51.
4 Greenberg, *British Trade and the Opening of China*, appendix 1.
5 Brennan, *Public Drinking and Popular Culture*, introduction.
6 Xu, *Sanyi Bitan*, pp. 48–9.
7 Diyi Lishi, *Dang'an Shiliao*, vol. 1, pp. 123–4.
8 Da Manzhoudiguo, *Da Qing Lichao Shilu: Xuanzong*, vol. CCLXIV, pp. 41–2.
9 Ibid., vol. CCCVII, p. 11A.
10 Ibid.
11 Brennan, *Public Drinking and Popular Culture*, introduction.
12 Lee Cassanelli, 'Qat: Changes in the Production and Consumption of a Quasilegal Commodity in Northeast Africa', in Appadurai (ed.), *Social Life of Things*, pp. 236–57.
13 Hao, *Commercial Revolution*, pp. 121–3.
14 Diyi Lishi, *Dang'an Shiliao*, vol. 1, pp. 284–6.
15 Da Manzhou diguo, *Shilu: Xuanzong*, vol. CCXVIII, p. 17A.
16 Ibid., vol. CCXVIII, pp. 28–9.
17 Yue Huang, 'Yinpeng', in Qi and Lin (eds.), *Yapian Zhanzheng*, p. 317.
18 Smedt (ed.), *Chinese Erotism*, p. 86.
19 Fairbank, *Trade and Diplomacy on the China Coast*, p. 63.
20 Hao, *Commercial Revolution*, pp. 1 and 112.
21 'Admonitory Pictures', *Chinese Repository*, V, 12 (1837), 571–3.
22 Fry, *Facts and Evidences*, p. 2.
23 Graham, *Right, Obligation and Interest of the Government of Great Britain to Request Redress from the Government of China*.
24 Warren, *Opium Question*, p. 107.
25 Diyi Lishi, *Dang'an Shiliao*, vol. 1, pp. 255–7.
26 Ibid., pp. 201–2.
27 'Journal of Occurrences', *Chinese Repository*, V, 3 (1836), 138.
28 Downing, *Fan-Qui's Visit to the Celestial Empire*, vol. III, p. 182.
29 Ouchterlony, *Chinese War*, p. 5.
30 Jiang, *Qijinglou Wenchao*, vol. IV, pp. 125–6.
31 Gong, *Gong Zizhen Quanji*, vol. 1, p. 106.

32 Gugong (ed.), *Daoguang Qijuzhu*, vol. LIII, pp. 031307–031308.
33 'Military Skill and Power of the Chinese', *Chinese Repository*, V, 5 (1836), 165–78.
34 Tiffany, *Canton Chinese*, pp. 178–9.
35 *Royal Commission on Opium*, vol. I, p. 503.
36 Williams, *Middle Kingdom: A Survey of the Chinese Empire*, vol. II, p. 383.
37 *Royal Commission on Opium*, vol. I, p. 532.
38 Liang, *Yingbingshi Heji*, vol. II, pp. 58–67.
39 Sun, *Sun Zhongshan Quanji*, vol. I, pp. 1–2.
40 R. Bin Wong, 'Opium and Modern Chinese State-Making', in Brook and Wakabayashi (eds.), *Opium Regimes*, pp. 189–211.
41 Mao, *Mao Zedong Xuanji*, vol. II, pp. 626–32.

CHAPTER 7   OUTWARD AND DOWNWARD
'LIQUIDATION'

1 The reference to 'liquidation' in the chapter title above is taken from Kopytoff, 'Cultural Biography of Things', pp. 64–91.
2 Hao, *Commercial Revolution*, pp. 121–3.
3 Holman, *Voyage Round the World*, vol. IV, pp. 89–90.
4 Diyi Lishi, *Dang'an Shiliao*, vol. I, pp. 77–9.
5 Da Manzhoudiguo, *Da Qing Lichao Shilu: Xuanzong*, vol. CXCI, pp. 32B–33A.
6 Ibid., vol. CXCVIII, pp. 2B–3A.
7 Ibid., vol. CXCVIII, pp. 1B–2A.
8 Zhang, *Daoxian Huanhai Jianwenlu*, p. 214.
9 Peng, *Yuzhou Jitan*, vol. I, p. 68.
10 Inspector General of Customs, *China Imperial Maritime Customs* II, special series no. 9, *Native Opium, 1887*, pp. 48–9.
11 Inspector General of Customs, *China Imperial Maritime Customs* II, special series no. 4, *Opium*, p. 79.
12 Litton to Principal Secretary of State for Foreign Affairs, 11 July 1903, PRO, Foreign Office Papers, 17/1728, fos. 1–2, 3–10, 13, 15, 16, 22–4, 29–30, 261–5, 266–9 and 307–9.
13 A correspondent, 'American Influence on the Destines of ultra-Malayan Asia', *Chinese Repository*, VII, 6 (1838), 80.
14 Owen, *British Opium Policy*, p. 192.
15 Allen, *Opium Trade*, pp. 14–15.
16 Smith, *Narrative of an Exploratory Visit*, p. 275.
17 Ibid., p. 130.
18 Davis, *China during the War*, vol. II, p. 204.
19 Christopher Munn, 'The Hong Kong Opium Revenue, 1845–1885', in Brook and Wakabayashi (eds.), *Opium Regimes*, pp. 105–26.
20 'Journal of occurrences', *Chinese Repository*, XIII, 10 (1844), 560; XIV, 11 (1845), 544; and XVI, 4 (1847), 179.
21 Hao, *Commercial Revolution*, pp. 123–34.

22 Owen, *British Opium Policy*, pp. 199–200.
23 Morse, *International Relations of the Chinese Empire*, p. 556.
24 Huc, *Chinese Empire*, vol. I, p. 27.
25 Giersch, 'Motley throng', 67–94.
26 Etherton, *Crisis in China*, p. 213.
27 Davis, *China during the War*, vol. II, pp. 202–3.
28 Hoppo to Ye Mingchen, 12 October 1852, PRO, Guangdong Provincial Archive, FO 931/1356, fo. 1.
29 Qi and Lin (eds.), *Di'erci Yapian Zhanzheng*, vol. I, p. 404.
30 Allen, *Opium Trade*, p. 42.
31 Ibid., p. 39.
32 Smith, *Narrative of an Exploratory Visit*, p. 431.
33 A correspondent, 'Men and Things from Shanghai', *Chinese Repository*, XIX, 2 (1850), 108–9.
34 Mao, *Moyu Lu*, vol. VII, pp. 104–5.
35 Wang, *Wang Tao Riji*, pp. 22–3.
36 Allen, *Opium Trade*, pp. 27–8.
37 Ibid., p. 42.
38 Sirr, *China and the Chinese*, vol. I, p. 221.
39 Smith, *Narrative of an Exploratory Visit*, p. 434.
40 Jocelyn, *Six Months with the Chinese Expedition*, p. 39.
41 Naquin, *Peking*, p. 600.
42 Jin and Zhang (eds.), *Nanhui Xianzhi*, vol. XX, p. 6A.
43 Liu and Chou (eds.), *Taigu Xianzhi*, vol. III, pp. 321–2.
44 Chen, *Bibin Zaji*, p. 33.
45 Davis, *China during the War*, vol. II, p. 202.

CHAPTER 8 'THE VOLUME OF SMOKE AND POWDER'

1 The quotation that forms the title of the chapter is taken from Lu (ed.), *Yanfen Juan*.
2 Henriot, *Prostitution and Sexuality in Shanghai*, pp. 73–98.
3 Kangnian Wang, 'Zhuangxie Xuanlu', in Wang (ed.), *Jindu Shijian*, pp. 24–5.
4 Little, *Intimate China*, pp. 178–9.
5 Penghua Sheng, 'Qinhuai Huafanglu', in Wang and Yu (ed.), *Yanshi Congchao*, p. 241.
6 Huanyuan Xu, 'Chennan Caotang Biji', in Lu (ed.), *Yanfen Juan*, p. 445.
7 Enshou Yang, 'Lanzhi Lingxianglu', in Lei (ed.), *Qingren Shuohui*, pp. 404–5.
8 Sheng Zhou, 'Yangzhou Meng', in Wang (ed.), *Shuo kuo* vol. I, p. 9B.
9 Antonia Finnane, 'Yangzhou, a Central Place in the Qing Empire', in Johnson (ed.), *Cities of Jiangnan*, pp. 117–49.
10 Xiao (ed.), *Shehui Baixiang*, pp. 47–8.
11 Tao Wang, 'Songying Manlu', in Lu (ed.), *Yanfen Juan*, pp. 388–9.
12 *Royal Commission on Opium*, vol. I, p. 519.
13 'Fulu Xiaoxiaoshanren Yanguan Yuejuan Jishi', *Shen Bao*, 19 April, 1897, 163.

14 Lu, *Beyond the Neon Lights*, p. 182.
15 Gamble, *Peking*, p. 247.
16 Sergeant, *Shanghai*, plate 37.
17 Yu, *Youtaixianguan Biji*, vol. XI, p. 292.
18 Mann, 'Widows in the Kinship, Class, and Community Structure', 37–56; Carlitz, 'Shrines, Governing-Class Identity', 612–40.
19 Yu, *Meng'an Zazhu*, vol. X, pp. 421–2.
20 Mann and Cheng (eds.), *Under Confucian Eyes*, p. 5.
21 Baiyi Jushi, 'Hutian Lu', in Lidai (ed.), *Biji Xiaoshuo Daguan*, vol. I, p. 27.
22 *Royal Commission on Opium*, vol. I, p. 1672.
23 Editorial, 'Jijiu tunfu shengshu yangyan qisihuisheng dan', *Shen Bao*, 14 and 15 June, 21 June 1872, 541, 549; editorial, 'Ji fu yangyan an', *Shen Bao*, 21 June 1872, 585–6; editorial, 'Quan funu wu qingsheng lun', *Shen Bao*, 18 August 1873, 3553 and 10 January 1875, 8581.

CHAPTER 9   'THE UNOFFICIAL HISTORY OF OPIUM'

1 The quotation that forms the title of the chapter is taken from Wuzhong Menghua Sheng (pseudonym), 'Furong Waishi', in A Ying (ed.), *Yapian Zhanzheng Wenxueji*, vol. I, pp. 536–7.
2 Evelyn Rawski, 'Concluding Perspectives', in Johnson, Nathan and Rawski (eds.), *Popular Culture in Late Imperial China*, pp. 399–417.
3 Zhixi Jushi, 'Yong Yantong', in Zhu and Gu (eds.), *Yancao Lu*, p. 14A.
4 Ziling Xu, 'Yandeng Xin', in Tan (ed.), *Ban'an Congshu*, p. 2514.
5 Shangchen Wang, 'Xiangsi Qu', in Tan (ed.), *Ban'an Congshu*, p. 2563.
6 Zhu and Gu (eds.), *Yancao Lu*, p. 188.
7 Weiping Zhang, 'Sanyuanli', in A Ying (ed.), *Yapian Zhanzheng Wenxueji*, vol. I, p. 1.
8 Li, *Qingmode Xiaceng Shehui Qimeng Yundong*, pp. 207–8. *Geng* and *dian* were the Chinese way of keeping time.
9 Wuzhong Menghua Sheng, 'Furong Waishi', in A Ying (ed.), *Yapian Zhanzheng Wenxueji*, vol. I, pp. 536–7.
10 Song (ed.), *Huihui Yaofang Kaoshi*, pp. 357 and 362.
11 Cui, *Bencao Mingkao*, pp. 624–6.
12 Fay, *Opium War*, p. 168.
13 Liang, *Liangban Qiuyu'an Suibi*, vol. IV, pp. 1A–B.
14 Pan, *Daoting Tushuo*, vol. V, pp. 113–19 and Tao Wang, 'Songying Manlu', in Lu (ed.), *Yanfen Juan*, pp. 388–9.
15 Wang, *Wang Tao Riji*, p. 45.
16 Inspector General of Customs, *Native Opium*, tabular.
17 Shen, Jiang and Zhu (eds.), *Jiu Shanghai*, p. 46.
18 Zhu Tianmu, 'Ye Yu', in Qi and Lin (eds.), *Yapian Zhanzheng*, p. 327.
19 Liedekerke, *Belle époque de l'opium*.
20 Ibid., pp. 165 and 169.
21 Ibid., pp. 174 and 163.
22 Ibid., p. 166.

23 Ibid., p. 59.
24 Hayter, *Opium and the Romantic Imagination*, p. 331.
25 Liedekerke, *Belle époque de l'opium*, p. 152.

CHAPTER 10   OPIATE OF THE PEOPLE

1 Feuerwerker, 'Presidential Address', 757–69.
2 Hao, *Commercial Revolution*, preface, and Gregory Blue, 'Opium for China: The British Connection', in Brook and Wakabayashi (eds.), *Opium Regimes*, pp. 31–54.
3 *Royal Commission on Opium*, vol. I, p. 611.
4 Cressy-Marcks, *Journey into China*, p. 72.
5 Giles, *Chinese Sketches*, pp. 114–15.
6 Morrison, *An Australian in China*, pp. 92–4.
7 Mintz, *Sweetness and Power*, p. 183.
8 Caine, 'Report on Trade at Hankow during 1868', *North China Herald and Market Report*, III, 124, 9 September 1869, 488.
9 Colquhoun, *Across Chryse*, vol. I, pp. 159–60.
10 Hosie, *Three Years in Western China*, p. 148.
11 Wu Binghuan, 30 April (no year), Cambridge University Library, Jardine Matheson Archive, large-sized Chinese letters.
12 A. G. Dallas (Shanghai) to David Jardine (Hong Kong), 3 May 1851, Cambridge University Library, Jardine Matheson Archive, B7/37, fo. 442.
13 Hao, *Commercial Revolution*, pp. 60–4.
14 M. A. Macleod (Foochow) to Alexander Perceval (Hong Kong), 11 May 1861, Cambridge University Library, Jardine Matheson Archive, B7/11, fo. 1236.
15 Jonathan Spence, 'Opium Smoking in Ch'ing China', in Wakeman and Grant (eds.), *Conflict and Control in Late Imperial China*, pp. 143–73.
16 Fairbank, Coolidge and Smith, *H. B. Morse*, p. 90.
17 Inspector General of Customs, *Native Opium*. The total is my own calculation.
18 Spector, *Li Hong-chang and Huai Army*, p. 216.
19 Van de Ven, 'Public Finance and the Rise of Warlordism', 829–68.
20 'Opium', *North China Herald*, III, 116, 15 July 1869, 374.
21 'Peking Hospital Report', *North China Herald*, III, 124, 9 September 1869, 488.
22 *Royal Commission on Opium*, vol. II, appendix XII.
23 Inspector General of Customs, *Native Opium*, pp. 1–4 and 60–3.
24 Xue, *Yong'an Suibi*, pp. 148–9.
25 Wang, *Jindu Shijian*, p. 163.
26 *Royal Commission on Opium*, vol. I, pp. 304–5.
27 Davis, *Yunnan*, pp. 311–12.
28 Colquhoun, *Across Chryse*, vol. II, p. 198.
29 Ibid., vol. I, pp. 191–2.
30 Kemp, *Face of China*, pp. 79–80.
31 Allen and Sachtleben, *Across Asia on a Bicycle*, pp. 164–7.
32 Conger, *Letters from China*, p. 315.

33 Inspector General of Customs, *Native Opium*, pp. 48–9.
34 Fairbank, Coolidge and Smith, *H. B. Morse*, p. 91.
35 Lin Manhong, 'Qingmo Shehui Liuxing Xishi Yapian Yanjiou', Ph.D. thesis, Taiwan Normal University, 1985.
36 Li, *Nanting Biji*, vol. XII, pp. 3A–B.
37 Fairbank, Coolidge and Smith, *H. B. Morse*, p. 137.
38 Xu, *Qingbei Leichao*, vol. XCII, pp. 163–4.
39 Inspector General of Customs, *Native Opium*, p. 22.
40 Ibid., p. 36.
41 Ibid., p. 53.
42 Ibid., p. 19.
43 'Opium', *North China Herald*, III, 116, 15 July 1869, 374.
44 Williams, *Middle Kingdom: A survey of the Chinese Empire*, vol. II, pp. 383–4.
45 Ibid.
46 Lee, *Big Smoke*, p. 76.
47 Inspector General of Customs, *Native Opium*, pp. 60–3.
48 Ibid., pp. 13 and 52.
49 Ibid., p. 35.
50 Ibid.
51 Ibid., pp. 9 and 22.
52 Xu, *Shiye Yewen*, p. 269.
53 Carl, *With the Empress Dowager of China*, p. 127.
54 Bland and Backhouse, *China under the Empress Dowager*, pp. 411 and 496–7.

CHAPTER II   THE ROAD TO ST LOUIS

1 Lee, *Big Smoke*, p. 7.
2 Emily Hahn, *Times and Places*, pp. 223–4.
3 Lee, *Big Smoke*, p. 34.
4 Ibid., p. 37.
5 Inspector General of Customs, *Native Opium*, p. 51.
6 Lee, *Big Smoke*, p. 45.
7 Sheng Zhou, 'Yangzhou Meng', in Wang (ed.), *Shuo Ku*, vol. III, p. 16A.
8 Lee, *Big Smoke*, pp. 42–3.
9 Wu and Yao (eds.), *Shanghaixian Xuzhi*, vol. I, p. 9A.
10 Zhaotang Li, 'Luanhou Jisuoji', in Zhongguo (ed.), *Jindaishi Zilao*, vol. XXXIV, pp. 177–86.
11 Shanghai (ed.), *Jiu Shanghai Shiliao Huibian*, vol. I, pp. 542–5.
12 Roche, *A History of Everyday Things*, p. 5.
13 *Royal Commission on Opium*, vol. I, p. 1739.
14 Ibid., vol. I, p. 2028.
15 Little, *Intimate China*, p. 179.
16 Headland, *Court Life in China*, p. 23.
17 Giles, *Chinese Sketches*, pp. 114–15.

18 *Royal Commission on Opium*, vol. I, p. 1637.
19 Ibid., vol. I, p. 1733.
20 Deborah Greenwald and David Harder, 'Domains of Shame: Evolutionary, Cultural, and Psychotherapeutic Aspects', in Gilbert and Andrews (eds.), *Shame*, pp. 225–45.
21 Veblen, *Theory of the Leisure Class*, p. 69.
22 Gay, *Consumption and Identity at Work*, p. 82.
23 *Royal Commission on Opium*, vol. IV, appendix, p. 342.
24 Wilson, Greenblatt and Wilson (eds.), *Moral Behavior in Chinese Society*, pp. 1–20 and 104–25.
25 *Royal Commission on Opium*, vol. I, p. 503.
26 Wang, *Wang Tao Riji*, p. 45.
27 Greenwald and Harder, 'Domains of Shame', pp. 225–45.
28 Wang, *Wang Tao Riji*, p. 21.
29 Cohen, *Between Tradition and Modernity*, p. 83.
30 Baudrillard, *Consumer Society*, pp. 49–68.
31 Ibid., pp. 60–1.
32 C. A. Bayly, '"Archaic" and "Modern" Globalisation in the Eurasian and African Arena, *c.* 1750–1850', in Hopkins (ed.), *Globalisation in World History*, pp. 47–73.
33 Special to the *New York Times*, LXXII, 23, 851, 14 May 1923, 9.
34 Kane, *Opium-Smoking in America and China*, p. 2.
35 McMahon, *Fall of the God of Money*, p. 181.
36 Rydell, *All the World's a Fair*, introduction.
37 Qiu, *Qingdai Yiwen*, vol. IV, pp. 27–8.

CHAPTER 12   'SHANGHAI VICE'

The title of this chapter is taken from the television documentary *Shanghai Vice*, which was made by Phil Agland and broadcast on Channel Four in the UK in 1999.
1 Wang, *Jindu Shijian*, p. 431 and Yuan (ed.), *Zhongguo Renkou*, p. 66.
2 Mary Rankin, John Fairbank, and Albert Feuerwerker, 'Introduction: Perspectives on Modern China's History', in Fairbank and Feuerwerker (eds.), *Cambridge History of China*, vol. XIII, pp. 3–6.
3 Chi Zhizheng, 'Huyou Mengying', in Shanghai (ed.), *Shanghai Tan*, p. 160.
4 Beaton, *Far East*, p. 57.
5 Maugham, *On a Chinese Screen*, p. 33–4.
6 Hu Xianghan, 'Shanghai Xiaozhi', in Shanghai (ed.), *Shanghai Tan*, p. 41.
7 Finch, *Shanghai and Beyond*, p. 277.
8 Brossollet, *Les Français de Shanghai 1849–1949*, p. 268.
9 Finch, *Shanghai and Beyond*, pp. 282–3.
10 Gavit, *Opium*, pp. 138–40.
11 Butel, *L'Opium*, pp. 320–5.
12 Brossollet, *Français de Shanghai*, p. 268.

13 Cressey, *China's Geographic Foundations*, p. 144.

14 Tawney, *Land and Labour in China*, p. 7.

15 Woodhead, *Adventures in Far Eastern Journalism*, p. 80.

16 Lary, *Warlord Soldiers*, p. 40.

17 Perry, *Rebels and Revolutionaries*, pp. 62–74.

18 Edward R. Slack Jr, 'The National Anti-Opium Association and the Guo-mindang State, 1924–1937' and Alan Baumler, 'Opium Control Versus Opium Suppression: The Origin of the 1935 Six-Year Plan to Eliminate Opium and Drugs', in Brook and Wakabayashi (eds.), *Opium Regimes*, pp. 248–69 and 270–91.

19 Finch, *Shanghai and Beyond*, p. 294.

20 Gavit, *Opium*, p. 120.

21 Xin Lin, 'Peiling Dabozhen de Yanpian Jingji', *Dongfang Zazhi*, 32, 14 (1935), 105–7.

22 Buck, *Land Utilization in China*, p. 325.

23 Ibid., pp. 231–3.

24 Perry, *Rebels and Revolutionaries*, pp. 180–1 and 211.

25 Morrison, *Australian in China*, pp. 48–9.

26 A Correspondent in China, 'Morphine in China', *Chemist and Druggist*, 61, 183 (1902), 560.

27 G. S. Muir, 'The Trade in Morphine to the East', *British Medical Journal*, 1 (1910), 240.

28 Woodhead, *Adventures in Far Eastern Journalism*, pp. 75–85.

29 Timothy Brook and Bob Tadashi Wakabayashi, 'Introduction: Opium's History in China', in Brook and Wakabayashi (eds.), *Opium Regimes*, pp. 1–27.

30 Frank W. Price, 'Japan's Continental Policy', in Nourse, *Four Hundred Million*, p. 352.

31 M. Searle Bates, 'The Narcotics Situation in Nanking and Other Occupied Areas', *Amerasia*, 3, 11 (1940), 525–7.

32 'Nantao refugee zone and the opium element in Sino-Japanese-Occidental relations', *China Weekly Review*, 83, 25 December 1937, 88–90.

33 Mark S. Eykholt, 'Resistance to Opium as a Social Evil in Wartime China', in Brook and Wakabayashi (eds.), *Opium Regimes*, pp. 360–9.

34 Nelson, *Journey to Chungking*, p. 133.

35 Han, *Destination Chungking*, pp. 232–3.

36 Meurville, *Chine du Yang-tsz*, pp. 150–2.

37 Yardley, *Chinese Black Chamber*, p. 155.

38 Ibid., p. 158.

39 Salisbury, *The Long March*, p. 181.

40 Ibid., p. 305.

41 Bertram, *Shadow of a War*, p. 25; Rattenbury, *China–Burma Vagabond*, p. 83.

42 League of Nations, *League of Nations Official Journal: October 1924*, appendix 4, p. 1434.

43 Snow, *Red Star over China*, pp. 54–5.

44 Yongfa Chen, 'Hongtaiyang Xia de Yingsu Hua', *Xin Shixue*, 1, 4 (1990), 41–117.

45 Xie, *Xie Juezai Riji*, vol. II, p. 734.
46 Vladimirov, *Diaries: Yenan, China*, pp. 43 and 183.
47 Su, *Zhongguo Dupingshi*, p. 530; Su, 'Woguo jindu taidu jianjue cuoshi deli', *Renmin Ribao*, 26 June 1992, 1, 'Yinianlai woguo pohuo dupinan wanyuqi', *Renmin Ribao*, 27 June 1992, 3, and 'Jiancha jiaqiang shehui zhi'an zonghe zhilide jueding zhixin qingkuang', *Renmin Ribao*, 30 August 1994, 3.
48 Wang, *Jindu Shijian*, p. 492.
49 Ignatius and Leung, 'What the revolution in China wiped out, reform brought back', *Wall Street Journal*, 15 November 1989, A1 and A23.

CONCLUSION

1 Finch, *Shanghai and Beyond*, p. 282.
2 Mary B. Rankin, John K. Fairbank and Albert Feuerwerker, 'Introduction: Perspectives on Modern China's History', in Fairbank and Feuerwerker (eds.), *Cambridge History of China*, vol. XIII, p. 6.
3 Little, *Intimate China*, pp. 95–6.
4 David Johnson, 'Communication, Class, and Consciousness in Late Imperial China', in Johnson, Nathan and Rawski (eds.), *Popular Culture in Late Imperial China*, pp. 34–72.
5 Joseph W. Esherick, 'Ten Theses on the Chinese Revolution', *Modern China*, 21, 1 (1995), 45–76.

Glossary

a fei rong	阿肥荣	*Hakka*	客家
a fu rong	阿芙蓉	*leng long gao*	冷笼膏
bai pi	白皮	*lianhuan hua*	连环画
beile	贝勒	*lijin/likin*	厘金
caizi jiaren	才子佳人	*liu jiao*	六角
Chenghua guimao	成化癸卯	*Liyuan zidi*	梨园子弟
chun fang	春方	*mei yao*	媚药
chunyao	春药	*minang*	米囊
Da jindan	大金丹	*minfeng chunpu*	民风淳朴
da tu	大土	*minnan*	闽南
da yan	大烟	*pian jie*	片疥
Daban/Taipan	大班	*piao ke*	嫖客
dangshan tu	碭山土	*piaohao*	票号
dong tu	东土	*qiao tu*	乔土
dou yan	斗烟	*Sandufu*	三都赋
fangzhong shu	房中术	*Sanyuanli*	三元里
Fu gao	福膏	*shizi yaotou*	狮子摇头
Fu jiang	福浆	*Shu Jiang*	蜀浆
gong ban	公班	*shua*	耍
guan tu	官土	*shuchang*	书场
han yan	旱烟	*shui yan*	水烟
hepurong	合甫融	*shuo chang*	说唱
hong pi	红皮	*su ke*	粟壳
hua hong	花红	*Tai jiang*	台浆
huafang	画舫	*Tai tu*	台土
huayan guan	花烟间	*Ti mian*	体面
Jian jiang	建浆	*tiaogao*	挑膏
jiepian	疥片	*tu jiang*	土浆
jisu	鸡苏	*xiang jiang*	象浆

223

Xiangfei zhu	湘妃竹	*yang* linen	洋锦
xiao tu	小土	*yang* marten	洋貂
xiaoren shu	小人书	*yang* money	洋钱
xin tu	新土	*yang* otter	洋獭
xingli	行李	*yang* paint	洋漆
Xiyu	西域	*yang* paper	洋纸
Wai yang	外洋	*yang* pen	洋笔
Wen jiang	温浆	*yang* pictures	洋画
wu xiang	乌香	*yang* red	洋红
yamen	衙门	*yang* tree	洋树
ya niao hong	鸭尿红	*yang* yan	洋烟
ya pian	鸦片	*yang* yao	洋药
yan hua	烟花	*yang* huo	洋货
yan fen	烟粉	*yang* huo jie	洋货街
yan xia	烟霞	*yao qian shu*	摇钱树
yan yun xi	烟云戏	*yincha*	饮茶
yang blue	洋青	*yingsu*	罂粟
yang bowl	洋碗	*yingsu fu*	罂粟腐
yang carpet	洋毯	*yingsu ke*	罂粟壳
yang china	洋瓷	*yingsu wan*	罂粟丸
yang copper	洋铜	*yingzisu*	罂子粟
yang cotton	洋布	*you hong*	油红
yang fans	洋扇	*yumi*	御米
yang glasses	洋玻璃	*yumi ke*	御米壳
yang guilds	洋行	*yunu shu*	御女术
yang handkerchiefs	洋帕	*zhugao*	煮膏
yang harp	洋琴	*zi xia gao*	紫霞膏

Bibliography

EUROPEAN LANGUAGE SOURCES

MANUSCRIPT SOURCES

Cambridge University Library, Jardine Matheson Archive

A. G. Dallas (Shanghai) to David Jardine (Hong Kong), 3 May 1851, B7/37, fo. 442.

James Matheson to B. C. Wilcocks, 8 March 1837, C5/2, fo. 51.

M. A. Macleod (Foochow) to Alexander Perceval (Hong Kong), 11 May 1861, B7/11, fo. 1236.

Robert Taylor to Cruttenden MacKillop, 4 November 1818, C1/1, fo. 10.

Public Record Office London, Foreign Office Papers

Litton to Principal Secretary of State for Foreign Affairs and other British Consuls, July 1903–December 1905, FO 17/1728, fos. 1–2, 3–10, 13, 15, 16, 22–4, 29–30, 261–5, 266–89 and 307–9.

British Library, East India Company Papers

East India Company Factory Records: China and Japan, 1596–1840. China super cargoes (ship's) diary, G/12/34, fos. 81–83, and G/12/35, fos. 1–2.

East India Company Factory Records: China and Japan, 1596–1840. Canton diary, G/12/75, 21 July, and Canton consultation, G/12/76, fos. 44–6, 46–8, 50–53, 53–56, 56–58, 58–61 and 61–2.

BOOKS AND JOURNALS

A Correspondent in China, 'Morphine in China', *Chemist and Druggist*, 61, 183 (1902), 560.

Abel, Clarke, *Narrative of a Journey in the Interior of China*, London: Longman, Hurst, Rees, Orme & Brown, 1818.

'Admonitory Pictures', *Chinese Repository*, V, 12 (1837), 571–3.

Allen, Nathan, *The Opium Trade*, Lowell, MA: James P. Walker, 1853.

Allen, Thomas Gaskell Jr and Sachtleben, William Lewis, *Across Asia on a Bicycle: The Journey of Two American Students from Constantinople to Peking*, London: T. Fisher Unwin, 1895.

'American Influence on the Destinies of Ultra-Malayan Asia', *Chinese Repository*, VII, 6 (1838), 80.

Appadurai, Arjun (ed.), *The Social Life of Things: Commodities in Culture Perspective*, Cambridge: Cambridge University Press, 1986.

Atkins, Peter and Bowler, Ian, *Food in Society: Economy, Culture, Geography*, London: Edward Arnold, 2001.

Barrow, John, *Travels in China*, London: T. Cadell & W. Davies, 1804.

Bates, M. Searle, 'The Narcotics Situation in Nanking and Other Occupied Areas', *Amerasia*, 3, II (1940), 525–7.

Baudrillard, Jean, *The Consumer Society: Myths and Structure*, London: Sage, 1998.

Beasley, W. G. and Pulleyblank, E. G. (eds.), *Historians of China and Japan*, Oxford: Oxford University Press, 1961.

Beaton, Cecil, *Far East*, London: B. T. Batsford, 1945.

Bell, John, *A Journey from St Petersburg to Pekin 1719–1722*, Glasgow: R. & A. Foulis, 1763.

Benedict, Ruth, *The Chrysanthemum and the Sword*, 2nd edn, London: Routledge & Kegan Paul, 1967.

Bertram, James, *The Shadow of a War: A New Zealander in the Far East 1939–1946*, London: Victor Gollancz, 1947.

Bland, J. O. P. and Backhouse, E., *China under the Empress Dowager: Being the History of the Life and Times of Tzu Hsi*, London: W. Heinemann, 1911.

Blusse, Leonard, *Strange Company: Chinese Settlers, Mestizo Women and the Dutch in VOC Batavia*, Dordrecht: Foris, 1986.

'No Boats to China: The Dutch East India Company and the Changing Pattern of the China Sea Trade, 1635–1690', *Modern Asian Studies*, 30, 1 (1996), 51–76.

Bourdieu, Pierre, *Distinction: A Social Critique of the Judgment of Taste*, Cambridge, MA: Harvard University Press, 1984.

Brennan, Thomas, *Public Drinking and Popular Culture in Eighteenth-Century Paris*, Princeton: Princeton University Press, 1988.

Brook, Timothy, *The Confusions of Pleasure: Commerce and Culture in Ming China*, Berkeley: University of California Press, 1998.

Brook, Timothy and Wakabayashi, Bob Tadashi (eds.), *Opium Regimes: China, Britain, and Japan, 1839–1952*, Berkeley: University of California Press, 2000.

Brossollet, Guy, *Les Français de Shanghai 1849–1949*, Paris: Belin, 1999.

Buck, John Lossing, *Land Utilization in China*, Nanjing: Jinling Daxue, 1937.

Butel, Paul, *L'Opium: histoire d'une fascination*, Paris: Perrin, 1995.

Caine, G. W., 'Report on Trade at Hankow during 1868', *North China Herald and Market Report*, III, 124, 9 September 1869, 488.

Carl, Katharine A., *With the Empress Dowager of China*, London: Nash, 1906.

Carlitz, Katherine, 'Shrines, Governing-Class Identity and the Cult of Widow Fidelity,' *Journal of Asian Studies*, 56, 3 (1997), 612–40.

Chang, Hsin-pao, *Commissioner Lin and the Opium War*, Cambridge, MA: Harvard University Press, 1964.

Ch'en, Jerome, *China and the West: Society and Culture 1815–1937*, Bloomington: Indiana University Press, 1979.

Cohen, Paul, *Between Tradition and Modernity: Wang T'ao and Reform in Late Ch'ing China*, Cambridge, MA: Harvard University Press, 1987.

Colenbrander, H. T. (ed.), *Dagh-Register Gehouden int Casteel Batavia vant Passerende als over Geheel Nederlandts-India Anno 1636*, Batavia: G. Kolff, 1899.

Colquhoun, Archibald R., *Across Chryse: Being the Narrative of a Journey of Exploration through the South China Border Lands from Canton to Mandalay*, 2 vols., London: S. Low, Marston, Searle & Rivington, 1883.

Conger, Mrs Sarah Pike, *Letters from China, with Particular Reference to the Empress Dowager and the Women of China*, Chicago: A. C. McClurg, 1909.

Cranmer-Byng, John L., *An Embassy to China: Being the Journal Kept by Lord Macartney during His Embassy to the Emperor of Ch'ien-lung 1793–1794*, London: Longman, 1962.

Cressey, George B., *China's Geographic Foundations: A Survey of the Land and its People*, New York: McGraw-Hill, 1934.

Cressy-Marcks, Violet, *Journey into China*, London: Hodder & Stoughton, 1940.

Davis, H. R., *Yunnan: The Link between India and the Yangtze*, Cambridge: Cambridge University Press, 1909.

Davis, John F., *China during the War and since the Peace*, 2 vols., London: Longman, Brown, Green & Longmans, 1852.

Dermigny, Louis (ed.), *Les Memoires de Charles de Contant sur le commerce à la Chine*, Paris: Ecole Pratique des Hautes Études, 1964.

Douglas, Mary (ed.), *Constructive Drinking: Perspectives on Drink from Anthropology*, Cambridge: Cambridge University Press, 1987.

Downing, C. Toogood, *The Fan-Qui's Visit to the Celestial Empire in 1836–7*, 3 vols., London: H. Colburn, 1838.

Esherick, Joseph W. 'Ten Theses on the Chinese Revolution', *Modern China*, 21 (1995), 45–76.

Etherton, P. T., *The Crisis in China*, Boston: Little Brown, 1927.

Fairbank, John K., *Trade and Diplomacy on the China Coast*, Cambridge, MA: Harvard University Press, 1953.

Fairbank, John K. Coolidge, Martha H. and Smith, Richard J., *H. B. Morse: Customs Commissioner and Historian of China*, Lexington: University Press of Kentucky, 1994.

Fairbank, John K., and Feuerwerker, Albert (eds.), *The Cambridge History of China*, vol. XIII, *Republican China 1912–1949, Part 1*, Cambridge: Cambridge University Press, 1986.

Fay, Peter W., *The Opium War 1840–1842*, 2nd edn, Chapel Hill: University of North Carolina Press, 1997.

Feuerwerker, Albert, 'Presidential Address: Questions about China's Early Modern Economic History that I wish I could Answer', *Journal of Asian Studies*, 51 (1992), 757–69.

Finch, Percy, *Shanghai and Beyond*, New York: Scribner, 1953.

Fry, William S., *Facts and Evidences Relating to the Opium Trade with China*, London: Pelham Richardson, 1840.

Gamble, Sidney D., *Peking: A Social Survey*, New York: George H. Doran, 1921.

Gavit, John Palmer, *Opium*, New York: Brentano's, 1927.

Gay, Paul du, *Consumption and Identity at Work*, London: Sage, 1996.

Giersch, C. Pat, 'A Motley Throng: Social Change on Southwest China's Early Modern Frontier, 1700–1880', *Journal of Asian Studies*, 60, 1 (February 2001), 67–94.

Gilbert, Paul and Andrews, Bernice (eds.), *Shame: Interpersonal Behaviour, Psychopathology, and Culture*, Oxford: Oxford University Press, 1998.

Giles, Herbert A., *Chinese Sketches*, London: Trubner, 1876.

Goodrich, Carrington and Chaoying, Fang (eds.), *Dictionary of Ming Biography 1368–1644*, New York: Columbia University Press, 1976.

Graham, Alexander, *The Right, Obligation and Interest of the Government of Great Britain to Request Redress from the Government of China*, London: Whittaker, 1840.

Greenberg, Michael, *British Trade and the Opening of China, 1800–1842*, Cambridge: Cambridge University Press, 1951.

Greenlee, William Brooks (trans.), *The Voyage of Pedro Alvares Cabral to Brazil and India*, London: Hakluyt Society, 1938.

Gulick, Robert Hans van, *Erotic Colour Prints of the Ming Period*, 3 vols., Tokyo: privately published, 1951.

Hahn, Emily, *Times and Places*, New York: Crowell, 1970.

Han, Suyin, *Destination Chungking*, Boston: Little Brown, 1942.

Hao, Yen-p'ing, *The Commercial Revolution in Nineteenth-Century China*, Berkeley: University of California Press, 1986.

Hayter, Alethea, *Opium and the Romantic Imagination*, Berkeley: University of California Press, 1968.

Headland, Isaac T., *Court Life in China: The Capital, its Officials and People*, New York: F. H. Revell, 1909.

Henriot, Christian, *Prostitution and Sexuality in Shanghai: A Social History, 1849–1949*, Cambridge: Cambridge University Press, 2001.

Hentzner, Paul, *Travels in England*, London: Edward Geffery, 1797.

Holman, James, *A Voyage Round the World, Including Travels in Africa, Asia, Australasia, America, etc. from 1827 to 1832*, 4 vols., London: Smith, Elder, 1834–5.

Holt, Edgar, *The Opium Wars in China*, London: Putnam, 1964.

Hopkins, Anthony (ed.), *Globalisation in World History*, London: Pimlico, 2002.

Hosie, Alexander, *Three Years in Western China*, 2nd edn, London: G. Philip, 1897.

Huang, Ray, *1587, A Year of no Significance: The Ming Dynasty in Decline*, New Haven: Yale University Press, 1981.

Huc, M., *The Chinese Empire*, 2 vols., London: Longman, Brown, Green & Longmans, 1855.

Ignatius, Adi and Leung, Julia, 'What the Revolution in China Wiped Out, Reform Brought Back', *Wall Street Journal*, 15 November 1989, A1 and A23.

Inspector General of Customs, *China Imperial Maritime Customs II*; special series no. 4, *Opium*, and no. 9, *Native Opium*, Shanghai: Statistical Department of the Inspectorate General, 1881 and 1888.

Jocelyn, Lord, *Six Months with the Chinese Expedition*, London: John Murray, 1841.

Johnson, David, Nathan, Andrew and Rawski, Evelyn S. (eds.) *Popular Culture in Late Imperial China*, Berkeley: University of California Press, 1985.

Johnson, Linda C. (ed.), 1993, *Cities of Jiangnan in Late Imperial China*, Albany: State University of New York Press.

'Journal of Occurrences', *Chinese Repository* II, 4 (1834), 574; II, 12 (1834), 574; V, 3 (1836), 138, 142, 143; XIV, 11 (1845), 544; XVI, 4 (1847), 179.

Kane, H. H., *Opium-Smoking in America and China: A Study of its Prevalence, and Effects, Immediate and Remote, on the Individual and the Nation*, New York: Arno Press, 1882.

Kemp, E. G., *The Face of China: Travels in East, North, Central and Western China*, London: Chatto & Windus, 1909.

Ko, Dorothy, *Teachers of the Inner Chamber: Women and Culture in Seventeenth-Century China*, Stanford: Stanford University Press, 1994.

Kopytoff, Igor, 'The Cultural Biography of Things: Commoditization as Process', in Appadurai (ed.), *Social Life of Things*, pp. 64–91.

Lary, Diana, *Warlord Soldiers*, Cambridge: Cambridge University Press, 1985.

League of Nations, *League of Nations Official Journal*, Geneva, October 1924.

Lee, John, 'Trade and Economy in Preindustrial East Asia, c. 1500–1800: East Asia in the Age of Global Integration', *Journal of Asian Studies*, 58, 1 (1999), 2–26.

Lee, Peter, *The Big Smoke: The Chinese Art and Craft of Opium*, Thailand: Lamplight Books, 1999.

Levi-Strauss, Claude, *The Raw and the Cooked: Introduction to a Science of Mythology*, New York: Harper & Row, 1969.

Liedekerke, Arnold de (ed.) *La Belle époque de l'opium: anthologie littéraire de la drogue de Charles Baudelaire à Jean Cocteau*, 3rd edn, Paris: Le Sphinx, 1984.

Linschoten, Jan Huygen van, *The Voyage of John Huyghen van Linschoten to the East Indies*, 1598, London: Hakluyt Society, 1885.

Little, Mrs Archibald, *Intimate China*, London: Hutchinson, 1899.

Lockyer, Charles, *An Account of the Trade in India: Containing Rules for Good Government in Trade, Price Courants, and Tables*, London: S. Crouch, 1711.

Lu, Hanchao, *Beyond the Neon Lights: Everyday Shanghai in the Early Twentieth Century*, Berkeley: University of California Press, 1999.

Lupton, Deborah, *Food, the Body and the Self*, London: Sage, 1996.

MacLeod, Murdo J. and Rawski, Evelyn S. (eds.), *European Intruders and Changes in Behaviour and Customs in Africa and Asia before 1800*, Brookfield, VT: Ashgate, 1998.

Mann, Susan, 'Widows in the Kinship, Class, and Community Structure of Qing Dynasty China', *Journal of Asian Studies*, 46, 1 (1987), 37–56.

Mann, Susan and Cheng, Yu-Yin (eds.), *Under Confucian Eyes: Writings on Gender in Chinese History*, Berkeley: University of California Press, 2001.

Maugham, Somerset W., *On a Chinese Screen*, London: Mandarin, 1990.

McMahon, Keith, *The Fall of the God of Money: Opium Smoking in Nineteenth-Century China*, Lanham, MD: Rowman & Littlefield, 2002.

Meurville, R. de, *La Chine du Yang-tsz*, Paris: Payot, 1946.

'Men and Things from Shanghai', *Chinese Repository*, XIX, 2 (1850), 108–9.

'Military Skill and Power of the Chinese', *Chinese Repository*, V, 5 (1836), 165–78.

Milburn, William, *Oriental Commerce: The Rise and Progress of the Trade of the Various European Nations with the Eastern World*, 2 vols., London: Black, Parry & Co., 1813.

Mintz, Sidney W., *Sweetness and Power: The Place of Sugar in Modern History*, New York: Knopf, 1985.

Morrison, George E., *An Australian in China: Being the Narrative of a Quiet Journey across China to Burma*, 3rd edn, London: H. Cox, 1902.

Morse, Hosea B., *The Chronicles of the East India Company Trading to China 1635–1834*, 5 vols., Oxford: Oxford University Press, 1926.
  The International Relations of the Chinese Empire, London: Longmans & Green, 1910.

Mote, Frederick W. and Twitchett, Denis (eds.), *The Cambridge History of China*, vol. VII, *The Ming Dynasty, 1368–1644, Part 1*, Cambridge: Cambridge University Press, 1988.

Muir, G. S., 'The Trade in Morphine to the East', *British Medical Journal*, 1 (1910), 240.

Mundy, Peter, *The Travels of Peter Mundy in Europe and Asia, 1608–1667*, 5 vols., London: Hakluyt Society, 1914.

Nagtegaal, Luc, *Riding the Dutch Tiger: The Dutch East India Company and the Northeast Coast of Java, 1680–1743*, Leiden: KITLV Press, 1996.

'Nantao Refugee Zone and the Opium Element in Sino-Japanese-Occidental Relations', *China Weekly Review*, 83, 25 December 1937, 88–90.

Naquin, Susan, *Peking: Temples and City Life, 1400–1900*, Berkeley: University of California Press, 2000.

Naquin, Susan and Rawski, Evelyn S., *Chinese Society in the Eighteenth Century*, New Haven: Yale University Press, 1987.

Needham, Joseph, *Science and Civilisation in China*, 7 vols. to date, Cambridge: Cambridge University Press, 1954.

Nelson, Daniel, *Journey to Chungking*, Minneapolis: Augsbury Publishing, 1945.

'Nest of Opium Smokers', *Chinese Repository*, IV, 7 (1835), 342.

Nourse, Mary A., *The Four Hundred Million: A Short History of the Chinese*, New York: Bobbs-Merrill, 1938.

'Opium', *North China Herald and Market Report*, III, 116, 15 July 1869, 374.

Ouchterlony, John, *The Chinese War: An Account of all the Operations of the British Forces from the Commencement to the Treaty of Nanking*, London: Saunders & Otley, 1844.

Owen, David E., *British Opium Policy in China and India*, New Haven: Yale University Press, 1934.

'Peking Hospital Report', *North China Herald and Market Report*, III, 124, 9 September 1869, 488.

Perry, Elizabeth J., *Rebels and Revolutionaries in North China 1845–1945*, Stanford: Stanford University Press, 1980.

Pires, Tome, *The Suma Oriental of Tome Pires*, 2 vols., London: Hakluyt Society, 1944.

Pomeranz, Kenneth, *The Great Divergence: China, Europe, and the Making of the Modern World Economy*, Princeton: Princeton University Press, 2000.

Prakash, Om, *The Dutch East India Company and the Economy of Bengal 1630–1720*, Princeton: Princeton University Press, 1985.

Rattenbury, Harold B., *China–Burma Vagabond*, London: F. Muller, 1946.

Rawski, Evelyn S., 'Research Themes in Ming-Qing Socioeconomic History – The State of the Field', *Journal of Asian Studies*, 50 (1991), 84–111.

Reid, Anthony, *Charting the Shape of Early Modern Southeast Asia*, Chiang Mai, Thailand: Silkworm Books, 1999.

Ritzer, George, *The McDonaldization of Society: An Investigation into the Changing Character of Contemporary Social Life*, Thousand Oaks, CA: Pine Forge, 1993.

Roche, Daniel, *A History of Everyday Things*, Cambridge: Cambridge University Press, 2000.

Royal Commission on Opium, vols. I, II and IV, London, 1893–4.

Rush, James R., 'Opium in Java: A Sinister Friend', *Journal of Asian Studies*, 44 (1985), 549–60.

Rydell, Robert W., *All the World's a Fair: Visions of Empire at American International Expositions, 1876–1916*, Chicago: University of Chicago Press, 1984.

Salisbury, Harrison E., *The Long March: The Untold Story*, London: Macmillan, 1985.

Scarth, John, *Twelve Years in China: The People, the Rebels, and the Mandarins*, Edinburgh: T. Constable, 1860.

Scott, Edmund, *An Exact Discourse of the Subtilties, Fashions, Policies, Religion, and Ceremonies of the East Indians, as well Chyneses as Javans*, 1606, London: Walter Burre, 1943.

Sergeant, Harriet, *Shanghai*, London: Crown, 1991.

Sirr, Henry Charles, *China and the Chinese: Their Religion, Character, Customs, and Manufactures, the Evils Arising from the Opium Trade*, 2 vols., London: W. S. Orr, 1849.

Skinner, G. William (ed.), *The City in Late Imperial China*, Stanford: Stanford University Press, 1977.

Smedt, Marc de (ed.), *Chinese Erotism*, New York: Crescent Books, 1981.

Smith, Joanna F. Handlin, 'Gardens in Ch'i Piao-chia's Social World: Wealth and Values in Late-Ming Kiangnan', *Journal of Asian Studies*, 51, 1 (1992), 55–81.

Smith, Rev. George, *A Narrative of an Exploratory Visit to Each of the Consular Cities of China, and to the Islands of Hong Kong and Chusan*, London: Seeley & Burnside, 1847.

Snow, Edgar, *Red Star over China*, 1st rev./enlarged edn, London: Victor Gollancz, 1968.

Special to the *New York Times*, LXXII, 23, 851, 14 May 1923, 9.

Spector, Stanley, *Li Hong-chang and the Huai Army: A Study in Nineteenth-Century Chinese Regionalism*, Seattle: University of Washington Press, 1964.

Staunton, Sir George L., *An Authentic Account of an Embassy from the King of Great Britain to the Emperor of China*, 2 vols., London: G. Nicol, 1797.

Stavorinus, John Splinter, *Voyages to the East-Indies*, 3 vols., London: G. G. & J. Robinson, 1798.

Tawney, Richard Henry, *Land and Labour in China*, London: Allen & Unwin, 1932.

Tiffany, Osmond, *The Canton Chinese*, Boston: James Munroe, 1849.

Trocki, Carl A., *Opium, Empire and the Global Political Economy: A Study of the Asian Opium Trade, 1750–1950*, London: Routledge, 1999.

Twitchett, Denis and Mote, Frederick W. (eds.), *The Cambridge History of China*, vol. VIII, *The Ming Dynasty, 1368–1644, Part 2*, Cambridge: Cambridge University Press, 1998.

Van de Ven, Hans, 'Public Finance and the Rise of Warlordism', *Modern Asian Studies*, 30, 1 (1996), 829–68.

Veblen, Thorstein, *Theory of the Leisure Class*, 1899, New York: A. M. Kelley, 1965.

Vladimirov, Peter, *The Vladimirov Diaries: Yenan, China, 1942–1945*, Garden City, NY: Doubleday, 1975.

Wakeman, Frederic Jr, *The Fall of Imperial China*, New York: Free Press, 1975.

Wakeman, Frederic Jr and Grant, Carolyn (eds.), *Conflict and Control in Late Imperial China*, Berkeley: University of California Press, 1975.

Waley-Cohen, Joanna, *The Sextants of Beijing*, New York: W. W. Norton, 1999.

Warren, Samuel, *The Opium Question*, London: James Ridgway, 1841.

Williams, S. Wells, *The Middle Kingdom: A Survey of the Geography, Government, Education, Social Life, Arts, Religion, & c., of the Chinese Empire and its Inhabitants*, 2 vols., London: W. H. Allen, 1883.

Wilson, Richard W., Greenblatt, Sidney L. and Wilson, Amy A. (eds.), *Moral Behavior in Chinese Society*, New York: Praeger, 1981.

Woodhead, H. G. W., *Adventures in Far Eastern Journalism: A Record of Thirty-Three Years' Experience*, Tokyo: Hokuseido Press, 1935.

Yardley, Herbert O., *Chinese Black Chamber: An Adventure in Espionage*, Boston: Houghton Mifflin, 1983.

CHINESE LANGUAGE SOURCES

MANUSCRIPT SOURCES

Cambridge University Library, Jardine Matheson Archive

Uncatalogued large-sized Chinese-language material:
Ahee, undated.
Wu Binghuan, 30 April (no year).

Public Record Office London, Foreign Office Papers

Hoppo to Ye Mingchen, 12 October 1852, Guangdong Provincial Archive, FO 931/1356, fo. 1.

BOOKS AND JOURNALS

A, Ying (ed.), *Yapian Zhanzheng Wenxueji*, Beijing: Zhonghua Shuju, 1957.
Aixinjueluo, Minning, *Yangzheng Shuwu Quanji Dingben*, 40 vols., Beijing: Nei Fu, 1822.
Bao, Shichen, *Anwu Sizong*, 36 vols., Taipei: Wenhai, 1968.
Chen, Jiamo, *Bencao Mengquan*, 12 vols., Shanghai: Zhongyiyao Daxue, 1994.
Chen, Shouxiang, *Jiumeng Chongjing: Fang Lin Bei Ning Cang Qingdai Mingxinpian Xuanji*, Nanning: Guangxi Meishu, 1998.
Chen, Xiqi, *Bibin Zaji*, Nanjing: Jinling Shuhuashe, 1983.
Chen, Yongfa, 'Hongtaiyang xia de *Yingsuhua*', *Xin Shixue*, 1, 4 (1990), 41–117.
Cheng, Enze, *Cheng Silang Yiji*, 10 vols., Taipei: Yiwen, 1965.
Cui, Yueli, *Bencao Mingkao*, Beijing: Zhongyi Guji, 2000.
Da Manzhoudiguo, Guowuyuan (ed.), *Da Qing Lichao Shilu: Gaozong*, 1, 500 vols., *Renzong*, 374 vols., *Xuanzong*, 476 vols., Taipei: Huanlian, 1964, 1964, 1964.
Dianshizhai (ed.), *Dianshizhai Huabao*, 58 vols., Shanghai: Dianshizhai, 1884.
Diyi Lishi, Dang'anguan (ed.), *Yapian Zhanzheng Dang'an Shiliao*, 7 vols., Tianjin: Guji, 1992.
Fang, Yizhi, *Wuli Xiaoshi*, 1785, 12 vols., Taipei: Commercial Press, 1981.
'Fulu Xiaoxiaoshanren Yanguan Yuejuan Jishi', *Shen Bao*, 19 April 1872, 163 and 178.
Gao, Lian, *Zunsheng Bajian*, 19 vols., Taipei: Commercial Press, 1979.
Gao, Shiqi, *Beishu Baowenglu*, Shanghai: Hanfenlou, 1860.
Gong, Zizhen, *Gong Zizhen Quanji*, 2 vols., Beijing: Zhonghua Shuju, 1959.
Gu, Yuanjiao, *Bencao Huijian*, 10 vols., Shanghai: Zhongyiyao Daxue, 1994.
Gugong, Bowuyuan (ed.), *Daoguang Qijuzhu*, 100 vols., Taipei: Palace Museum, 1985.
  Gongzhongdang Yongzhengchao Zouzhe, 27 vols., Taipei: Palace Museum, 1977.
Hu, Shiyu, *Dou Cun*, 4 vols., Beijing: Xinhua Shudian, 1985.
Huang, Shujing, *Taihai Shicha Lu*, 8 vols., Taipei: Wenhai, 1980.

Huang, Yuanyu, *Yuqiu Yaojie*, 8 vols., Beijing: Zhongyiyao, 1999.
'Ji Fu Yangyan An', *Shen Bao*, 21 June 1872.
Jiang, Xiangnan, *Qijinglou Wenchao*, 6 vols., Zhengzhou: Zhongguo Guji, 1991.
'Jijiu Tunfu Shengshu Yangyan Qisihuisheng Dan', *Shen Bao*, 14 and 15 June 1872.
Jin, Fuceng and Zhang, Wenhu (eds.), *Nanhui Xianzhi*, 22 vols., Taipei: Chengwen,
    1970.
Lan, Dingyuan, *Pingtai Jilue*, Taipei: Taiwan Yinhang, 1958.
Lei, Jin (ed.), *Qingren Shuohui*, Shanghai: Saoye Shanfang, 1928.
Lei, Mengshui (ed.), *Zhonghua Zhuzhici*, 2 vols., Shanghai: Guji, 1997.
Li, Boyuan, *Nanting Biji*, 16 vols., Shanghai: Guji, 1983.
Li, Dongyang and Shen, Shixing (eds.), *Da Ming Huidian*, 228 vols., Beijing: Nei
    Fu, 1587.
Li, Shizhen, *Bencao Gangmu*, 52 vols., Beijing: Renmin Weisheng, 1978.
Li, Xiaoti, *Qingmode Xiaceng Shehui Qimeng Yundong*, Shijiaozhaung: Hebei Jiayu,
    2001.
Li Xin, 'Peiling Dabozhen de Yanpian Jingying', *Dongfang Zazhi*, 32, 14 (1935),
    105–7.
Liang, Qichao, *Yingbingshi Heji*, 2nd edn, 24 vols., Shanghai: Zhonghua Shuji,
    1936.
Liang, Shaoren, *Liangban Qiuyu'an Suibi*, 8 vols., Taipeixian: Wenhai, 1975.
Liang, Zhangju, *Tui'an Suibi*, 22 vols., Taipei: Wenhai, 1971.
Lidai, Mingren, *Biji Xiaoshuo Daguan*, 4 vols., Taipei: Xinxing, 1962.
Lin, Manhong, 'Qingmo Shehui Liuxing Xishi Yapian Yanjiou', unpublished Ph.D.
    thesis, Taiwan Normal University, 1985.
Liu, Yuji and Chou, Zenghu (eds.), *Taigu Xianzhi*, 8 vols. Taipei: Chengwen, 1976.
Lu, Lin (ed.), *Yanfen Juan*, Hefei: Huangshan Shushe, 1994.
Mao, Xianglin, *Moyu Lu*, 16 vols., Shanghai: Guji, 1985.
Mao, Zedong, *Mao Zedong Xuanji*, 4 vols., Beijing: Renmin, 1991.
Pan, Lun'en, *Daoting Tushuo*, 12 vols., Hefei: Huangshan Shushe, 1996.
Peng, Songyu, *Yuzhou Jitan*, 2 vols., Taipei: Dahua Yinshuguan, 1968.
Peng, Yulin (ed.), *Hengyang Xianzhi*, 12 vols., Taipei: Chengwen, 1970.
Qi, Sihe and Lin, Shuhui (eds.), *Di'erci Yapian Zhanzheng*, Shanghai: Renmin,
    1978.
    Yapian Zhanzheng, 6 vols., Shanghai: Renmin, 1954.
Qian, Yong, *Luyuan Conghua*, Beijing: Zhonghua Shuju, 1979.
Qiu, Yulin, *Qingdai Yiwen*, 10 vols., Shanghai: Zhonghua Shuju, 1989.
Qu, Tuiyuan (ed.), *Beijing Lishi Fengtuo Congshu*, Beijing: Guangye Shushe, 1925.
'Quan Funu Wu Qingsheng Lun', *Shen Bao*, 18 August 1873, 3553.
Shanghai, Guji (ed.), *Shanghai Tan yu Shanghai Ren*, Shanghai: Guji, 1989.
Shanghai, Tongxunshe (ed.), *Jiu Shanghai Shiliao Huibian*, 2 vols., Beijing: Beijing
    Tushuguan, 1998.
Shen, Defu, *Wanli Yehuo Bian*, 1827, 3 vols., Beijing: Zhonghua Shuju, 1959.
Shen, Feide, Jiang, Hao and Zhu, Wengaung (eds.), *Jiu Shanghai de YanDuChang*,
    Shanghai: Baijia, 1988.
Shen, Fu, *Fusheng Liuji*, 4 vols., Hong Kong: Shanghai Yinshuguan, 1970.

Shi, Hongbao, *Min Zaji*, Taipei: Minyue Shuju, 1968.

Song, Xian (ed.), *Huihui Yaofang Kaoshi*, Beijing: Zhonghua Shuju, 2000.

Su, Ning, 'Jiancha JiaQiang Shehui Zhi'an Zonghe Zhilide Jueding Zhixing Qingkuang', *Renmin Ribao*, 30 August 1994, 3.

    'Woguo Jindu Taidu Jianjue Chuoshi Deli', *Renmin Ribao*, 26 June 1992, 1.

    'Yinianlai Woguo Pohuo Duping'an Wanyuqi', *Renmin Ribao*, 27 June 1992, 3.

Su, Shi, *Su Shi Shiji*, 50 vols., Beijing: Zhonghua Shuju, 1982.

Su, Zhiliang, *Zhongguo Dupingshi*, Shanghai: Renmin, 1997.

Sun, Zhongshan, *Sun Zhongshan Quanji*, 11 vols., Beijing: Zhonghua Shuju, 1981.

Tan, Xian (ed.), *Ban'an Congshu*, Taipei: Huawen Shuju, 1970.

Tang, Bin, *Sanxian Zhengshu*, 5 vols., Taipei: Xuesheng Shuju, 1976.

Wang, Ang, *Yifang Jijie*, 21 vols., Beijing: Zhongyiyao, 1997.

Wang, Hongbin, *Jindu Shijian*, Changsha: Yuelu Shushe, 1997.

Wang, Peixun (ed.), *Tingyulou Suibi*, Chongqing: Chubanshe, 1996.

Wang, Shizhen, *Gubugu Lu*, Shanghai: Commercial Press, 1937.

    Xiangzu Biji, 12 vols., Shanghai: Guji, 1982.

Wang, Tao, *Wang Tao Riji*, Beijing: Zhonghua Shuju, 1987.

Wang, Tao and Yu, Chensheng, *Yanshi Congchao*, Taipei: Guangwen Shuju, 1976.

Wang, Wenru (ed.), *Shuo Ku*, 4 vols., Shanghai: Wenmin Shuju, 1915.

Wu, Xin and Yao, Wendan (eds.), *Shanghaixian Xuzhi*, 30 vols., Taipei: Chengwen, 1970.

Xiao, Qian (ed.), *Shehui Baixiang*, Taipei: Commercial Press, 1992.

Xiao, Yuanke (ed.), *Qingshuo Qizhong*, Shanghai: Wenyi, 1992.

Xie, Juezai, *Xie Juezai Riji*, 2 vols., Beijing: Renmin, 1984.

Xu, Boling, *Yinjing Juan*, 1776, 12 vols., Taipei: Commercial Press, 1971.

Xu, Chunfu, *Gujin Yitong Daquan*, 100 vols., Taipei: Xinwenfeng, 1978.

Xu, Ke, *Qingpai Leichao*, 92 vols., Taipei: Commercial Press, 1966.

Xu, Zhiyan, *Shiye Yewen*, Taiyuan: Shanxi Guji, 1995.

Xu, Zhongyuan, *Sanyi Bitan*, Chongqing: Chubanshe, 1996.

Xue, Fucheng, *Yong'an Suibi*, Beijing: Zhongyang Dangxiao, 1998.

Ye, Mengzhu, *Yueshi Bian*, 10 vols., Shanghai: Guji, 1981.

Yin, Guangren and Zhang, Rulin, *Aomen Zhilue*, Taipei: Guangwen, 1968.

Yu, Jiao, *Meng'an Zazhu*, 10 vols., Beijing: Wenhua Yishu, 1988.

Yu, Yue, *Youtaixianguan Biji*, 16 vols., Shanghai: Guji, 1986.

Yu, Zhengxie, *Guisi Leigao*, 1879, 15 vols., Taipei : Shijie Shuju, 1965.

Yuan, Tingdong (ed.), *Zhongguo Xiyan Shihua*, Taipei: Commercial Press, 1998.

Yuan, Yongxi (ed.), *Zhongguo Renkou: Zonglun*, Beijing: Caizheng Jingji, 1991.

Zeng, Yuwang, *Zeng Yuwang Riji*, Shanghai: Renmin, 1982.

Zhang, Dai, *Tan'an Mengyi*, 8 vols., Shanghai: Shanghai Shudian, 1982.

Zhang, Jingyue, *Jingyue Quanshu*, 64 vols., Beijing: Zhongyiyao, 1999.

Zhang, Jixin, *Daoxian Huanhai Jiwenlu*, Beijing: Zhonghua Shuju, 1981.

Zhang, Lu, *Benjing Fengyuan*, 4 vols., Beijing: Zhongyiyao, 1999.

Zhang, Tingyu (ed.), *Ming Shi*, 1740, 332 vols., Beijing: Zhonghua Shuju, 1974.

Zhang, Xie, *Dong Xi Yang Kao*, Taipei: Commercial Press, 1965.

Zhang, Zuyi, *Qingdai Yesji*, 3 vols., Taiyuan: Shanxi Guji, 1996.

Zhao, Xuemin, *Bencao Gangmu Shiyi*, 10 vols., Taipei: Hongye Shuju, 1985.

Zhao, Yi, *Yanpu Zaji*, 7 vols., Beijing: Zhonghua Shuju, 1982.

Zheng, Chaoxiong, 'Cong Guangxi Hepu Mingdai Yaozhinie Faxian Ciyandou Tanji Yancao Chuanru Woguo de Shijian Wenti', *Nongye Kaogu*, 12, 2 (1986), 383–7 and 391.

Zhongguo, Kexueyuan Jinshisuo (ed.), *Jindaishi Zilao*, vol. XXXIV, Beijing: Zhonghua Shuju, 1964.

Zhonghua, Shuju (ed.), *Quan Tang Shi*, 900 vols., Beijing: Zhonghua Shuju, 1960.

Zhongyang, Yanjiuyuan (ed.), *Ming Shenzong Shilu*, 596 vols., Taipei: Academic Sinica, 1966.

Ming Xiaozong Shilu, 224 vols., Taipei: Academic Sinica, 1964.

Zhou, Shouchang, *Siyitang Rizha*, Changsha: Yuelu Shushe, 1985.

Zhou, Yi, *QiZhen Yecheng*, 16 vols., Taipei: Mingwen Shuju, 1991.

Zhu, Fengchun and Gu, Lu (eds.), *Yancao Lu*, Suzhou: Yisu Caotang, 1820.

Zhu, Jingying, *Haidong Zhaji*, Taipei: Taiwan Yinhang, 1958.

Index

For EU product safety concerns, contact us at Calle de José Abascal, 56–1°,
28003 Madrid, Spain or eugpsr@cambridge.org.

www.ingramcontent.com/pod-product-compliance
Ingram Content Group UK Ltd.
Pitfield, Milton Keynes, MK11 3LW, UK
UKHW020331140625

459647UK00018B/2105